# Category Theory for Programmers

*By* **Bartosz Milewski**

*compiled and edited by*
**Igal Tabachnik**

CATEGORY THEORY FOR PROGRAMMERS

Bartosz Milewski

Version v1.0.0-0-g41e0fc3
October 21, 2018

Converted from a series of blog posts by Bartosz Milewski.
PDF and book compiled by Igal Tabachnik.

LaTeX source code is available on GitHub:
https://github.com/hmemcpy/milewski-ctfp-pdf

# Contents

# Preface

For some time now I've been floating the idea of writing a book about category theory that would be targeted at programmers. Mind you, not computer scientists but programmers — engineers rather than scientists. I know this sounds crazy and I am properly scared. I can't deny that there is a huge gap between science and engineering because I have worked on both sides of the divide. But I've always felt a very strong compulsion to explain things. I have tremendous admiration for Richard Feynman who was the master of simple explanations. I know I'm no Feynman, but I will try my best. I'm starting by publishing this preface — which is supposed to motivate the reader to learn category theory — in hopes of starting a discussion and soliciting feedback.[1]

I WILL ATTEMPT, in the space of a few paragraphs, to convince you that this book is written for you, and whatever objections you might have to learning one of the most abstract branches of mathematics in your "copious spare time" are totally unfounded.

My optimism is based on several observations. First, category theory is a treasure trove of extremely useful programming ideas. Haskell programmers have been tapping this resource for a long time, and the ideas are slowly percolating into other languages, but this process is too slow. We need to speed it up.

Second, there are many different kinds of math, and they appeal to different audiences. You might be allergic to calculus or algebra, but it doesn't mean you won't enjoy category theory. I would go as far as to argue that category theory is the kind of math that is particularly well

---

[1] You may also watch me teach this material to a live audience, at https://goo.gl/GT2UWU (or search "bartosz milewski category theory" on YouTube.)

suited for the minds of programmers. That's because category theory — rather than dealing with particulars — deals with structure. It deals with the kind of structure that makes programs composable.

Composition is at the very root of category theory — it's part of the definition of the category itself. And I will argue strongly that composition is the essence of programming. We've been composing things forever, long before some great engineer came up with the idea of a subroutine. Some time ago the principles of structural programming revolutionized programming because they made blocks of code composable. Then came object oriented programming, which is all about composing objects. Functional programming is not only about composing functions and algebraic data structures — it makes concurrency composable — something that's virtually impossible with other programming paradigms.

Third, I have a secret weapon, a butcher's knife, with which I will butcher math to make it more palatable to programmers. When you're a professional mathematician, you have to be very careful to get all your assumptions straight, qualify every statement properly, and construct all your proofs rigorously. This makes mathematical papers and books extremely hard to read for an outsider. I'm a physicist by training, and in physics we made amazing advances using informal reasoning. Mathematicians laughed at the Dirac delta function, which was made up on the spot by the great physicist P. A. M. Dirac to solve some differential equations. They stopped laughing when they discovered a completely new branch of calculus called distribution theory that formalized Dirac's insights.

Of course when using hand-waving arguments you run the risk of saying something blatantly wrong, so I will try to make sure that there is solid mathematical theory behind informal arguments in this book. I do have a worn-out copy of Saunders Mac Lane's *Category Theory for the Working Mathematician* on my nightstand.

Since this is category theory *for programmers* I will illustrate all major concepts using computer code. You are probably aware that functional languages are closer to math than the more popular imperative languages. They also offer more abstracting power. So a natural temptation would be to say: You must learn Haskell before the bounty of category theory becomes available to you. But that would imply that category theory has no application outside of functional programming and that's simply not true. So I will provide a lot of C++ examples. Granted,

you'll have to overcome some ugly syntax, the patterns might not stand out from the background of verbosity, and you might be forced to do some copy and paste in lieu of higher abstraction, but that's just the lot of a C++ programmer.

But you're not off the hook as far as Haskell is concerned. You don't have to become a Haskell programmer, but you need it as a language for sketching and documenting ideas to be implemented in C++. That's exactly how I got started with Haskell. I found its terse syntax and powerful type system a great help in understanding and implementing C++ templates, data structures, and algorithms. But since I can't expect the readers to already know Haskell, I will introduce it slowly and explain everything as I go.

If you're an experienced programmer, you might be asking yourself: I've been coding for so long without worrying about category theory or functional methods, so what's changed? Surely you can't help but notice that there's been a steady stream of new functional features invading imperative languages. Even Java, the bastion of object-oriented programming, let the lambdas in. C++ has recently been evolving at a frantic pace — a new standard every few years — trying to catch up with the changing world. All this activity is in preparation for a disruptive change or, as we physicist call it, a phase transition. If you keep heating water, it will eventually start boiling. We are now in the position of a frog that must decide if it should continue swimming in increasingly hot water, or start looking for some alternatives.

One of the forces that are driving the big change is the multicore revolution. The prevailing programming paradigm, object oriented programming, doesn't buy you anything in the realm of concurrency and parallelism, and instead encourages dangerous and buggy design. Data hiding, the basic premise of object orientation, when combined with sharing and mutation, becomes a recipe for data races. The idea of combining a mutex with the data it protects is nice but, unfortunately, locks don't compose, and lock hiding makes deadlocks more likely and harder to debug.

But even in the absence of concurrency, the growing complexity of software systems is testing the limits of scalability of the imperative paradigm. To put it simply, side effects are getting out of hand. Granted, functions that have side effects are often convenient and easy to write. Their effects can in principle be encoded in their names and in the comments. A function called SetPassword or WriteFile is obviously mutating some state and generating side effects, and we are used to dealing with that. It's only when we start composing functions that have side effects on top of other functions that have side effects, and so on, that things start getting hairy. It's not that side effects are inherently bad — it's the fact that they are hidden from view that makes them impossible to manage at larger scales. Side effects don't scale, and imperative programming is all about side effects.

Changes in hardware and the growing complexity of software are forcing us to rethink the foundations of programming. Just like the builders of Europe's great gothic cathedrals we've been honing our craft to the limits of material and structure. There is an unfinished gothic cathedral in Beauvais[2], France, that stands witness to this deeply human struggle with limitations. It was intended to beat all previous records of height and lightness, but it suffered a series of collapses. Ad hoc measures like iron rods and wooden supports keep it from disintegrating, but obviously a lot of things went wrong. From a modern perspective, it's a miracle that so many gothic structures had been successfully completed without the help of modern material science, computer modelling, finite element analysis, and general math and physics. I hope future generations will be as admiring of the programming skills we've been displaying in building complex operating systems, web servers, and the internet infrastructure. And, frankly, they should, because we've done all this based on very flimsy theoretical foundations. We have to fix those foundations if we want to move forward.

---

[2]http://en.wikipedia.org/wiki/Beauvais_Cathedral

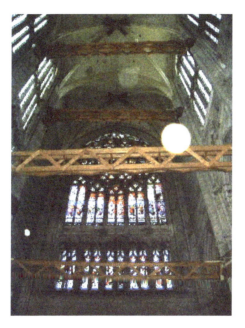

Ad hoc measures preventing the Beauvais cathedral from collapsing.

# Part One

# 1

# Category: The Essence of Composition

A CATEGORY is an embarrassingly simple concept. A category consists of *objects* and *arrows* that go between them. That's why categories are so easy to represent pictorially. An object can be drawn as a circle or a point, and an arrow... is an arrow. (Just for variety, I will occasionally draw objects as piggies and arrows as fireworks.) But the essence of a category is *composition*. Or, if you prefer, the essence of composition is a category. Arrows compose, so if you have an arrow from object $A$ to object $B$, and another arrow from object $B$ to object $C$, then there must be an arrow — their composition — that goes from $A$ to $C$.

## 1.1  Arrows as Functions

Is this already too much abstract nonsense? Do not despair. Let's talk concretes. Think of arrows, which are also called *morphisms*, as functions. You have a function $f$ that takes an argument of type $A$ and returns a $B$. You have another function $g$ that takes a $B$ and returns a $C$. You can compose them by passing the result of $f$ to $g$. You have just defined a new function that takes an $A$ and returns a $C$.

In math, such composition is denoted by a small circle between functions: $g \circ f$. Notice the right to left order of composition. For some people this is confusing. You may be familiar with the pipe notation in Unix, as in:

```
lsof | grep Chrome
```

In a category, if there is an arrow going from *A* to *B* and an arrow going from *B* to *C* then there must also be a direct arrow from *A* to *C* that is their composition. This diagram is not a full category because it's missing identity morphisms (see later).

or the chevron >> in F#, which both go from left to right. But in mathematics and in Haskell functions compose right to left. It helps if you read g ∘ f as "g *after* f."

Let's make this even more explicit by writing some C code. We have one function f that takes an argument of type A and returns a value of type B:

```
B f(A a);
```

and another:

```
C g(B b);
```

Their composition is:

```
C g_after_f(A a)
{
    return g(f(a));
}
```

Here, again, you see right-to-left composition: g(f(a)); this time in C.

I wish I could tell you that there is a template in the C++ Standard Library that takes two functions and returns their composition, but there isn't one. So let's try some Haskell for a change. Here's the declaration of a function from A to B:

```
f :: A -> B
```

Similarly:

4

```
g :: B -> C
```

Their composition is:

```
g . f
```

Once you see how simple things are in Haskell, the inability to express straightforward functional concepts in C++ is a little embarrassing. In fact, Haskell will let you use Unicode characters so you can write composition as:

```
g ∘ f
```

You can even use Unicode double colons and arrows:

```
f :: A → B
```

So here's the first Haskell lesson: Double colon means "has the type of..." A function type is created by inserting an arrow between two types. You compose two functions by inserting a period between them (or a Unicode circle).

## 1.2 Properties of Composition

There are two extremely important properties that the composition in any category must satisfy.

1. Composition is associative. If you have three morphisms, $f$, $g$, and $h$, that can be composed (that is, their objects match end-to-end), you don't need parentheses to compose them. In math notation this is expressed as:

$$h \circ (g \circ f) = (h \circ g) \circ f = h \circ g \circ f$$

   In (pseudo) Haskell:

```
f :: A -> B
g :: B -> C
h :: C -> D
h . (g . f) == (h . g) . f == h . g . f
```

   (I said "pseudo," because equality is not defined for functions.)

   Associativity is pretty obvious when dealing with functions, but it may be not as obvious in other categories.

5

2. For every object $A$ there is an arrow which is a unit of composition. This arrow loops from the object to itself. Being a unit of composition means that, when composed with any arrow that either starts at $A$ or ends at $A$, respectively, it gives back the same arrow. The unit arrow for object A is called $\text{id}_A$ (*identity* on *A*). In math notation, if $f$ goes from $A$ to $B$ then

$$f \circ \text{id}_A = f$$

and

$$\text{id}_B \circ f = f$$

When dealing with functions, the identity arrow is implemented as the identity function that just returns back its argument. The implementation is the same for every type, which means this function is universally polymorphic. In C++ we could define it as a template:

```
template<class T> T id(T x) { return x; }
```

Of course, in C++ nothing is that simple, because you have to take into account not only what you're passing but also how (that is, by value, by reference, by const reference, by move, and so on).

In Haskell, the identity function is part of the standard library (called Prelude). Here's its declaration and definition:

```
id :: a -> a
id x = x
```

As you can see, polymorphic functions in Haskell are a piece of cake. In the declaration, you just replace the type with a type variable. Here's the trick: names of concrete types always start with a capital letter, names of type variables start with a lowercase letter. So here a stands for all types.

Haskell function definitions consist of the name of the function followed by formal parameters — here just one, x. The body of the function follows the equal sign. This terseness is often shocking to newcomers but you will quickly see that it makes perfect sense. Function definition and function call are the bread and butter of functional programming so their syntax is reduced to the bare minimum. Not only are there no parentheses around the argument list but there are no commas between arguments (you'll see that later, when we define functions of multiple arguments).

The body of a function is always an expression — there are no statements in functions. The result of a function is this expression — here, just x.

This concludes our second Haskell lesson.

The identity conditions can be written (again, in pseudo-Haskell) as:

```
f . id == f
id . f == f
```

You might be asking yourself the question: Why would anyone bother with the identity function — a function that does nothing? Then again, why do we bother with the number zero? Zero is a symbol for nothing. Ancient Romans had a number system without a zero and they were able to build excellent roads and aqueducts, some of which survive to this day.

Neutral values like zero or id are extremely useful when working with symbolic variables. That's why Romans were not very good at algebra, whereas the Arabs and the Persians, who were familiar with the concept of zero, were. So the identity function becomes very handy as an argument to, or a return from, a higher-order function. Higher order functions are what make symbolic manipulation of functions possible. They are the algebra of functions.

To summarize: A category consists of objects and arrows (morphisms). Arrows can be composed, and the composition is associative. Every object has an identity arrow that serves as a unit under composition.

## 1.3   Composition is the Essence of Programming

Functional programmers have a peculiar way of approaching problems. They start by asking very Zen-like questions. For instance, when designing an interactive program, they would ask: What is interaction? When implementing Conway's Game of Life, they would probably ponder about the meaning of life. In this spirit, I'm going to ask: What is programming? At the most basic level, programming is about telling the computer what to do. "Take the contents of memory address x and add it to the contents of the register EAX." But even when we program in assembly, the instructions we give the computer are an expression of something more meaningful. We are solving a non-trivial problem (if it were trivial, we wouldn't need the help of the computer). And how do we solve problems? We decompose bigger problems into smaller problems. If the smaller problems are still too big, we decompose them further, and so on. Finally, we write code that solves all the small problems. And then comes the essence of programming: we compose those pieces of code to create solutions to larger problems. Decomposition wouldn't make sense if we weren't able to put the pieces back together.

This process of hierarchical decomposition and recomposition is not imposed on us by computers. It reflects the limitations of the human mind. Our brains can only deal with a small number of concepts at a time. One of the most cited papers in psychology, The Magical Number Seven, Plus or Minus Two[1], postulated that we can only keep $7 \pm 2$ "chunks" of information in our minds. The details of our understanding of the human short-term memory might be changing, but we know for sure that it's limited. The bottom line is that we are unable to deal with the soup of objects or the spaghetti of code. We need structure not because well-structured programs are pleasant to look at, but because otherwise our brains can't process them efficiently. We often describe some piece of code as elegant or beautiful, but what we really mean is that it's easy to process by our limited human minds. Elegant code creates chunks that are just the right size and come in just the right number for our mental digestive system to assimilate them.

So what are the right chunks for the composition of programs? Their surface area has to increase slower than their volume. (I like this analogy because of the intuition that the surface area of a geometric object grows with the square of its size — slower than the volume, which grows with the cube of its size.) The surface area is the information we need in order to compose chunks. The volume is the information we need in order to implement them. The idea is that, once a chunk is implemented, we can forget about the details of its implementation and concentrate on how it interacts with other chunks. In object-oriented programming, the surface is the class declaration of the object, or its abstract interface. In functional programming, it's the declaration of a function. (I'm simplifying things a bit, but that's the gist of it.)

Category theory is extreme in the sense that it actively discourages us from looking inside the objects. An object in category theory is an abstract nebulous entity. All you can ever know about it is how it re-

---

[1] http://en.wikipedia.org/wiki/The_Magical_Number_Seven,_Plus_or_ Minus_Two

lates to other objects — how it connects with them using arrows. This is how internet search engines rank web sites by analyzing incoming and outgoing links (except when they cheat). In object-oriented programming, an idealized object is only visible through its abstract interface (pure surface, no volume), with methods playing the role of arrows. The moment you have to dig into the implementation of the object in order to understand how to compose it with other objects, you've lost the advantages of your programming paradigm.

## 1.4  Challenges

1. Implement, as best as you can, the identity function in your favorite language (or the second favorite, if your favorite language happens to be Haskell).
2. Implement the composition function in your favorite language. It takes two functions as arguments and returns a function that is their composition.
3. Write a program that tries to test that your composition function respects identity.
4. Is the world-wide web a category in any sense? Are links morphisms?
5. Is Facebook a category, with people as objects and friendships as morphisms?
6. When is a directed graph a category?

# 2

# Types and Functions

THE CATEGORY OF TYPES AND FUNCTIONS plays an important role in programming, so let's talk about what types are and why we need them.

## 2.1  Who Needs Types?

There seems to be some controversy about the advantages of static vs. dynamic and strong vs. weak typing. Let me illustrate these choices with a thought experiment. Imagine millions of monkeys at computer keyboards happily hitting random keys, producing programs, compiling, and running them.

With machine language, any combination of bytes produced by monkeys would be accepted and run. But with higher level languages, we do appreciate the fact that a compiler is able to detect lexical and

grammatical errors. Lots of monkeys will go without bananas, but the remaining programs will have a better chance of being useful. Type checking provides yet another barrier against nonsensical programs. Moreover, whereas in a dynamically typed language, type mismatches would be discovered at runtime, in strongly typed statically checked languages type mismatches are discovered at compile time, eliminating lots of incorrect programs before they have a chance to run.

So the question is, do we want to make monkeys happy, or do we want to produce correct programs?

The usual goal in the typing monkeys thought experiment is the production of the complete works of Shakespeare. Having a spell checker and a grammar checker in the loop would drastically increase the odds. The analog of a type checker would go even further by making sure that, once Romeo is declared a human being, he doesn't sprout leaves or trap photons in his powerful gravitational field.

## 2.2  Types Are About Composability

Category theory is about composing arrows. But not any two arrows can be composed. The target object of one arrow must be the same as the source object of the next arrow. In programming we pass the results of one function to another. The program will not work if the target function is not able to correctly interpret the data produced by the source function. The two ends must fit for the composition to work. The stronger the type system of the language, the better this match can be described and mechanically verified.

The only serious argument I hear against strong static type checking is that it might eliminate some programs that are semantically correct. In practice, this happens extremely rarely and, in any case, every language provides some kind of a backdoor to bypass the type system when that's really necessary. Even Haskell has unsafeCoerce. But such devices should be used judiciously. Franz Kafka's character, Gregor Samsa, breaks the type system when he metamorphoses into a giant bug, and we all know how it ends.

Another argument I hear a lot is that dealing with types imposes too much burden on the programmer. I could sympathize with this sentiment after having to write a few declarations of iterators in C++ myself, except that there is a technology called *type inference* that lets the compiler deduce most of the types from the context in which they are used. In C++, you can now declare a variable auto and let the compiler figure out its type.

In Haskell, except on rare occasions, type annotations are purely optional. Programmers tend to use them anyway, because they can tell a lot about the semantics of code, and they make compilation errors easier to understand. It's a common practice in Haskell to start a project by designing the types. Later, type annotations drive the implementation and become compiler-enforced comments.

Strong static typing is often used as an excuse for not testing the code. You may sometimes hear Haskell programmers saying, "If it compiles, it must be correct." Of course, there is no guarantee that a type-correct program is correct in the sense of producing the right output. The result of this cavalier attitude is that in several studies Haskell didn't come as strongly ahead of the pack in code quality as one would expect. It seems that, in the commercial setting, the pressure to fix bugs is applied only up to a certain quality level, which has everything to do with the economics of software development and the tolerance of the end user, and very little to do with the programming language or methodology. A better criterion would be to measure how many projects fall behind schedule or are delivered with drastically reduced functionality.

As for the argument that unit testing can replace strong typing, consider the common refactoring practice in strongly typed languages: changing the type of an argument of a particular function. In a strongly typed language, it's enough to modify the declaration of that function and then fix all the build breaks. In a weakly typed language, the fact that a function now expects different data cannot be propagated to call sites. Unit testing may catch some of the mismatches, but testing is almost always a probabilistic rather than a deterministic process. Testing is a poor substitute for proof.

## 2.3  What Are Types?

The simplest intuition for types is that they are sets of values. The type Bool (remember, concrete types start with a capital letter in Haskell) is a two element set of True and False. Type Char is a set of all Unicode characters like a or ą.

Sets can be finite or infinite. The type of String, which is a synonym for a list of Char, is an example of an infinite set.

When we declare x to be an `Integer`:

```
x :: Integer
```

we are saying that it's an element of the set of integers. `Integer` in Haskell is an infinite set, and it can be used to do arbitrary precision arithmetic. There is also a finite-set `Int` that corresponds to machine type, just like the C++ `int`.

There are some subtleties that make this identification of types and sets tricky. There are problems with polymorphic functions that involve circular definitions, and with the fact that you can't have a set of all sets; but as I promised, I won't be a stickler for math. The great thing is that there is a category of sets, which is called **Set**, and we'll just work with it. In **Set**, objects are sets and morphisms (arrows) are functions.

**Set** is a very special category, because we can actually peek inside its objects and get a lot of intuitions from doing that. For instance, we know that an empty set has no elements. We know that there are special one-element sets. We know that functions map elements of one set to elements of another set. They can map two elements to one, but not one element to two. We know that an identity function maps each element of a set to itself, and so on. The plan is to gradually forget all this information and instead express all those notions in purely categorical terms, that is in terms of objects and arrows.

In the ideal world we would just say that Haskell types are sets and Haskell functions are mathematical functions between sets. There is just one little problem: A mathematical function does not execute any code — it just knows the answer. A Haskell function has to calculate the answer. It's not a problem if the answer can be obtained in a finite number of steps — however big that number might be. But there are some calculations that involve recursion, and those might never terminate. We can't just ban non-terminating functions from Haskell because distinguishing between terminating and non-terminating functions is undecidable — the famous halting problem. That's why computer scientists came up with a brilliant idea, or a major hack, depending on your point of view, to extend every type by one more special value called the *bottom* and denoted by _|_, or Unicode ⊥. This "value" corresponds to a non-terminating computation. So a function declared as:

```
f :: Bool -> Bool
```

may return `True`, `False`, or `_|_`; the latter meaning that it would never terminate.

Interestingly, once you accept the bottom as part of the type system, it is convenient to treat every runtime error as a bottom, and even allow functions to return the bottom explicitly. The latter is usually done using the expression `undefined`, as in:

```
f :: Bool -> Bool
f x = undefined
```

This definition type checks because `undefined` evaluates to bottom, which is a member of any type, including `Bool`. You can even write:

```
f :: Bool -> Bool
f = undefined
```

(without the x) because the bottom is also a member of the type `Bool -> Bool`.

Functions that may return bottom are called partial, as opposed to total functions, which return valid results for every possible argument.

Because of the bottom, you'll see the category of Haskell types and functions referred to as Hask rather than **Set**. From the theoretical point of view, this is the source of never-ending complications, so at this point I will use my butcher's knife and terminate this line of reasoning. From the pragmatic point of view, it's okay to ignore non-terminating functions and bottoms, and treat Hask as bona fide **Set**.[1]

## 2.4   Why Do We Need a Mathematical Model?

As a programmer you are intimately familiar with the syntax and grammar of your programming language. These aspects of the language are usually described using formal notation at the very beginning of the language spec. But the meaning, or semantics, of the language is much harder to describe; it takes many more pages, is rarely formal enough, and almost never complete. Hence the never ending discussions among language lawyers, and a whole cottage industry of books dedicated to the exegesis of the finer points of language standards.

---

[1]Nils Anders Danielsson, John Hughes, Patrik Jansson, Jeremy Gibbons, Fast and Loose Reasoning is Morally Correct. This paper provides justification for ignoring bottoms in most contexts.

There are formal tools for describing the semantics of a language but, because of their complexity, they are mostly used with simplified academic languages, not real-life programming behemoths. One such tool called *operational semantics* describes the mechanics of program execution. It defines a formalized idealized interpreter. The semantics of industrial languages, such as C++, is usually described using informal operational reasoning, often in terms of an "abstract machine."

The problem is that it's very hard to prove things about programs using operational semantics. To show a property of a program you essentially have to "run it" through the idealized interpreter.

It doesn't matter that programmers never perform formal proofs of correctness. We always "think" that we write correct programs. Nobody sits at the keyboard saying, "Oh, I'll just throw a few lines of code and see what happens." We think that the code we write will perform certain actions that will produce desired results. We are usually quite surprised when it doesn't. That means we do reason about programs we write, and we usually do it by running an interpreter in our heads. It's just really hard to keep track of all the variables. Computers are good at running programs — humans are not! If we were, we wouldn't need computers.

But there is an alternative. It's called *denotational semantics* and it's based on math. In denotational semantics every programming construct is given its mathematical interpretation. With that, if you want to prove a property of a program, you just prove a mathematical theorem. You might think that theorem proving is hard, but the fact is that we humans have been building up mathematical methods for thousands of years, so there is a wealth of accumulated knowledge to tap into. Also, as compared to the kind of theorems that professional mathematicians prove, the problems that we encounter in programming are usually quite simple, if not trivial.

Consider the definition of a factorial function in Haskell, which is a language quite amenable to denotational semantics:

```
fact n = product [1..n]
```

The expression [1..n] is a list of integers from 1 to n. The function product multiplies all elements of a list. That's just like a definition of factorial taken from a math text. Compare this with C:

```
int fact(int n) {
    int i;
```

```
    int result = 1;
    for (i = 2; i <= n; ++i)
        result *= i;
    return result;
}
```

Need I say more?

Okay, I'll be the first to admit that this was a cheap shot! A factorial function has an obvious mathematical denotation. An astute reader might ask: What's the mathematical model for reading a character from the keyboard or sending a packet across the network? For the longest time that would have been an awkward question leading to a rather convoluted explanation. It seemed like denotational semantics wasn't the best fit for a considerable number of important tasks that were essential for writing useful programs, and which could be easily tackled by operational semantics. The breakthrough came from category theory. Eugenio Moggi discovered that computational effect can be mapped to monads. This turned out to be an important observation that not only gave denotational semantics a new lease on life and made pure functional programs more usable, but also shed new light on traditional programming. I'll talk about monads later, when we develop more categorical tools.

One of the important advantages of having a mathematical model for programming is that it's possible to perform formal proofs of correctness of software. This might not seem so important when you're writing consumer software, but there are areas of programming where the price of failure may be exorbitant, or where human life is at stake. But even when writing web applications for the health system, you may appreciate the thought that functions and algorithms from the Haskell standard library come with proofs of correctness.

## 2.5  Pure and Dirty Functions

The things we call functions in C++ or any other imperative language, are not the same things mathematicians call functions. A mathematical function is just a mapping of values to values.

We can implement a mathematical function in a programming language: Such a function, given an input value will calculate the output value. A function to produce a square of a number will probably multiply the input value by itself. It will do it every time it's called, and it's guaranteed to produce the same output every time it's called with the same input. The square of a number doesn't change with the phases of the Moon.

Also, calculating the square of a number should not have a side effect of dispensing a tasty treat for your dog. A "function" that does that cannot be easily modelled as a mathematical function.

In programming languages, functions that always produce the same result given the same input and have no side effects are called *pure functions*. In a pure functional language like Haskell all functions are pure. Because of that, it's easier to give these languages denotational semantics and model them using category theory. As for other languages, it's always possible to restrict yourself to a pure subset, or reason about side effects separately. Later we'll see how monads let us model all kinds of effects using only pure functions. So we really don't lose anything by restricting ourselves to mathematical functions.

## 2.6   Examples of Types

Once you realize that types are sets, you can think of some rather exotic types. For instance, what's the type corresponding to an empty set? No, it's not C++ void, although this type *is* called Void in Haskell. It's a type that's not inhabited by any values. You can define a function that takes Void, but you can never call it. To call it, you would have to provide a value of the type Void, and there just aren't any. As for what this function can return, there are no restrictions whatsoever. It can return any type (although it never will, because it can't be called). In other words it's a function that's polymorphic in the return type. Haskellers have a name for it:

```
absurd :: Void -> a
```

(Remember, a is a type variable that can stand for any type.) The name is not coincidental. There is deeper interpretation of types and functions in terms of logic called the Curry-Howard isomorphism. The type Void represents falsity, and the type of the function absurd corresponds to the statement that from falsity follows anything, as in the Latin adage "ex falso sequitur quodlibet."

Next is the type that corresponds to a singleton set. It's a type that has only one possible value. This value just "is." You might not immediately recognise it as such, but that is the C++ void. Think of functions from and to this type. A function from void can always be called. If it's a pure function, it will always return the same result. Here's an example of such a function:

```
int f44() { return 44; }
```

You might think of this function as taking "nothing", but as we've just seen, a function that takes "nothing" can never be called because there is no value representing "nothing." So what does this function take? Conceptually, it takes a dummy value of which there is only one instance ever, so we don't have to mention it explicitly. In Haskell, however, there is a symbol for this value: an empty pair of parentheses, (). So, by a funny coincidence (or is it a coincidence?), the call to a function of void looks the same in C++ and in Haskell. Also, because of the Haskell's love of terseness, the same symbol () is used for the type, the constructor, and the only value corresponding to a singleton set. So here's this function in Haskell:

```
f44 :: () -> Integer
f44 () = 44
```

The first line declares that f44 takes the type (), pronounced "unit," into the type Integer. The second line defines f44 by pattern matching the only constructor for unit, namely (), and producing the number 44. You call this function by providing the unit value ():

```
f44 ()
```

Notice that every function of unit is equivalent to picking a single element from the target type (here, picking the Integer 44). In fact you could think of f44 as a different representation for the number 44. This is an example of how we can replace explicit mention of elements of a set by talking about functions (arrows) instead. Functions from unit to any type *A* are in one-to-one correspondence with the elements of that set *A*.

What about functions with the void return type, or, in Haskell, with the unit return type? In C++ such functions are used for side effects, but we know that these are not real functions in the mathematical sense of the word. A pure function that returns unit does nothing: it discards its argument.

Mathematically, a function from a set $A$ to a singleton set maps every element of $A$ to the single element of that singleton set. For every $A$ there is exactly one such function. Here's this function for Integer:

```
fInt :: Integer -> ()
fInt x = ()
```

You give it any integer, and it gives you back a unit. In the spirit of terseness, Haskell lets you use the wildcard pattern, the underscore, for an argument that is discarded. This way you don't have to invent a name for it. So the above can be rewritten as:

```
fInt :: Integer -> ()
fInt _ = ()
```

Notice that the implementation of this function not only doesn't depend on the value passed to it, but it doesn't even depend on the type of the argument.

Functions that can be implemented with the same formula for any type are called parametrically polymorphic. You can implement a whole family of such functions with one equation using a type parameter instead of a concrete type. What should we call a polymorphic function from any type to unit type? Of course we'll call it unit:

```
unit :: a -> ()
unit _ = ()
```

In C++ you would write this function as:

```
template<class T>
void unit(T) {}
```

Next in the typology of types is a two-element set. In C++ it's called bool and in Haskell, predictably, Bool. The difference is that in C++ bool is a built-in type, whereas in Haskell it can be defined as follows:

```
data Bool = True | False
```

(The way to read this definition is that Bool is either True or False.) In principle, one should also be able to define a Boolean type in C++ as an enumeration:

```
enum bool {
    true,
    false
};
```

but C++ `enum` is secretly an integer. The C++11 "`enum class`" could have been used instead, but then you would have to qualify its values with the class name, as in `bool::true` and `bool::false`, not to mention having to include the appropriate header in every file that uses it.

Pure functions from `Bool` just pick two values from the target type, one corresponding to `True` and another to `False`.

Functions to `Bool` are called *predicates*. For instance, the Haskell library `Data.Char` is full of predicates like `isAlpha` or `isDigit`. In C++ there is a similar library that defines, among others, `isalpha` and `isdigit`, but these return an `int` rather than a Boolean. The actual predicates are defined in `std::ctype` and have the form `ctype::is(alpha, c)`, `ctype::is(digit, c)`, etc.

## 2.7 Challenges

1. Define a higher-order function (or a function object) `memoize` in your favorite language. This function takes a pure function `f` as an argument and returns a function that behaves almost exactly like `f`, except that it only calls the original function once for every argument, stores the result internally, and subsequently returns this stored result every time it's called with the same argument. You can tell the memoized function from the original by watching its performance. For instance, try to memoize a function that takes a long time to evaluate. You'll have to wait for the result the first time you call it, but on subsequent calls, with the same argument, you should get the result immediately.
2. Try to memoize a function from your standard library that you normally use to produce random numbers. Does it work?
3. Most random number generators can be initialized with a seed. Implement a function that takes a seed, calls the random number generator with that seed, and returns the result. Memoize that function. Does it work?
4. Which of these C++ functions are pure? Try to memoize them and observe what happens when you call them multiple times: memoized and not.

(a) The factorial function from the example in the text.

(b) `std::getchar()`

(c)
```
bool f() {
        std::cout << "Hello!" << std::endl;
        return true;
}
```

(d)
```
int f(int x) {
        static int y = 0;
        y += x;
        return y;
}
```

5. How many different functions are there from `Bool` to `Bool`? Can you implement them all?

6. Draw a picture of a category whose only objects are the types `Void`, `()` (unit), and `Bool`; with arrows corresponding to all possible functions between these types. Label the arrows with the names of the functions.

# 3

# Categories Great and Small

YOU CAN GET real appreciation for categories by studying a variety of examples. Categories come in all shapes and sizes and often pop up in unexpected places. We'll start with something really simple.

## 3.1  No Objects

The most trivial category is one with zero objects and, consequently, zero morphisms. It's a very sad category by itself, but it may be important in the context of other categories, for instance, in the category of all categories (yes, there is one). If you think that an empty set makes sense, then why not an empty category?

## 3.2  Simple Graphs

You can build categories just by connecting objects with arrows. You can imagine starting with any directed graph and making it into a category by simply adding more arrows. First, add an identity arrow at each node. Then, for any two arrows such that the end of one coincides with the beginning of the other (in other words, any two *composable* arrows), add a new arrow to serve as their composition. Every time you add a new arrow, you have to also consider its composition with any other arrow (except for the identity arrows) and itself. You usually end up with infinitely many arrows, but that's okay.

Another way of looking at this process is that you're creating a category, which has an object for every node in the graph, and all possible *chains* of composable graph edges as morphisms. (You may even consider identity morphisms as special cases of chains of length zero.)

Such a category is called a *free category* generated by a given graph. It's an example of a free construction, a process of completing a given structure by extending it with a minimum number of items to satisfy its laws (here, the laws of a category). We'll see more examples of it in the future.

## 3.3 Orders

And now for something completely different! A category where a morphism is a relation between objects: the relation of being less than or equal. Let's check if it indeed is a category. Do we have identity morphisms? Every object is less than or equal to itself: check! Do we have composition? If $a \leq b$ and $b \leq c$ then $a \leq c$: check! Is composition associative? Check! A set with a relation like this is called a *preorder*, so a preorder is indeed a category.

You can also have a stronger relation, that satisfies an additional condition that, if $a \leq b$ and $b \leq a$ then $a$ must be the same as $b$. That's called a *partial order*.

Finally, you can impose the condition that any two objects are in a relation with each other, one way or another; and that gives you a *linear order* or *total order*.

Let's characterize these ordered sets as categories. A preorder is a category where there is at most one morphism going from any object $a$ to any object $b$. Another name for such a category is "thin." A preorder is a thin category.

A set of morphisms from object $a$ to object $b$ in a category $\mathbf{C}$ is called a *hom-set* and is written as $\mathbf{C}(a, b)$ (or, sometimes, $\text{Hom}_\mathbf{C}(a, b)$). So every hom-set in a preorder is either empty or a singleton. That includes the hom-set $\mathbf{C}(a, a)$, the set of morphisms from $a$ to $a$, which must be a singleton, containing only the identity, in any preorder. You may, however, have cycles in a preorder. Cycles are forbidden in a partial order.

It's very important to be able to recognize preorders, partial orders, and total orders because of sorting. Sorting algorithms, such as

24

quicksort, bubble sort, merge sort, etc., can only work correctly on total orders. Partial orders can be sorted using topological sort.

## 3.4  Monoid as Set

Monoid is an embarrassingly simple but amazingly powerful concept. It's the concept behind basic arithmetics: Both addition and multiplication form a monoid. Monoids are ubiquitous in programming. They show up as strings, lists, foldable data structures, futures in concurrent programming, events in functional reactive programming, and so on.

Traditionally, a monoid is defined as a set with a binary operation. All that's required from this operation is that it's associative, and that there is one special element that behaves like a unit with respect to it.

For instance, natural numbers with zero form a monoid under addition. Associativity means that:

$$(a + b) + c = a + (b + c)$$

(In other words, we can skip parentheses when adding numbers.)

The neutral element is zero, because:

$$0 + a = a$$

and

$$a + 0 = a$$

The second equation is redundant, because addition is commutative ($a + b = b + a$), but commutativity is not part of the definition of a monoid. For instance, string concatenation is not commutative and yet it forms a monoid. The neutral element for string concatenation, by the way, is an empty string, which can be attached to either side of a string without changing it.

In Haskell we can define a type class for monoids — a type for which there is a neutral element called mempty and a binary operation called mappend:

```
class Monoid m where
    mempty  :: m
    mappend :: m -> m -> m
```

The type signature for a two-argument function, m -> m -> m, might look strange at first, but it will make perfect sense after we talk about currying. You may interpret a signature with multiple arrows in two basic ways: as a function of multiple arguments, with the rightmost type being the return type; or as a function of one argument (the leftmost one), returning a function. The latter interpretation may be emphasized by adding parentheses (which are redundant, because the arrow is right-associative), as in: `m -> (m -> m)`. We'll come back to this interpretation in a moment.

Notice that, in Haskell, there is no way to express the monoidal properties of `mempty` and `mappend` (i.e., the fact that `mempty` is neutral and that `mappend` is associative). It's the responsibility of the programmer to make sure they are satisfied.

Haskell classes are not as intrusive as C++ classes. When you're defining a new type, you don't have to specify its class up front. You are free to procrastinate and declare a given type to be an instance of some class much later. As an example, let's declare `String` to be a monoid by providing the implementation of `mempty` and `mappend` (this is, in fact, done for you in the standard Prelude):

```
instance Monoid String where
    mempty = ""
    mappend = (++)
```

Here, we have reused the list concatenation operator (++), because a `String` is just a list of characters.

A word about Haskell syntax: Any infix operator can be turned into a two-argument function by surrounding it with parentheses. Given two strings, you can concatenate them by inserting ++ between them:

```
"Hello " ++ "world!"
```

or by passing them as two arguments to the parenthesized (++):

```
(++) "Hello " "world!"
```

Notice that arguments to a function are not separated by commas or surrounded by parentheses. (This is probably the hardest thing to get used to when learning Haskell.)

It's worth emphasizing that Haskell lets you express equality of functions, as in:

```
mappend = (++)
```

Conceptually, this is different than expressing the equality of values produced by functions, as in:

```
mappend s1 s2 = (++) s1 s2
```

The former translates into equality of morphisms in the category Hask (or **Set**, if we ignore bottoms, which is the name for never-ending calculations). Such equations are not only more succinct, but can often be generalized to other categories. The latter is called *extensional* equality, and states the fact that for any two input strings, the outputs of mappend and (++) are the same. Since the values of arguments are sometimes called *points* (as in: the value of $f$ at point $x$), this is called pointwise equality. Function equality without specifying the arguments is described as *point-free*. (Incidentally, point-free equations often involve composition of functions, which is symbolized by a point, so this might be a little confusing to the beginner.)

The closest one can get to declaring a monoid in C++ would be to use the (proposed) syntax for concepts.

```
template<class T>
  T mempty = delete;

template<class T>
  T mappend(T, T) = delete;

template<class M>
  concept bool Monoid = requires (M m) {
    { mempty<M> } -> M;
    { mappend(m, m); } -> M;
  };
```

The first definition uses a value template (also proposed). A polymorphic value is a family of values — a different value for every type.

The keyword delete means that there is no default value defined: It will have to be specified on a case-by-case basis. Similarly, there is no default for mappend.

The concept Monoid is a predicate (hence the bool type) that tests whether there exist appropriate definitions of mempty and mappend for a given type M.

An instantiation of the Monoid concept can be accomplished by providing appropriate specializations and overloads:

```
template<>
std::string mempty<std::string> = {""};

std::string mappend(std::string s1, std::string s2) {
    return s1 + s2;
}
```

## 3.5 Monoid as Category

That was the "familiar" definition of the monoid in terms of elements of a set. But as you know, in category theory we try to get away from sets and their elements, and instead talk about objects and morphisms. So let's change our perspective a bit and think of the application of the binary operator as "moving" or "shifting" things around the set.

For instance, there is the operation of adding 5 to every natural number. It maps 0 to 5, 1 to 6, 2 to 7, and so on. That's a function defined on the set of natural numbers. That's good: we have a function and a set. In general, for any number n there is a function of adding $n$ — the "adder" of $n$.

How do adders compose? The composition of the function that adds 5 with the function that adds 7 is a function that adds 12. So the composition of adders can be made equivalent to the rules of addition. That's good too: we can replace addition with function composition.

But wait, there's more: There is also the adder for the neutral element, zero. Adding zero doesn't move things around, so it's the identity function in the set of natural numbers.

Instead of giving you the traditional rules of addition, I could as well give you the rules of composing adders, without any loss of information. Notice that the composition of adders is associative, because the composition of functions is associative; and we have the zero adder corresponding to the identity function.

An astute reader might have noticed that the mapping from integers to adders follows from the second interpretation of the type signature of `mappend` as `m -> (m -> m)`. It tells us that `mappend` maps an element of a monoid set to a function acting on that set.

Now I want you to forget that you are dealing with the set of natural numbers and just think of it as a single object, a blob with a bunch of morphisms — the adders. A monoid is a single object category. In fact the name monoid comes from Greek *mono*, which means single.

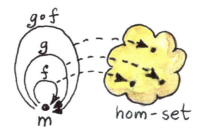

Monoid hom-set seen as morphisms and as points in a set.

Every monoid can be described as a single object category with a set of morphisms that follow appropriate rules of composition.

String concatenation is an interesting case, because we have a choice of defining right appenders and left appenders (or *prependers*, if you will). The composition tables of the two models are a mirror reverse of each other. You can easily convince yourself that appending "bar" after "foo" corresponds to prepending "foo" after prepending "bar".

You might ask the question whether every categorical monoid — a one-object category — defines a unique set-with-binary-operator monoid. It turns out that we can always extract a set from a single-object category. This set is the set of morphisms — the adders in our example. In other words, we have the hom-set $M(m, m)$ of the single object $m$ in the category $M$. We can easily define a binary operator in this set: The monoidal product of two set-elements is the element corresponding to the composition of the corresponding morphisms. If you give me two elements of $M(m, m)$ corresponding to $f$ and $g$, their product will correspond to the composition $f \circ g$. The composition always exists, because the source and the target for these morphisms are the same object. And it's associative by the rules of category. The identity morphism is the neutral element of this product. So we can always recover a set monoid from a category monoid. For all intents and purposes they are one and the same.

There is just one little nit for mathematicians to pick: morphisms don't have to form a set. In the world of categories there are things larger than sets. A category in which morphisms between any two objects form a set is called locally small. As promised, I will be mostly ignoring such subtleties, but I thought I should mention them for the record.

A lot of interesting phenomena in category theory have their root in the fact that elements of a hom-set can be seen both as morphisms, which follow the rules of composition, and as points in a set. Here, composition of morphisms in **M** translates into monoidal product in the set $\mathbf{M}(m, m)$.

## 3.6 Challenges

1. Generate a free category from:

   (a) A graph with one node and no edges
   (b) A graph with one node and one (directed) edge (hint: this edge can be composed with itself)
   (c) A graph with two nodes and a single arrow between them
   (d) A graph with a single node and 26 arrows marked with the letters of the alphabet: a, b, c ... z.

2. What kind of order is this?

   (a) A set of sets with the inclusion relation: $A$ is included in $B$ if every element of $A$ is also an element of $B$.
   (b) C++ types with the following subtyping relation: T1 is a subtype of T2 if a pointer to T1 can be passed to a function that expects a pointer to T2 without triggering a compilation error.

3. Considering that Bool is a set of two values True and False, show that it forms two (set-theoretical) monoids with respect to, respectively, operator && (AND) and || (OR).

4. Represent the Bool monoid with the AND operator as a category: List the morphisms and their rules of composition.

5. Represent addition modulo 3 as a monoid category.

# Kleisli Categories

You've seen how to model types and pure functions as a category. I also mentioned that there is a way to model side effects, or non-pure functions, in category theory. Let's have a look at one such example: functions that log or trace their execution. Something that, in an imperative language, would likely be implemented by mutating some global state, as in:

```
string logger;

bool negate(bool b) {
    logger += "Not so! ";
    return !b;
}
```

You know that this is not a pure function, because its memoized version would fail to produce a log. This function has *side effects*.

In modern programming, we try to stay away from global mutable state as much as possible — if only because of the complications of concurrency. And you would never put code like this in a library.

Fortunately for us, it's possible to make this function pure. You just have to pass the log explicitly, in and out. Let's do that by adding a string argument, and pairing regular output with a string that contains the updated log:

```
pair<bool, string> negate(bool b, string logger) {
    return make_pair(!b, logger + "Not so! ");
}
```

This function is pure, it has no side effects, it returns the same pair every time it's called with the same arguments, and it can be memoized if necessary. However, considering the cumulative nature of the log, you'd have to memoize all possible histories that can lead to a given call. There would be a separate memo entry for:

```
negate(true, "It was the best of times. ");
```

and

```
negate(true, "It was the worst of times. ");
```

and so on.

It's also not a very good interface for a library function. The callers are free to ignore the string in the return type, so that's not a huge burden; but they are forced to pass a string as input, which might be inconvenient.

Is there a way to do the same thing less intrusively? Is there a way to separate concerns? In this simple example, the main purpose of the function negate is to turn one Boolean into another. The logging is secondary. Granted, the message that is logged is specific to the function, but the task of aggregating the messages into one continuous log is a separate concern. We still want the function to produce a string, but we'd like to unburden it from producing a log. So here's the compromise solution:

```
pair<bool, string> negate(bool b) {
    return make_pair(!b, "Not so! ");
}
```

The idea is that the log will be aggregated *between* function calls.

To see how this can be done, let's switch to a slightly more realistic example. We have one function from string to string that turns lower case characters to upper case:

```
string toUpper(string s) {
    string result;
    int (*toupperp)(int) = &toupper; // toupper is overloaded
    transform(begin(s), end(s), back_inserter(result), toupperp);
    return result;
}
```

and another that splits a string into a vector of strings, breaking it on whitespace boundaries:

```
vector<string> toWords(string s) {
    return words(s);
}
```

The actual work is done in the auxiliary function words:

```
vector<string> words(string s) {
    vector<string> result{""};
    for (auto i = begin(s); i != end(s); ++i)
    {
        if (isspace(*i))
            result.push_back("");
        else
            result.back() += *i;
    }
    return result;
}
```

We want to modify the functions toUpper and toWords so that they piggyback a message string on top of their regular return values.

We will "embellish" the return values of these functions. Let's do it in a generic way by defining a template Writer that encapsulates a pair whose first component is a value of arbitrary type A and the second component is a string:

```
template<class A>
using Writer = pair<A, string>;
```

Here are the embellished functions:

```
Writer<string> toUpper(string s) {
    string result;
    int (*toupperp)(int) = &toupper;
    transform(begin(s), end(s), back_inserter(result), toupperp);
    return make_pair(result, "toUpper ");
```

```
}

Writer<vector<string>> toWords(string s) {
    return make_pair(words(s), "toWords ");
}
```

We want to compose these two functions into another embellished
function that uppercases a string and splits it into words, all the while
producing a log of those actions. Here's how we may do it:

```
Writer<vector<string>> process(string s) {
    auto p1 = toUpper(s);
    auto p2 = toWords(p1.first);
    return make_pair(p2.first, p1.second + p2.second);
}
```

We have accomplished our goal: The aggregation of the log is no longer
the concern of the individual functions. They produce their own messages, which are then, externally, concatenated into a larger log.

Now imagine a whole program written in this style. It's a nightmare
of repetitive, error-prone code. But we are programmers. We know how
to deal with repetitive code: we abstract it! This is, however, not your
run of the mill abstraction — we have to abstract *function composition*
itself. But composition is the essence of category theory, so before we
write more code, let's analyze the problem from the categorical point
of view.

## 4.1  The Writer Category

The idea of embellishing the return types of a bunch of functions in
order to piggyback some additional functionality turns out to be very
fruitful. We'll see many more examples of it. The starting point is our
regular category of types and functions. We'll leave the types as objects,
but redefine our morphisms to be the embellished functions.

For instance, suppose that we want to embellish the function isEven
that goes from int to bool. We turn it into a morphism that is represented by an embellished function. The important point is that this
morphism is still considered an arrow between the objects int and bool,
even though the embellished function returns a pair:

```
pair<bool, string> isEven(int n) {
    return make_pair(n % 2 == 0, "isEven ");
}
```

By the laws of a category, we should be able to compose this morphism with another morphism that goes from the object `bool` to whatever. In particular, we should be able to compose it with our earlier `negate`:

```
pair<bool, string> negate(bool b) {
    return make_pair(!b, "Not so! ");
}
```

Obviously, we cannot compose these two morphisms the same way we compose regular functions, because of the input/output mismatch. Their composition should look more like this:

```
pair<bool, string> isOdd(int n) {
    pair<bool, string> p1 = isEven(n);
    pair<bool, string> p2 = negate(p1.first);
    return make_pair(p2.first, p1.second + p2.second);
}
```

So here's the recipe for the composition of two morphisms in this new category we are constructing:

1. Execute the embellished function corresponding to the first morphism
2. Extract the first component of the result pair and pass it to the embellished function corresponding to the second morphism
3. Concatenate the second component (the string) of the first result and the second component (the string) of the second result
4. Return a new pair combining the first component of the final result with the concatenated string.

If we want to abstract this composition as a higher order function in C++, we have to use a template parameterized by three types corresponding to three objects in our category. It should take two embellished functions that are composable according to our rules, and return a third embellished function:

```
template<class A, class B, class C>
function<Writer<C>(A)> compose(function<Writer<B>(A)> m1,
                               function<Writer<C>(B)> m2)
{
    return [m1, m2](A x) {
        auto p1 = m1(x);
```

```
        auto p2 = m2(p1.first);
        return make_pair(p2.first, p1.second + p2.second);
    };
}
```

Now we can go back to our earlier example and implement the composition of toUpper and toWords using this new template:

```
Writer<vector<string>> process(string s) {
    return compose<string, string, vector<string>>(toUpper,
    ↪  toWords)(s);
}
```

There is still a lot of noise with the passing of types to the compose template. This can be avoided as long as you have a C++14-compliant compiler that supports generalized lambda functions with return type deduction (credit for this code goes to Eric Niebler):

```
auto const compose = [](auto m1, auto m2) {
    return [m1, m2](auto x) {
        auto p1 = m1(x);
        auto p2 = m2(p1.first);
        return make_pair(p2.first, p1.second + p2.second);
    };
};
```

In this new definition, the implementation of process simplifies to:

```
Writer<vector<string>> process(string s) {
    return compose(toUpper, toWords)(s);
}
```

But we are not finished yet. We have defined composition in our new category, but what are the identity morphisms? These are not our regular identity functions! They have to be morphisms from type A back to type A, which means they are embellished functions of the form:

```
Writer<A> identity(A);
```

They have to behave like units with respect to composition. If you look at our definition of composition, you'll see that an identity morphism should pass its argument without change, and only contribute an empty string to the log:

```
template<class A> Writer<A> identity(A x) {
    return make_pair(x, "");
}
```

You can easily convince yourself that the category we have just defined is indeed a legitimate category. In particular, our composition is trivially associative. If you follow what's happening with the first component of each pair, it's just a regular function composition, which is associative. The second components are being concatenated, and concatenation is also associative.

An astute reader may notice that it would be easy to generalize this construction to any monoid, not just the string monoid. We would use mappend inside compose and mempty inside identity (in place of + and ""). There really is no reason to limit ourselves to logging just strings. A good library writer should be able to identify the bare minimum of constraints that make the library work — here the logging library's only requirement is that the log have monoidal properties.

## 4.2  Writer in Haskell

The same thing in Haskell is a little more terse, and we also get a lot more help from the compiler. Let's start by defining the Writer type:

```
type Writer a = (a, String)
```

Here I'm just defining a type alias, an equivalent of a typedef (or using) in C++. The type Writer is parameterized by a type variable a and is equivalent to a pair of a and String. The syntax for pairs is minimal: just two items in parentheses, separated by a comma.

Our morphisms are functions from an arbitrary type to some Writer type:

```
a -> Writer b
```

We'll declare the composition as a funny infix operator, sometimes called the "fish":

```
(>=>) :: (a -> Writer b) -> (b -> Writer c) -> (a -> Writer c)
```

It's a function of two arguments, each being a function on its own, and returning a function. The first argument is of the type (a -> Writer b), the second is (b -> Writer c), and the result is (a -> Writer c).

Here's the definition of this infix operator — the two arguments m1 and m2 appearing on either side of the fishy symbol:

```
m1 >=> m2 = \x ->
    let (y, s1) = m1 x
        (z, s2) = m2 y
    in (z, s1 ++ s2)
```

The result is a lambda function of one argument x. The lambda is written as a backslash — think of it as the Greek letter λ with an amputated leg.

The `let` expression lets you declare auxiliary variables. Here the result of the call to m1 is pattern matched to a pair of variables (y, s1); and the result of the call to m2, with the argument y from the first pattern, is matched to (z, s2).

It is common in Haskell to pattern match pairs, rather than use accessors, as we did in C++. Other than that there is a pretty straightforward correspondence between the two implementations.

The overall value of the `let` expression is specified in its `in` clause: here it's a pair whose first component is z and the second component is the concatenation of two strings, s1++s2.

I will also define the identity morphism for our category, but for reasons that will become clear much later, I will call it `return`.

```
return :: a -> Writer a
return x = (x, "")
```

For completeness, let's have the Haskell versions of the embellished functions upCase and toWords:

```
upCase :: String -> Writer String
upCase s = (map toUpper s, "upCase ")

toWords :: String -> Writer [String]
toWords s = (words s, "toWords ")
```

The function map corresponds to the C++ transform. It applies the character function toUpper to the string s. The auxiliary function words is defined in the standard Prelude library.

Finally, the composition of the two functions is accomplished with the help of the fish operator:

```
process :: String -> Writer [String]
process = upCase >=> toWords
```

## 4.3　Kleisli Categories

You might have guessed that I haven't invented this category on the spot. It's an example of the so called Kleisli category — a category based on a monad. We are not ready to discuss monads yet, but I wanted to give you a taste of what they can do. For our limited purposes, a Kleisli category has, as objects, the types of the underlying programming language. Morphisms from type *A* to type *B* are functions that go from *A* to a type derived from *B* using the particular embellishment. Each Kleisli category defines its own way of composing such morphisms, as well as the identity morphisms with respect to that composition. (Later we'll see that the imprecise term "embellishment" corresponds to the notion of an endofunctor in a category.)

The particular monad that I used as the basis of the category in this post is called the *writer monad* and it's used for logging or tracing the execution of functions. It's also an example of a more general mechanism for embedding effects in pure computations. You've seen previously that we could model programming-language types and functions in the category of sets (disregarding bottoms, as usual). Here we have extended this model to a slightly different category, a category where morphisms are represented by embellished functions, and their composition does more than just pass the output of one function to the input of another. We have one more degree of freedom to play with: the composition itself. It turns out that this is exactly the degree of freedom which makes it possible to give simple denotational semantics to programs that in imperative languages are traditionally implemented using side effects.

## 4.4　Challenge

A function that is not defined for all possible values of its argument is called a partial function. It's not really a function in the mathematical sense, so it doesn't fit the standard categorical mold. It can, however, be represented by a function that returns an embellished type `optional`:

```
template<class A> class optional {
    bool _isValid;
    A _value;
public:
    optional()      : _isValid(false) {}
```

```
    optional(A v) : _isValid(true), _value(v) {}
    bool isValid() const { return _isValid; }
    A value() const { return _value; }
};
```

As an example, here's the implementation of the embellished function safe_root:

```
optional<double> safe_root(double x) {
    if (x >= 0) return optional<double>{sqrt(x)};
    else return optional<double>{};
}
```

Here's the challenge:

1. Construct the Kleisli category for partial functions (define composition and identity).
2. Implement the embellished function safe_reciprocal that returns a valid reciprocal of its argument, if it's different from zero.
3. Compose safe_root and safe_reciprocal to implement safe_root_reciprocal that calculates sqrt(1/x) whenever possible.

# 5

# Products and Coproducts

T HE ANCIENT GREEK playwright Euripides once said: "Every man is like the company he is wont to keep." We are defined by our relationships. Nowhere is this more true than in category theory. If we want to single out a particular object in a category, we can only do this by describing its pattern of relationships with other objects (and itself). These relationships are defined by morphisms.

There is a common construction in category theory called the *universal construction* for defining objects in terms of their relationships. One way of doing this is to pick a pattern, a particular shape constructed from objects and morphisms, and look for all its occurrences in the category. If it's a common enough pattern, and the category is large, chances are you'll have lots and lots of hits. The trick is to establish some kind of ranking among those hits, and pick what could be considered the best fit.

This process is reminiscent of the way we do web searches. A query is like a pattern. A very general query will give you large *recall*: lots of hits. Some may be relevant, others not. To eliminate irrelevant hits, you refine your query. That increases its *precision*. Finally, the search engine will rank the hits and, hopefully, the one result that you're interested in will be at the top of the list.

## 5.1 Initial Object

The simplest shape is a single object. Obviously, there are as many instances of this shape as there are objects in a given category. That's a lot to choose from. We need to establish some kind of ranking and try to find the object that tops this hierarchy. The only means at our disposal are morphisms. If you think of morphisms as arrows, then it's possible that there is an overall net flow of arrows from one end of the category to another. This is true in ordered categories, for instance in partial orders. We could generalize that notion of object precedence by saying that object *a* is "more initial" than object *b*, if there is an arrow (a morphism) going from *a* to *b*. We would then define *the* initial object as one that has arrows going to all other objects. Obviously there is no guarantee that such an object exists, and that's okay. A bigger problem is that there may be too many such objects: The recall is good, but precision is lacking. The solution is to take a hint from ordered categories — they allow at most one arrow between any two objects: there is only one way of being less-than or equal-to another object. Which leads us to this definition of the initial object:

> The **initial object** is the object that has one and only one morphism going to any object in the category.

However, even that doesn't guarantee the uniqueness of the initial object (if one exists). But it guarantees the next best thing: uniqueness *up to isomorphism*. Isomorphisms are very important in category theory, so I'll talk about them shortly. For now, let's just agree that uniqueness up to isomorphism justifies the use of "the" in the definition of the initial object.

Here are some examples: The initial object in a partially ordered set (often called a *poset*) is its least element. Some posets don't have an initial object — like the set of all integers, positive and negative, with less-than-or-equal relation for morphisms.

In the category of sets and functions, the initial object is the empty set. Remember, an empty set corresponds to the Haskell type Void (there is no corresponding type in C++) and the unique polymorphic function from Void to any other type is called absurd:

```
absurd :: Void -> a
```

It's this family of morphisms that makes Void the initial object in the category of types.

## 5.2  Terminal Object

Let's continue with the single-object pattern, but let's change the way we rank the objects. We'll say that object *a* is "more terminal" than object *b* if there is a morphism going from *b* to *a* (notice the reversal of direction). We'll be looking for an object that's more terminal than any other object in the category. Again, we will insist on uniqueness:

> The **terminal object** is the object with one and only one morphism coming to it from any object in the category.

And again, the terminal object is unique, up to isomorphism, which I will show shortly. But first let's look at some examples. In a poset, the terminal object, if it exists, is the biggest object. In the category of sets, the terminal object is a singleton. We've already talked about singletons — they correspond to the void type in C++ and the unit type

43

() in Haskell. It's a type that has only one value — implicit in C++ and explicit in Haskell, denoted by (). We've also established that there is one and only one pure function from any type to the unit type:

```
unit :: a -> ()
unit _ = ()
```

so all the conditions for the terminal object are satisfied.

Notice that in this example the uniqueness condition is crucial, because there are other sets (actually, all of them, except for the empty set) that have incoming morphisms from every set. For instance, there is a Boolean-valued function (a predicate) defined for every type:

```
yes :: a -> Bool
yes _ = True
```

But Bool is not a terminal object. There is at least one more Bool-valued function from every type:

```
no :: a -> Bool
no _ = False
```

Insisting on uniqueness gives us just the right precision to narrow down the definition of the terminal object to just one type.

## 5.3  Duality

You can't help but to notice the symmetry between the way we defined the initial object and the terminal object. The only difference between the two was the direction of morphisms. It turns out that for any category C we can define the *opposite category* $C^{op}$ just by reversing all the arrows. The opposite category automatically satisfies all the requirements of a category, as long as we simultaneously redefine composition. If original morphisms $f :: a \rightarrow b$ and $g :: b \rightarrow c$ composed to $h :: a \rightarrow c$ with $h = g \circ f$, then the reversed morphisms $f^{op} :: b \rightarrow a$ and $g^{op} :: c \rightarrow b$ will compose to $h^{op} :: c \rightarrow a$ with $h^{op} = f^{op} \circ g^{op}$. And reversing the identity arrows is a (pun alert!) no-op.

Duality is a very important property of categories because it doubles the productivity of every mathematician working in category theory. For every construction you come up with, there is its opposite; and for every theorem you prove, you get one for free. The constructions in the opposite category are often prefixed with "co", so you have products and coproducts, monads and comonads, cones and cocones, limits and colimits, and so on. There are no cocomonads though, because reversing the arrows twice gets us back to the original state.

It follows then that a terminal object is the initial object in the opposite category.

## 5.4 Isomorphisms

As programmers, we are well aware that defining equality is a non-trivial task. What does it mean for two objects to be equal? Do they have to occupy the same location in memory (pointer equality)? Or is it enough that the values of all their components are equal? Are two complex numbers equal if one is expressed as the real and imaginary part, and the other as modulus and angle? You'd think that mathematicians would have figured out the meaning of equality, but they haven't. They have the same problem of multiple competing definitions for equality. There is the propositional equality, intensional equality, extensional equality, and equality as a path in homotopy type theory. And then there are the weaker notions of isomorphism, and even weaker of equivalence.

The intuition is that isomorphic objects look the same — they have the same shape. It means that every part of one object corresponds to some part of another object in a one-to-one mapping. As far as our instruments can tell, the two objects are a perfect copy of each other. Mathematically it means that there is a mapping from object $a$ to object $b$, and there is a mapping from object $b$ back to object $a$, and they are the inverse of each other. In category theory we replace mappings with morphisms. An isomorphism is an invertible morphism; or a pair of morphisms, one being the inverse of the other.

We understand the inverse in terms of composition and identity: Morphism $g$ is the inverse of morphism $f$ if their composition is the identity morphism. These are actually two equations because there are two ways of composing two morphisms:

```
f . g = id
g . f = id
```

When I said that the initial (terminal) object was unique up to isomorphism, I meant that any two initial (terminal) objects are isomorphic.

That's actually easy to see. Let's suppose that we have two initial objects $i_1$ and $i_2$. Since $i_1$ is initial, there is a unique morphism $f$ from $i_1$ to $i_2$. By the same token, since $i_2$ is initial, there is a unique morphism $g$ from $i_2$ to $i_1$. What's the composition of these two morphisms?

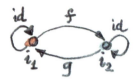

All morphisms in this diagram are unique.

The composition $g \circ f$ must be a morphism from $i_1$ to $i_1$. But $i_1$ is initial so there can only be one morphism going from $i_1$ to $i_1$. Since we are in a category, we know that there is an identity morphism from $i_1$ to $i_1$, and since there is room for only one, that must be it. Therefore $g \circ f$ is equal to identity. Similarly, $f \circ g$ must be equal to identity, because there can be only one morphism from $i_2$ back to $i_2$. This proves that $f$ and $g$ must be the inverse of each other. Therefore any two initial objects are isomorphic.

Notice that in this proof we used the uniqueness of the morphism from the initial object to itself. Without that we couldn't prove the "up to isomorphism" part. But why do we need the uniqueness of $f$ and $g$? Because not only is the initial object unique up to isomorphism, it is unique up to *unique* isomorphism. In principle, there could be more than one isomorphism between two objects, but that's not the case here. This "uniqueness up to unique isomorphism" is the important property of all universal constructions.

## 5.5 Products

The next universal construction is that of a product. We know what a Cartesian product of two sets is: it's a set of pairs. But what's the pattern that connects the product set with its constituent sets? If we can figure that out, we'll be able to generalize it to other categories.

All we can say is that there are two functions, the projections, from the product to each of the constituents. In Haskell, these two functions are called `fst` and `snd` and they pick, respectively, the first and the second component of a pair:

```
fst :: (a, b) -> a
fst (x, y) = x

snd :: (a, b) -> b
snd (x, y) = y
```

Here, the functions are defined by pattern matching their arguments: the pattern that matches any pair is (x, y), and it extracts its components into variables x and y.

These definitions can be simplified even further with the use of wildcards:

```
fst (x, _) = x
snd (_, y) = y
```

In C++, we would use template functions, for instance:

```
template<class A, class B> A
fst(pair<A, B> const & p) {
    return p.first;
}
```

Equipped with this seemingly very limited knowledge, let's try to define a pattern of objects and morphisms in the category of sets that will lead us to the construction of a product of two sets, *a* and *b*. This pattern consists of an object *c* and two morphisms *p* and *q* connecting it to *a* and *b*, respectively:

```
p :: c -> a
q :: c -> b
```

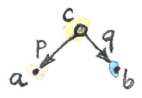

All *cs* that fit this pattern will be considered candidates for the product. There may be lots of them.

For instance, let's pick, as our constituents, two Haskell types, Int and
Bool, and get a sampling of candidates for their product.

Here's one: Int. Can Int be considered a candidate for the product
of Int and Bool? Yes, it can — and here are its projections:

```
p :: Int -> Int
p x = x

q :: Int -> Bool
q _ = True
```

That's pretty lame, but it matches the criteria.

Here's another one: (Int, Int, Bool). It's a tuple of three elements,
or a triple. Here are two morphisms that make it a legitimate candidate
(we are using pattern matching on triples):

```
p :: (Int, Int, Bool) -> Int
p (x, _, _) = x

q :: (Int, Int, Bool) -> Bool
q (_, _, b) = b
```

You may have noticed that while our first candidate was too small — it
only covered the Int dimension of the product; the second was too big
— it spuriously duplicated the Int dimension.

But we haven't explored yet the other part of the universal construction: the ranking. We want to be able to compare two instances
of our pattern. We want to compare one candidate object $c$ and its two
projections $p$ and $q$ with another candidate object $c'$ and its two projections $p'$ and $q'$. We would like to say that $c$ is "better" than $c'$ if there
is a morphism $m$ from $c'$ to $c$ — but that's too weak. We also want its
projections to be "better," or "more universal," than the projections of
$c'$. What it means is that the projections $p'$ and $q'$ can be reconstructed
from $p$ and $q$ using $m$:

```
p' = p . m
q' = q . m
```

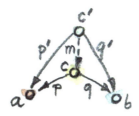

Another way of looking at these equations is that *m factorizes p'* and *q'*. Just pretend that these equations are in natural numbers, and the dot is multiplication: *m* is a common factor shared by *p'* and *q'*.

Just to build some intuitions, let me show you that the pair (Int, Bool) with the two canonical projections, fst and snd is indeed *better* than the two candidates I presented before.

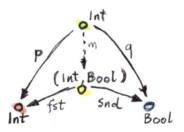

The mapping m for the first candidate is:

```
m :: Int -> (Int, Bool)
m x = (x, True)
```

Indeed, the two projections, p and q can be reconstructed as:

```
p x = fst (m x) = x
q x = snd (m x) = True
```

The m for the second example is similarly uniquely determined:

```
m (x, _, b) = (x, b)
```

We were able to show that (Int, Bool) is better than either of the two candidates. Let's see why the opposite is not true. Could we find some m' that would help us reconstruct fst and snd from p and q?

```
fst = p . m'
snd = q . m'
```

In our first example, q always returned True and we know that there are pairs whose second component is False. We can't reconstruct snd from q.

The second example is different: we retain enough information after running either p or q, but there is more than one way to factorize fst and snd. Because both p and q ignore the second component of the triple, our m' can put anything in it. We can have:

```
m' (x, b) = (x, x, b)
```

or

```
m' (x, b) = (x, 42, b)
```

and so on.

Putting it all together, given any type c with two projections p and q, there is a unique m from c to the Cartesian product (a, b) that factorizes them. In fact, it just combines p and q into a pair.

```
m :: c -> (a, b)
m x = (p x, q x)
```

That makes the Cartesian product (a, b) our best match, which means that this universal construction works in the category of sets. It picks the product of any two sets.

Now let's forget about sets and define a product of two objects in any category using the same universal construction. Such a product doesn't always exist, but when it does, it is unique up to a unique isomorphism.

> A **product** of two objects $a$ and $b$ is the object $c$ equipped
> with two projections such that for any other object $c'$ equipped
> with two projections there is a unique morphism $m$ from
> $c'$ to $c$ that factorizes those projections.

A (higher order) function that produces the factorizing function m from two candidates is sometimes called the *factorizer*. In our case, it would be the function:

```
factorizer :: (c -> a) -> (c -> b) -> (c -> (a, b))
factorizer p q = \x -> (p x, q x)
```

## 5.6 Coproduct

Like every construction in category theory, the product has a dual, which is called the coproduct. When we reverse the arrows in the product pattern, we end up with an object *c* equipped with two *injections*, i and j: morphisms from *a* and *b* to *c*.

```
i :: a -> c
j :: b -> c
```

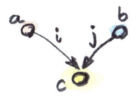

The ranking is also inverted: object *c* is "better" than object *c'* that is equipped with the injections *i'* and *j'* if there is a morphism *m* from *c* to *c'* that factorizes the injections:

```
i' = m . i
j' = m . j
```

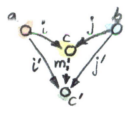

The "best" such object, one with a unique morphism connecting it to any other pattern, is called a coproduct and, if it exists, is unique up to unique isomorphism.

> A **coproduct** of two objects *a* and *b* is the object *c* equipped with two injections such that for any other object *c'* equipped with two injections there is a unique morphism *m* from *c* to *c'* that factorizes those injections.

In the category of sets, the coproduct is the *disjoint union* of two sets. An element of the disjoint union of *a* and *b* is either an element of *a* or an element of *b*. If the two sets overlap, the disjoint union contains two copies of the common part. You can think of an element of a disjoint union as being tagged with an identifier that specifies its origin.

For a programmer, it's easier to understand a coproduct in terms of types: it's a tagged union of two types. C++ supports unions, but they are not tagged. It means that in your program you have to somehow keep track which member of the union is valid. To create a tagged union, you have to define a tag — an enumeration — and combine it with the union. For instance, a tagged union of an `int` and a `char const *` could be implemented as:

```
struct Contact {
    enum { isPhone, isEmail } tag;
    union { int phoneNum; char const * emailAddr; };
};
```

The two injections can either be implemented as constructors or as functions. For instance, here's the first injection as a function `PhoneNum`:

```
Contact PhoneNum(int n) {
    Contact c;
    c.tag = isPhone;
    c.phoneNum = n;
    return c;
}
```

It injects an integer into `Contact`.

A tagged union is also called a *variant*, and there is a very general implementation of a variant in the boost library, `boost::variant`.

In Haskell, you can combine any data types into a tagged union by separating data constructors with a vertical bar. The `Contact` example translates into the declaration:

```
data Contact = PhoneNum Int | EmailAddr String
```

Here, `PhoneNum` and `EmailAddr` serve both as constructors (injections), and as tags for pattern matching (more about this later). For instance, this is how you would construct a contact using a phone number:

```
helpdesk :: Contact
helpdesk = PhoneNum 2222222
```

Unlike the canonical implementation of the product that is built into Haskell as the primitive pair, the canonical implementation of the co-product is a data type called Either, which is defined in the standard Prelude as:

```
data Either a b = Left a | Right b
```

It is parameterized by two types, a and b and has two constructors: Left that takes a value of type a, and Right that takes a value of type b.

Just as we've defined the factorizer for a product, we can define one for the coproduct. Given a candidate type c and two candidate injections i and j, the factorizer for Either produces the factoring function:

```
factorizer :: (a -> c) -> (b -> c) -> Either a b -> c
factorizer i j (Left a)  = i a
factorizer i j (Right b) = j b
```

## 5.7 Asymmetry

We've seen two sets of dual definitions: The definition of a terminal object can be obtained from the definition of the initial object by reversing the direction of arrows; in a similar way, the definition of the coproduct can be obtained from that of the product. Yet in the category of sets the initial object is very different from the final object, and coproduct is very different from product. We'll see later that product behaves like multiplication, with the terminal object playing the role of one; whereas coproduct behaves more like the sum, with the initial object playing the role of zero. In particular, for finite sets, the size of the product is the product of the sizes of individual sets, and the size of the coproduct is the sum of the sizes.

This shows that the category of sets is not symmetric with respect to the inversion of arrows.

Notice that while the empty set has a unique morphism to any set (the absurd function), it has no morphisms coming back. The singleton set has a unique morphism coming to it from any set, but it *also* has outgoing morphisms to every set (except for the empty one). As we've seen before, these outgoing morphisms from the terminal object play a very important role of picking elements of other sets (the empty set has no elements, so there's nothing to pick).

It's the relationship of the singleton set to the product that sets it apart from the coproduct. Consider using the singleton set, represented by the unit type (), as yet another — vastly inferior — candidate for the product pattern. Equip it with two projections p and q: functions from the singleton to each of the constituent sets. Each selects a concrete element from either set. Because the product is universal, there is also a (unique) morphism m from our candidate, the singleton, to the product. This morphism selects an element from the product set — it selects a concrete pair. It also factorizes the two projections:

```
p = fst . m
q = snd . m
```

When acting on the singleton value (), the only element of the singleton set, these two equations become:

```
p () = fst (m ())
q () = snd (m ())
```

Since m () is the element of the product picked by m, these equations tell us that the element picked by p from the first set, p (), is the first component of the pair picked by m. Similarly, q () is equal to the second component. This is in total agreement with our understanding that elements of the product are pairs of elements from the constituent sets.

There is no such simple interpretation of the coproduct. We could try the singleton set as a candidate for a coproduct, in an attempt to extract the elements from it, but there we would have two injections going into it rather than two projections coming out of it. They'd tell us nothing about their sources (in fact, we've seen that they ignore the input parameter). Neither would the unique morphism from the coproduct to our singleton. The category of sets just looks very different when seen from the direction of the initial object than it does when seen from the terminal end.

This is not an intrinsic property of sets, it's a property of functions, which we use as morphisms in **Set**. Functions are, in general, asymmetric. Let me explain.

A function must be defined for every element of its domain set (in programming, we call it a *total* function), but it doesn't have to cover the whole codomain. We've seen some extreme cases of it: functions from a singleton set — functions that select just a single element in the codomain. (Actually, functions from an empty set are the real extremes.) When the size of the domain is much smaller than the size of the codomain, we often think of such functions as embedding the domain in the codomain. For instance, we can think of a function from a singleton set as embedding its single element in the codomain. I call them *embedding* functions, but mathematicians prefer to give a name to the opposite: functions that tightly fill their codomains are called *surjective* or *onto*.

The other source of asymmetry is that functions are allowed to map many elements of the domain set into one element of the codomain. They can collapse them. The extreme case are functions that map whole sets into a singleton. You've seen the polymorphic `unit` function that does just that. The collapsing can only be compounded by composition. A composition of two collapsing functions is even more collapsing than the individual functions. Mathematicians have a name for non-collapsing functions: they call them *injective* or *one-to-one*.

Of course there are some functions that are neither embedding nor collapsing. They are called *bijections* and they are truly symmetric, because they are invertible. In the category of sets, an isomorphism is the same as a bijection.

## 5.8  Challenges

1. Show that the terminal object is unique up to unique isomorphism.
2. What is a product of two objects in a poset? Hint: Use the universal construction.
3. What is a coproduct of two objects in a poset?
4. Implement the equivalent of Haskell `Either` as a generic type in your favorite language (other than Haskell).
5. Show that `Either` is a "better" coproduct than `int` equipped with two injections:

   ```
   int i(int n) { return n; }
   int j(bool b) { return b ? 0: 1; }
   ```

   Hint: Define a function

   ```
   int m(Either const & e);
   ```

   that factorizes i and j.
6. Continuing the previous problem: How would you argue that `int` with the two injections i and j cannot be "better" than `Either`?

7. Still continuing: What about these injections?

```
int i(int n) {
    if (n < 0) return n;
    return n + 2;
}

int j(bool b) { return b ? 0: 1; }
```

8. Come up with an inferior candidate for a coproduct of int and bool that cannot be better than Either because it allows multiple acceptable morphisms from it to Either.

## 5.9 Bibliography

1. The Catsters, Products and Coproducts[1] video.

---

[1]https://www.youtube.com/watch?v=upCSDIO9pjc

# 6

# Simple Algebraic Data Types

W E'VE SEEN TWO BASIC ways of combining types: using a product and a coproduct. It turns out that a lot of data structures in everyday programming can be built using just these two mechanisms. This fact has important practical consequences. Many properties of data structures are composable. For instance, if you know how to compare values of basic types for equality, and you know how to generalize these comparisons to product and coproduct types, you can automate the derivation of equality operators for composite types. In Haskell you can automatically derive equality, comparison, conversion to and from string, and more, for a large subset of composite types.

Let's have a closer look at product and sum types as they appear in programming.

## 6.1  Product Types

The canonical implementation of a product of two types in a programming language is a pair. In Haskell, a pair is a primitive type constructor; in C++ it's a relatively complex template defined in the Standard Library.

Pairs are not strictly commutative: a pair (Int, Bool) cannot be substituted for a pair (Bool, Int), even though they carry the same information. They are, however, commutative up to isomorphism — the isomorphism being given by the swap function (which is its own inverse):

```
swap :: (a, b) -> (b, a)
swap (x, y) = (y, x)
```

You can think of the two pairs as simply using a different format for storing the same data. It's just like big endian vs. little endian.

You can combine an arbitrary number of types into a product by nesting pairs inside pairs, but there is an easier way: nested pairs are equivalent to tuples. It's the consequence of the fact that different ways of nesting pairs are isomorphic. If you want to combine three types in a product, a, b, and c, in this order, you can do it in two ways:

```
((a, b), c)
```

or

```
(a, (b, c))
```

These types are different — you can't pass one to a function that expects the other — but their elements are in one-to-one correspondence. There is a function that maps one to another:

```
alpha :: ((a, b), c) -> (a, (b, c))
alpha ((x, y), z) = (x, (y, z))
```

and this function is invertible:

```
alpha_inv :: (a, (b, c)) -> ((a, b), c)
alpha_inv (x, (y, z)) = ((x, y), z)
```

so it's an isomorphism. These are just different ways of repackaging the same data.

You can interpret the creation of a product type as a binary operation on types. From that perspective, the above isomorphism looks very much like the associativity law we've seen in monoids:

$$(a * b) * c = a * (b * c)$$

Except that, in the monoid case, the two ways of composing products were equal, whereas here they are only equal "up to isomorphism."

If we can live with isomorphisms, and don't insist on strict equality, we can go even further and show that the unit type, (), is the unit of the product the same way 1 is the unit of multiplication. Indeed, the pairing of a value of some type a with a unit doesn't add any information. The type:

```
(a, ())
```

is isomorphic to a. Here's the isomorphism:

```
rho :: (a, ()) -> a
rho (x, ()) = x

rho_inv :: a -> (a, ())
rho_inv x = (x, ())
```

These observations can be formalized by saying that **Set** (the category of sets) is a *monoidal category*. It's a category that's also a monoid, in the sense that you can multiply objects (here, take their Cartesian product). I'll talk more about monoidal categories, and give the full definition in the future.

There is a more general way of defining product types in Haskell — especially, as we'll see soon, when they are combined with sum types. It uses named constructors with multiple arguments. A pair, for instance, can be defined alternatively as:

```
data Pair a b = P a b
```

Here, Pair a b is the name of the type parameterized by two other types, a and b; and P is the name of the data constructor. You define a pair type by passing two types to the Pair type constructor. You construct a pair value by passing two values of appropriate types to the constructor P. For instance, let's define a value stmt as a pair of String and Bool:

```
stmt :: Pair String Bool
stmt = P "This statements is" False
```

The first line is the type declaration. It uses the type constructor Pair, with String and Bool replacing a and the b in the generic definition of `Pair`. The second line defines the actual value by passing a concrete string and a concrete Boolean to the data constructor `P`. Type constructors are used to construct types; data constructors, to construct values.

Since the name spaces for type and data constructors are separate in Haskell, you will often see the same name used for both, as in:

```
data Pair a b = Pair a b
```

And if you squint hard enough, you may even view the built-in pair type as a variation on this kind of declaration, where the name `Pair` is replaced with the binary operator `(,)`. In fact you can use `(,)` just like any other named constructor and create pairs using prefix notation:

```
stmt = (,) "This statement is" False
```

Similarly, you can use `(,,)` to create triples, and so on.

Instead of using generic pairs or tuples, you can also define specific named product types, as in:

```
data Stmt = Stmt String Bool
```

which is just a product of `String` and `Bool`, but it's given its own name and constructor. The advantage of this style of declaration is that you may define many types that have the same content but different meaning and functionality, and which cannot be substituted for each other.

Programming with tuples and multi-argument constructors can get messy and error prone — keeping track of which component represents what. It's often preferable to give names to components. A product type with named fields is called a record in Haskell, and a `struct` in C.

## 6.2  Records

Let's have a look at a simple example. We want to describe chemical elements by combining two strings, name and symbol; and an integer, the atomic number; into one data structure. We can use a tuple `(String, String, Int)` and remember which component represents what. We would extract components by pattern matching, as in this function that checks if the symbol of the element is the prefix of its name (as in **He** being the prefix of **Helium**):

```
startsWithSymbol :: (String, String, Int) -> Bool
startsWithSymbol (name, symbol, _) = isPrefixOf symbol name
```

This code is error prone, and is hard to read and maintain. It's much better to define a record:

```
data Element = Element { name :: String
                       , symbol :: String
                       , atomicNumber :: Int }
```

The two representations are isomorphic, as witnessed by these two conversion functions, which are the inverse of each other:

```
tupleToElem :: (String, String, Int) -> Element
tupleToElem (n, s, a) = Element { name = n
                                , symbol = s
                                , atomicNumber = a }

elemToTuple :: Element -> (String, String, Int)
elemToTuple e = (name e, symbol e, atomicNumber e)
```

Notice that the names of record fields also serve as functions to access these fields. For instance, atomicNumber e retrieves the atomicNumber field from e. We use atomicNumber as a function of the type:

```
atomicNumber :: Element -> Int
```

With the record syntax for Element, our function startsWithSymbol becomes more readable:

```
startsWithSymbol :: Element -> Bool
startsWithSymbol e = isPrefixOf (symbol e) (name e)
```

We could even use the Haskell trick of turning the function isPrefixOf into an infix operator by surrounding it with backquotes, and make it read almost like a sentence:

```
startsWithSymbol e = symbol e `isPrefixOf` name e
```

The parentheses could be omitted in this case, because an infix operator has lower precedence than a function call.

## 6.3 Sum Types

Just as the product in the category of sets gives rise to product types, the coproduct gives rise to sum types. The canonical implementation of a sum type in Haskell is:

```
data Either a b = Left a | Right b
```

And like pairs, `Either`s are commutative (up to isomorphism), can be nested, and the nesting order is irrelevant (up to isomorphism). So we can, for instance, define a sum equivalent of a triple:

```
data OneOfThree a b c = Sinistral a | Medial b | Dextral c
```

and so on.

It turns out that **Set** is also a (symmetric) monoidal category with respect to coproduct. The role of the binary operation is played by the disjoint sum, and the role of the unit element is played by the initial object. In terms of types, we have `Either` as the monoidal operator and `Void`, the uninhabited type, as its neutral element. You can think of `Either` as plus, and `Void` as zero. Indeed, adding `Void` to a sum type doesn't change its content. For instance:

```
Either a Void
```

is isomorphic to a. That's because there is no way to construct a `Right` version of this type — there isn't a value of type `Void`. The only inhabitants of `Either a Void` are constructed using the `Left` constructors and they simply encapsulate a value of type a. So, symbolically, $a + 0 = a$.

Sum types are pretty common in Haskell, but their C++ equivalents, unions or variants, are much less common. There are several reasons for that.

First of all, the simplest sum types are just enumerations and are implemented using `enum` in C++. The equivalent of the Haskell sum type:

```
data Color = Red | Green | Blue
```

is the C++:

```
enum { Red, Green, Blue };
```

An even simpler sum type:

```
data Bool = True | False
```

is the primitive bool in C++.

Simple sum types that encode the presence or absence of a value are variously implemented in C++ using special tricks and "impossible" values, like empty strings, negative numbers, null pointers, etc. This kind of optionality, if deliberate, is expressed in Haskell using the Maybe type:

```
data Maybe a = Nothing | Just a
```

The Maybe type is a sum of two types. You can see this if you separate the two constructors into individual types. The first one would look like this:

```
data NothingType = Nothing
```

It's an enumeration with one value called Nothing. In other words, it's a singleton, which is equivalent to the unit type (). The second part:

```
data JustType a = Just a
```

is just an encapsulation of the type a. We could have encoded Maybe as:

```
data Maybe a = Either () a
```

More complex sum types are often faked in C++ using pointers. A pointer can be either null, or point to a value of specific type. For instance, a Haskell list type, which can be defined as a (recursive) sum type:

```
data List a = Nil | Cons a (List a)
```

can be translated to C++ using the null pointer trick to implement the empty list:

```
template<class A>
class List {
    Node<A> * _head;
public:
    List() : _head(nullptr) {} // Nil
    List(A a, List<A> l)        // Cons
      : _head(new Node<A>(a, l))
    {}
};
```

Notice that the two Haskell constructors Nil and Cons are translated into two overloaded List constructors with analogous arguments (none, for Nil; and a value and a list for Cons). The List class doesn't need a tag to distinguish between the two components of the sum type. Instead it uses the special nullptr value for _head to encode Nil.

The main difference, though, between Haskell and C++ types is that Haskell data structures are immutable. If you create an object using one particular constructor, the object will forever remember which constructor was used and what arguments were passed to it. So a Maybe object that was created as Just "energy" will never turn into Nothing. Similarly, an empty list will forever be empty, and a list of three elements will always have the same three elements.

It's this immutability that makes construction reversible. Given an object, you can always disassemble it down to parts that were used in its construction. This deconstruction is done with pattern matching and it reuses constructors as patterns. Constructor arguments, if any, are replaced with variables (or other patterns).

The List data type has two constructors, so the deconstruction of an arbitrary List uses two patterns corresponding to those constructors. One matches the empty Nil list, and the other a Cons-constructed list. For instance, here's the definition of a simple function on Lists:

```
maybeTail :: List a -> Maybe (List a)
maybeTail Nil = Nothing
maybeTail (Cons _ t) = Just t
```

The first part of the definition of maybeTail uses the Nil constructor as pattern and returns Nothing. The second part uses the Cons constructor as pattern. It replaces the first constructor argument with a wildcard, because we are not interested in it. The second argument to Cons is bound to the variable t (I will call these things variables even though, strictly speaking, they never vary: once bound to an expression, a variable never changes). The return value is Just t. Now, depending on how your List was created, it will match one of the clauses. If it was created using Cons, the two arguments that were passed to it will be retrieved (and the first discarded).

Even more elaborate sum types are implemented in C++ using polymorphic class hierarchies. A family of classes with a common ancestor may be understood as one variant type, in which the vtable serves as a hidden tag. What in Haskell would be done by pattern matching on the constructor, and by calling specialized code, in C++ is accomplished by dispatching a call to a virtual function based on the vtable pointer.

You will rarely see `union` used as a sum type in C++ because of severe limitations on what can go into a union. You can't even put a `std::string` into a union because it has a copy constructor.

## 6.4  Algebra of Types

Taken separately, product and sum types can be used to define a variety of useful data structures, but the real strength comes from combining the two. Once again we are invoking the power of composition.

Let's summarize what we've discovered so far. We've seen two commutative monoidal structures underlying the type system: We have the sum types with `Void` as the neutral element, and the product types with the unit type, (), as the neutral element. We'd like to think of them as analogous to addition and multiplication. In this analogy, `Void` would correspond to zero, and unit, (), to one.

Let's see how far we can stretch this analogy. For instance, does multiplication by zero give zero? In other words, is a product type with one component being `Void` isomorphic to `Void`? For example, is it possible to create a pair of, say `Int` and `Void`?

To create a pair you need two values. Although you can easily come up with an integer, there is no value of type `Void`. Therefore, for any type a, the type (a, `Void`) is uninhabited — has no values — and is therefore equivalent to `Void`. In other words, $a \times 0 = 0$.

Another thing that links addition and multiplication is the distributive property:

$$a \times (b + c) = a \times b + a \times c$$

Does it also hold for product and sum types? Yes, it does — up to isomorphisms, as usual. The left hand side corresponds to the type:

```
(a, Either b c)
```

and the right hand side corresponds to the type:

```
Either (a, b) (a, c)
```

Here's the function that converts them one way:

```
prodToSum :: (a, Either b c) -> Either (a, b) (a, c)
prodToSum (x, e) =
    case e of
      Left  y -> Left  (x, y)
      Right z -> Right (x, z)
```

and here's one that goes the other way:

```
sumToProd :: Either (a, b) (a, c) -> (a, Either b c)
sumToProd e =
    case e of
      Left  (x, y) -> (x, Left  y)
      Right (x, z) -> (x, Right z)
```

The case of statement is used for pattern matching inside functions. Each pattern is followed by an arrow and the expression to be evaluated when the pattern matches. For instance, if you call prodToSum with the value:

```
prod1 :: (Int, Either String Float)
prod1 = (2, Left "Hi!")
```

the e in case e of will be equal to Left "Hi!". It will match the pattern Left y, substituting "Hi!" for y. Since the x has already been matched to 2, the result of the case of clause, and the whole function, will be Left (2, "Hi!"), as expected.

I'm not going to prove that these two functions are the inverse of each other, but if you think about it, they must be! They are just trivially re-packing the contents of the two data structures. It's the same data, only different format.

Mathematicians have a name for two such intertwined monoids: it's called a *semiring*. It's not a full *ring*, because we can't define subtraction of types. That's why a semiring is sometimes called a *rig*, which is a pun on "ring without an *n*" (negative). But barring that, we can get a lot of mileage from translating statements about, say, natural numbers, which form a rig, to statements about types. Here's a translation table with some entries of interest:

| Numbers | Types |
| --- | --- |
| 0 | Void |
| 1 | () |

| Numbers | Types |
| --- | --- |
| $a + b$ | `Either a b = Left a | Right b` |
| $a \times b$ | `(a, b)` or `Pair a b = Pair a b` |
| $2 = 1 + 1$ | `data Bool = True | False` |
| $1 + a$ | `data Maybe = Nothing | Just a` |

The list type is quite interesting, because it's defined as a solution to an equation. The type we are defining appears on both sides of the equation:

```
data List a = Nil | Cons a (List a)
```

If we do our usual substitutions, and also replace `List a` with x, we get the equation:

```
x = 1 + a * x
```

We can't solve it using traditional algebraic methods because we can't subtract or divide types. But we can try a series of substitutions, where we keep replacing x on the right hand side with (1 + a*x), and use the distributive property. This leads to the following series:

```
x = 1 + a*x
x = 1 + a*(1 + a*x) = 1 + a + a*a*x
x = 1 + a + a*a*(1 + a*x) = 1 + a + a*a + a*a*a*x
...
x = 1 + a + a*a + a*a*a + a*a*a*a...
```

We end up with an infinite sum of products (tuples), which can be interpreted as: A list is either empty, 1; or a singleton, a; or a pair, a*a; or a triple, a*a*a; etc... Well, that's exactly what a list is — a string of as!

There's much more to lists than that, and we'll come back to them and other recursive data structures after we learn about functors and fixed points.

Solving equations with symbolic variables — that's algebra! It's what gives these types their name: algebraic data types.

Finally, I should mention one very important interpretation of the algebra of types. Notice that a product of two types a and b must contain both a value of type a *and* a value of type b, which means both types must be inhabited. A sum of two types, on the other hand, contains either a value of type a *or* a value of type b, so it's enough if one of them is inhabited. Logical *and* and *or* also form a semiring, and it too can be mapped into type theory:

| Logic | Types |
|-------|-------|
| false | `Void` |
| true | `()` |
| $a \parallel b$ | `Either a b = Left a | Right b` |
| $a \&\& b$ | `(a, b)` |

This analogy goes deeper, and is the basis of the Curry-Howard isomorphism between logic and type theory. We'll come back to it when we talk about function types.

## 6.5  Challenges

1. Show the isomorphism between `Maybe` a and `Either` `()` a.
2. Here's a sum type defined in Haskell:

```
data Shape = Circle Float
           | Rect Float Float
```

When we want to define a function like `area` that acts on a `Shape`, we do it by pattern matching on the two constructors:

```
area :: Shape -> Float
area (Circle r) = pi * r * r
area (Rect d h) = d * h
```

Implement `Shape` in C++ or Java as an interface and create two classes: `Circle` and `Rect`. Implement `area` as a virtual function.

3. Continuing with the previous example: We can easily add a new function `circ` that calculates the circumference of a `Shape`. We can do it without touching the definition of `Shape`:

```
circ :: Shape -> Float
circ (Circle r) = 2.0 * pi * r
circ (Rect d h) = 2.0 * (d + h)
```

Add `circ` to your C++ or Java implementation. What parts of the original code did you have to touch?

4. Continuing further: Add a new shape, Square, to Shape and make all the necessary updates. What code did you have to touch in Haskell vs. C++ or Java? (Even if you're not a Haskell programmer, the modifications should be pretty obvious.)

5. Show that $a + a = 2 \times a$ holds for types (up to isomorphism). Remember that 2 corresponds to Bool, according to our translation table.

# 7

# Functors

$A$T THE RISK OF SOUNDING like a broken record, I will say this about
functors: A functor is a very simple but powerful idea. Category
theory is just full of those simple but powerful ideas. A functor is a
mapping between categories. Given two categories, **C** and **D**, a functor
$F$ maps objects in **C** to objects in **D** — it's a function on objects. If $a$ is
an object in **C**, we'll write its image in **D** as $Fa$ (no parentheses). But a
category is not just objects — it's objects and morphisms that connect
them. A functor also maps morphisms — it's a function on morphisms.
But it doesn't map morphisms willy-nilly — it preserves connections.
So if a morphism $f$ in **C** connects object $a$ to object $b$,

$$f :: a \rightarrow b$$

the image of $f$ in **D**, $Ff$, will connect the image of $a$ to the image of $b$:

$$Ff :: Fa \rightarrow Fb$$

(This is a mixture of mathematical and
Haskell notation that hopefully makes sense by
now. I won't use parentheses when applying
functors to objects or morphisms.)

As you can see, a functor preserves the
structure of a category: what's connected in
one category will be connected in the other category. But there's something more to the struc-
ture of a category: there's also the composition of morphisms. If $h$ is a

composition of $f$ and $g$:

$$h = g.f$$

we want its image under $F$ to be a composition of the images of $f$ and $g$:

$$Fh = Fg \cdot Ff$$

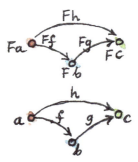

Finally, we want all identity morphisms in C to be mapped to identity morphisms in **D**:

$$Fid_a = id_{Fa}$$

Here, $id_a$ is the identity at the object $a$, and $id_{Fa}$ the identity at $Fa$. Note that these conditions make functors much more restrictive than regular functions. Functors must preserve the structure of a category. If you picture a category as a collection of objects held together by a network of morphisms, a functor is not allowed to introduce any tears into this fabric. It may smash objects together, it may glue multiple morphisms into one, but it may never break things apart. This no-tearing constraint is similar to the continuity condition you might know from calculus. In this

sense functors are "continuous" (although there exists an even more restrictive notion of continuity for functors). Just like functions, functors may do both collapsing and embedding. The embedding aspect is more prominent when the source category is much smaller than the target category. In the extreme, the source can be the trivial singleton category — a category with one object and one morphism (the identity). A functor from the singleton category to any other category simply selects an object in that category. This is fully analogous to the property of morphisms from singleton sets selecting elements in target sets. The maximally collapsing functor is called the constant functor $\Delta_c$. It maps every object in the source category to one selected object $c$ in the target category. It also maps every morphism in the source category to the identity morphism $id_c$. It acts like a black hole, compacting everything into one singularity. We'll see more of this functor when we discuss limits and colimits.

## 7.1 Functors in Programming

Let's get down to earth and talk about programming. We have our category of types and functions. We can talk about functors that map this category into itself — such functors are called endofunctors. So what's an endofunctor in the category of types? First of all, it maps types to types. We've seen examples of such mappings, maybe without realizing that they were just that. I'm talking about definitions of types that were parameterized by other types. Let's see a few examples.

### 7.1.1 The Maybe Functor

The definition of `Maybe` is a mapping from type a to type `Maybe a`:

```
data Maybe a = Nothing | Just a
```

Here's an important subtlety: `Maybe` itself is not a type, it's a *type constructor*. You have to give it a type argument, like `Int` or `Bool`, in order to turn it into a type. `Maybe` without any argument represents a function on types. But can we turn `Maybe` into a functor? (From now on, when I speak of functors in the context of programming, I will almost always mean endofunctors.) A functor is not only a mapping of objects (here, types) but also a mapping of morphisms (here, functions). For any function from a to b:

```
f :: a -> b
```

we would like to produce a function from `Maybe a` to `Maybe b`. To define such a function, we'll have two cases to consider, corresponding to the two constructors of `Maybe`. The `Nothing` case is simple: we'll just return `Nothing` back. And if the argument is `Just`, we'll apply the function f to its contents. So the image of f under `Maybe` is the function:

```
f' :: Maybe a -> Maybe b
f' Nothing = Nothing
f' (Just x) = Just (f x)
```

(By the way, in Haskell you can use apostrophes in variables names, which is very handy in cases like these.) In Haskell, we implement the morphism-mapping part of a functor as a higher order function called fmap. In the case of Maybe, it has the following signature:

```
fmap :: (a -> b) -> (Maybe a -> Maybe b)
```

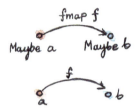

We often say that fmap *lifts* a function. The lifted function acts on Maybe values. As usual, because of currying, this signature may be interpreted in two ways: as a function of one argument — which itself is a function (a -> b) — returning a function (Maybe a -> Maybe b); or as a function of two arguments returning Maybe b:

```
fmap :: (a -> b) -> Maybe a -> Maybe b
```

Based on our previous discussion, this is how we implement fmap for Maybe:

```
fmap _ Nothing = Nothing
fmap f (Just x) = Just (f x)
```

To show that the type constructor Maybe together with the function fmap form a functor, we have to prove that fmap preserves identity and composition. These are called "the functor laws," but they simply ensure the preservation of the structure of the category.

## 7.1.2  Equational Reasoning

To prove the functor laws, I will use *equational reasoning*, which is a common proof technique in Haskell. It takes advantage of the fact that

74

Haskell functions are defined as equalities: the left hand side equals the right hand side. You can always substitute one for another, possibly renaming variables to avoid name conflicts. Think of this as either inlining a function, or the other way around, refactoring an expression into a function. Let's take the identity function as an example:

```
id x = x
```

If you see, for instance, id y in some expression, you can replace it with y (inlining). Further, if you see id applied to an expression, say id (y + 2), you can replace it with the expression itself (y + 2). And this substitution works both ways: you can replace any expression e with id e (refactoring). If a function is defined by pattern matching, you can use each sub-definition independently. For instance, given the above definition of fmap you can replace fmap f Nothing with Nothing, or the other way around. Let's see how this works in practice. Let's start with the preservation of identity:

```
fmap id = id
```

There are two cases to consider: Nothing and Just. Here's the first case (I'm using Haskell pseudo-code to transform the left hand side to the right hand side):

```
  fmap id Nothing
= { definition of fmap }
  Nothing
= { definition of id }
  id Nothing
```

Notice that in the last step I used the definition of id backwards. I replaced the expression Nothing with id Nothing. In practice, you carry out such proofs by "burning the candle at both ends," until you hit the same expression in the middle — here it was Nothing. The second case is also easy:

```
  fmap id (Just x)
= { definition of fmap }
  Just (id x)
= { definition of id }
  Just x
= { definition of id }
  id (Just x)
```

Now, lets show that `fmap` preserves composition:

```
fmap (g . f) = fmap g . fmap f
```

First the Nothing case:

```
  fmap (g . f) Nothing
= { definition of fmap }
  Nothing
= { definition of fmap }
  fmap g Nothing
= { definition of fmap }
  fmap g (fmap f Nothing)
```

And then the Just case:

```
  fmap (g . f) (Just x)
= { definition of fmap }
  Just ((g . f) x)
= { definition of composition }
  Just (g (f x))
= { definition of fmap }
  fmap g (Just (f x))
= { definition of fmap }
  fmap g (fmap f (Just x))
= { definition of composition }
  (fmap g . fmap f) (Just x)
```

It's worth stressing that equational reasoning doesn't work for C++ style "functions" with side effects. Consider this code:

```
int square(int x) {
    return x * x;
}

int counter() {
    static int c = 0;
    return c++;
}

double y = square(counter());
```

Using equational reasoning, you would be able to inline square to get:

```
double y = counter() * counter();
```

This is definitely not a valid transformation, and it will not produce the same result. Despite that, the C++ compiler will try to use equational reasoning if you implement square as a macro, with disastrous results.

### 7.1.3 Optional

Functors are easily expressed in Haskell, but they can be defined in any language that supports generic programming and higher-order functions. Let's consider the C++ analog of Maybe, the template type optional. Here's a sketch of the implementation (the actual implementation is much more complex, dealing with various ways the argument may be passed, with copy semantics, and with the resource management issues characteristic of C++):

```
template<class T>
class optional {
    bool _isValid; // the tag
    T _v;
public:
    optional()    : _isValid(false) {}         // Nothing
    optional(T x) : _isValid(true) , _v(x) {} // Just
    bool isValid() const { return _isValid; }
    T val() const { return _v; } };
```

This template provides one part of the definition of a functor: the mapping of types. It maps any type T to a new type optional<T>. Let's define its action on functions:

```
template<class A, class B>
std::function<optional<B>(optional<A>)>
fmap(std::function<B(A)> f) {
    return [f](optional<A> opt) {
        if (!opt.isValid())
            return optional<B>{};
        else
            return optional<B>{ f(opt.val()) };
    };
}
```

This is a higher order function, taking a function as an argument and returning a function. Here's the uncurried version of it:

```
template<class A, class B>
optional<B> fmap(std::function<B(A)> f, optional<A> opt) {
```

```
    if (!opt.isValid())
        return optional<B>{};
    else
        return optional<B>{ f(opt.val()) };
}
```

There is also an option of making `fmap` a template method of `optional`. This embarrassment of choices makes abstracting the functor pattern in C++ a problem. Should functor be an interface to inherit from (unfortunately, you can't have template virtual functions)? Should it be a curried or an uncurried free template function? Can the C++ compiler correctly infer the missing types, or should they be specified explicitly? Consider a situation where the input function f takes an `int` to a `bool`. How will the compiler figure out the type of g:

```
auto g = fmap(f);
```

especially if, in the future, there are multiple functors overloading `fmap`? (We'll see more functors soon.)

### 7.1.4 Typeclasses

So how does Haskell deal with abstracting the functor? It uses the typeclass mechanism. A typeclass defines a family of types that support a common interface. For instance, the class of objects that support equality is defined as follows:

```
class Eq a where
    (==) :: a -> a -> Bool
```

This definition states that type a is of the class `Eq` if it supports the operator (==) that takes two arguments of type a and returns a `Bool`. If you want to tell Haskell that a particular type is `Eq`, you have to declare it an *instance* of this class and provide the implementation of (==). For example, given the definition of a 2D `Point` (a product type of two `Floats`):

```
data Point = Pt Float Float
```

you can define the equality of points:

```
instance Eq Point where
    (Pt x y) == (Pt x' y') = x == x' && y == y'
```

Here I used the operator (==) (the one I'm defining) in the infix position between the two patterns (Pt x y) and (Pt x' y'). The body of the function follows the single equal sign. Once Point is declared an instance of Eq, you can directly compare points for equality. Notice that, unlike in C++ or Java, you don't have to specify the Eq class (or interface) when defining Point — you can do it later in client code. Typeclasses are also Haskell's only mechanism for overloading functions (and operators). We will need that for overloading fmap for different functors. There is one complication, though: a functor is not defined as a type but as a mapping of types, a type constructor. We need a typeclass that's not a family of types, as was the case with Eq, but a family of type constructors. Fortunately a Haskell typeclass works with type constructors as well as with types. So here's the definition of the Functor class:

```
class Functor f where
    fmap :: (a -> b) -> f a -> f b
```

It stipulates that f is a Functor if there exists a function fmap with the specified type signature. The lowercase f is a type variable, similar to type variables a and b. The compiler, however, is able to deduce that it represents a type constructor rather than a type by looking at its usage: acting on other types, as in f a and f b. Accordingly, when declaring an instance of Functor, you have to give it a type constructor, as is the case with Maybe:

```
instance Functor Maybe where
    fmap _ Nothing = Nothing
    fmap f (Just x) = Just (f x)
```

By the way, the Functor class, as well as its instance definitions for a lot of simple data types, including Maybe, are part of the standard Prelude library.

### 7.1.5  Functor in C++

Can we try the same approach in C++? A type constructor corresponds to a template class, like optional, so by analogy, we would parameterize fmap with a *template template parameter* F. This is the syntax for it:

```
template<template<class> F, class A, class B>
F<B> fmap(std::function<B(A)>, F<A>);
```

We would like to be able to specialize this template for different functors. Unfortunately, there is a prohibition against partial specialization of template functions in C++. You can't write:

```
template<class A, class B>
optional<B> fmap<optional>(std::function<B(A)> f, optional<A> opt)
```

Instead, we have to fall back on function overloading, which brings us back to the original definition of the uncurried fmap:

```
template<class A, class B>
optional<B> fmap(std::function<B(A)> f, optional<A> opt) {
    if (!opt.isValid())
        return optional<B>{};
    else
        return optional<B>{ f(opt.val()) };
}
```

This definition works, but only because the second argument of fmap selects the overload. It totally ignores the more generic definition of fmap.

### 7.1.6 The List Functor

To get some intuition as to the role of functors in programming, we need to look at more examples. Any type that is parameterized by another type is a candidate for a functor. Generic containers are parameterized by the type of the elements they store, so let's look at a very simple container, the list:

```
data List a = Nil | Cons a (List a)
```

We have the type constructor List, which is a mapping from any type a to the type List a. To show that List is a functor we have to define the lifting of functions: Given a function a -> b define a function List a -> List b:

```
fmap :: (a -> b) -> (List a -> List b)
```

A function acting on List a must consider two cases corresponding to the two list constructors. The Nil case is trivial — just return Nil — there isn't much you can do with an empty list. The Cons case is a bit tricky, because it involves recursion. So let's step back for a moment

and consider what we are trying to do. We have a list of a, a function f
that turns a to b, and we want to generate a list of b. The obvious thing
is to use f to turn each element of the list from a to b. How do we do
this in practice, given that a (non-empty) list is defined as the Cons of a
head and a tail? We apply f to the head and apply the lifted (fmapped) f
to the tail. This is a recursive definition, because we are defining lifted
f in terms of lifted f:

```
fmap f (Cons x t) = Cons (f x) (fmap f t)
```

Notice that, on the right hand side, fmap f is applied to a list that's
shorter than the list for which we are defining it — it's applied to its
tail. We recurse towards shorter and shorter lists, so we are bound to
eventually reach the empty list, or Nil. But as we've decided earlier,
fmap f acting on Nil returns Nil, thus terminating the recursion. To
get the final result, we combine the new head (f x) with the new tail
(fmap f t) using the Cons constructor. Putting it all together, here's the
instance declaration for the list functor:

```
instance Functor List where
    fmap _ Nil = Nil
    fmap f (Cons x t) = Cons (f x) (fmap f t)
```

If you are more comfortable with C++, consider the case of a std::vector,
which could be considered the most generic C++ container. The implementation of fmap for std::vector is just a thin encapsulation of
std::transform:

```
template<class A, class B>
std::vector<B> fmap(std::function<B(A)> f, std::vector<A> v) {
    std::vector<B> w;
    std::transform( std::begin(v)
                  , std::end(v)
                  , std::back_inserter(w)
                  , f);
    return w;
}
```

We can use it, for instance, to square the elements of a sequence of
numbers:

```
std::vector<int> v{ 1, 2, 3, 4 };
auto w = fmap([](int i) { return i*i; }, v);
```

```
std::copy( std::begin(w)
         , std::end(w)
         , std::ostream_iterator(std::cout, ", "));
```

Most C++ containers are functors by virtue of implementing iterators
that can be passed to std::transform, which is the more primitive cousin
of fmap. Unfortunately, the simplicity of a functor is lost under the
usual clutter of iterators and temporaries (see the implementation of
fmap above). I'm happy to say that the new proposed C++ range library
makes the functorial nature of ranges much more pronounced.

### 7.1.7  The Reader Functor

Now that you might have developed some intuitions — for instance,
functors being some kind of containers — let me show you an example
which at first sight looks very different. Consider a mapping of type a
to the type of a function returning a. We haven't really talked about
function types in depth — the full categorical treatment is coming —
but we have some understanding of those as programmers. In Haskell,
a function type is constructed using the arrow type constructor (->)
which takes two types: the argument type and the result type. You've
already seen it in infix form, a -> b, but it can equally well be used in
prefix form, when parenthesized:

```
(->) a b
```

Just like with regular functions, type functions of more than one argument can be partially applied. So when we provide just one type
argument to the arrow, it still expects another one. That's why:

```
(->) a
```

is a type constructor. It needs one more type b to produce a complete
type a -> b. As it stands, it defines a whole family of type constructors parameterized by a. Let's see if this is also a family of functors.
Dealing with two type parameters can get a bit confusing, so let's do
some renaming. Let's call the argument type r and the result type a,
in line with our previous functor definitions. So our type constructor
takes any type a and maps it into the type r -> a. To show that it's
a functor, we want to lift a function a -> b to a function that takes
r -> a and returns r -> b. These are the types that are formed using

the type constructor (->) r acting on, respectively, a and b. Here's the type signature of fmap applied to this case:

```
fmap :: (a -> b) -> (r -> a) -> (r -> b)
```

We have to solve the following puzzle: given a function f :: a -> b and a function g :: r -> a, create a function r -> b. There is only one way we can compose the two functions, and the result is exactly what we need. So here's the implementation of our fmap:

```
instance Functor ((->) r) where
    fmap f g = f . g
```

It just works! If you like terse notation, this definition can be reduced further by noticing that composition can be rewritten in prefix form:

```
fmap f g = (.) f g
```

and the arguments can be omitted to yield a direct equality of two functions:

```
fmap = (.)
```

This combination of the type constructor (->) r with the above implementation of fmap is called the reader functor.

## 7.2 Functors as Containers

We've seen some examples of functors in programming languages that define general-purpose containers, or at least objects that contain some value of the type they are parameterized over. The reader functor seems to be an outlier, because we don't think of functions as data. But we've seen that pure functions can be memoized, and function execution can be turned into table lookup. Tables are data. Conversely, because of Haskell's laziness, a traditional container, like a list, may actually be implemented as a function. Consider, for instance, an infinite list of natural numbers, which can be compactly defined as:

```
nats :: [Integer]
nats = [1..]
```

In the first line, a pair of square brackets is Haskell's built-in type constructor for lists. In the second line, square brackets are used to create a list literal. Obviously, an infinite list like this cannot be stored in memory. The compiler implements it as a function that generates Integers on demand. Haskell effectively blurs the distinction between data and code. A list could be considered a function, and a function could be considered a table that maps arguments to results. The latter can even be practical if the domain of the function is finite and not too large. It would not be practical, however, to implement strlen as table lookup, because there are infinitely many different strings. As programmers, we don't like infinities, but in category theory you learn to eat infinities for breakfast. Whether it's a set of all strings or a collection of all possible states of the Universe, past, present, and future — we can deal with it! So I like to think of the functor object (an object of the type generated by an endofunctor) as containing a value or values of the type over which it is parameterized, even if these values are not physically present there. One example of a functor is a C++ std::future, which may at some point contain a value, but it's not guaranteed it will; and if you want to access it, you may block waiting for another thread to finish execution. Another example is a Haskell IO object, which may contain user input, or the future versions of our Universe with "Hello World!" displayed on the monitor. According to this interpretation, a functor object is something that may contain a value or values of the type it's parameterized upon. Or it may contain a recipe for generating those values. We are not at all concerned about being able to access the values — that's totally optional, and outside of the scope of the functor. All we are interested in is to be able to manipulate those values using functions. If the values can be accessed, then we should be able to see the results of this manipulation. If they can't, then all we care about is that the manipulations compose correctly and that the manipulation with an identity function doesn't change anything. Just to show you how much we don't care about being able to access the values inside a functor object, here's a type constructor that ignores completely its argument a:

```
data Const c a = Const c
```

The Const type constructor takes two types, c and a. Just like we did with the arrow constructor, we are going to partially apply it to create a functor. The data constructor (also called Const) takes just one value of type c. It has no dependence on a. The type of fmap for this type constructor is:

```
fmap :: (a -> b) -> Const c a -> Const c b
```

Because the functor ignores its type argument, the implementation of fmap is free to ignore its function argument — the function has nothing to act upon:

```
instance Functor (Const c) where
    fmap _ (Const v) = Const v
```

This might be a little clearer in C++ (I never thought I would utter those words!), where there is a stronger distinction between type arguments — which are compile-time — and values, which are run-time:

```
template<class C, class A>
struct Const {
    Const(C v) : _v(v) {}
    C _v;
};
```

The C++ implementation of fmap also ignores the function argument and essentially re-casts the Const argument without changing its value:

```
template<class C, class A, class B>
Const<C, B> fmap(std::function<B(A)> f, Const<C, A> c) {
    return Const<C, B>{c._v};
}
```

Despite its weirdness, the Const functor plays an important role in many constructions. In category theory, it's a special case of the $\Delta_c$ functor I mentioned earlier — the endo-functor case of a black hole. We'll be seeing more of it in the future.

## 7.3 Functor Composition

It's not hard to convince yourself that functors between categories compose, just like functions between sets compose. A composition of two functors, when acting on objects, is just the composition of their respective object mappings; and similarly when acting on morphisms. After jumping through two functors, identity morphisms end up as identity morphisms, and compositions of morphisms finish up as compositions of morphisms. There's really nothing much to it. In particular, it's easy to compose endofunctors. Remember the function maybeTail? I'll rewrite it using Haskell's built in implementation of lists:

```
maybeTail :: [a] -> Maybe [a]
maybeTail [] = Nothing
maybeTail (x:xs) = Just xs
```

(The empty list constructor that we used to call Nil is replaced with the empty pair of square brackets []. The Cons constructor is replaced with the infix operator : (colon).) The result of maybeTail is of a type that's a composition of two functors, Maybe and [], acting on a. Each of these functors is equipped with its own version of fmap, but what if we want to apply some function f to the contents of the composite: a Maybe list? We have to break through two layers of functors. We can use fmap to break through the outer Maybe. But we can't just send f inside Maybe because f doesn't work on lists. We have to send (fmap f) to operate on the inner list. For instance, let's see how we can square the elements of a Maybe list of integers:

```
square x = x * x

mis :: Maybe [Int]
mis = Just [1, 2, 3]

mis2 = fmap (fmap square) mis
```

The compiler, after analyzing the types, will figure out that, for the outer fmap, it should use the implementation from the Maybe instance, and for the inner one, the list functor implementation. It may not be immediately obvious that the above code may be rewritten as:

```
mis2 = (fmap . fmap) square mis
```

But remember that fmap may be considered a function of just one argument:

```
fmap :: (a -> b) -> (f a -> f b)
```

In our case, the second fmap in (fmap . fmap) takes as its argument:

```
square :: Int -> Int
```

and returns a function of the type:

```
[Int] -> [Int]
```

The first `fmap` then takes that function and returns a function:

```
Maybe [Int] -> Maybe [Int]
```

Finally, that function is applied to `mis`. So the composition of two functors is a functor whose `fmap` is the composition of the corresponding `fmaps`. Going back to category theory: It's pretty obvious that functor composition is associative (the mapping of objects is associative, and the mapping of morphisms is associative). And there is also a trivial identity functor in every category: it maps every object to itself, and every morphism to itself. So functors have all the same properties as morphisms in some category. But what category would that be? It would have to be a category in which objects are categories and morphisms are functors. It's a category of categories. But a category of *all* categories would have to include itself, and we would get into the same kinds of paradoxes that made the set of all sets impossible. There is, however, a category of all *small* categories called **Cat** (which is big, so it can't be a member of itself). A small category is one in which objects form a set, as opposed to something larger than a set. Mind you, in category theory, even an infinite uncountable set is considered "small." I thought I'd mention these things because I find it pretty amazing that we can recognize the same structures repeating themselves at many levels of abstraction. We'll see later that functors form categories as well.

## 7.4 Challenges

1. Can we turn the `Maybe` type constructor into a functor by defining:

   ```
   fmap _ _ = Nothing
   ```

   which ignores both of its arguments? (Hint: Check the functor laws.)
2. Prove functor laws for the reader functor. Hint: it's really simple.
3. Implement the reader functor in your second favorite language (the first being Haskell, of course).

4. Prove the functor laws for the list functor. Assume that the laws are true for the tail part of the list you're applying it to (in other words, use *induction*).

# 8

# Functoriality

Now THAT YOU KNOW what a functor is, and have seen a few examples, let's see how we can build larger functors from smaller ones. In particular it's interesting to see which type constructors (which correspond to mappings between objects in a category) can be extended to functors (which include mappings between morphisms).

## 8.1 Bifunctors

Since functors are morphisms in **Cat** (the category of categories), a lot of intuitions about morphisms — and functions in particular — apply to functors as well. For instance, just like you can have a function of two arguments, you can have a functor of two arguments, or a *bifunctor*. On objects, a bifunctor maps every pair of objects, one from category C, and one from category D, to an object in category E. Notice that this is just saying that it's a mapping from a *Cartesian product* of categories C × D to E.

That's pretty straightforward. But functoriality means that a bifunctor has to map morphisms as well. This time, though, it must map a pair of morphisms, one from C and one from D, to a morphism in E.

Again, a pair of morphisms is just a single morphism in the product category C × D to E. We define a morphism in a Cartesian product of categories as a pair of morphisms which goes from one pair of objects to another pair of objects. These pairs of morphisms can be composed in the obvious way:

$$(f, g) \circ (f', g') = (f \circ f', g \circ g')$$

The composition is associative and it has an identity — a pair of identity morphisms $(\mathrm{id}, \mathrm{id})$. So a Cartesian product of categories is indeed a category.

But an easier way to think about bifunctors is that they are functors in both arguments. So instead of translating functorial laws — associativity and identity preservation — from functors to bifunctors, it's enough to check them separately for each argument. If you have a mapping from a pair of categories to a third category, and you prove

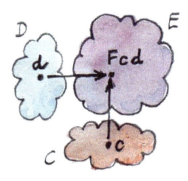

that it is functorial in each argument separately (i.e., keeping the other argument constant), then the mapping is automatically a bifunctor. By *functorial* I mean that it acts on morphisms like an honest functor.

Let's define a bifunctor in Haskell. In this case all three categories are the same: the category of Haskell types. A bifunctor is a type constructor that takes two type arguments. Here's the definition of the `Bifunctor` typeclass taken directly from the library `Control.Bifunctor`:

```
class Bifunctor f where
    bimap :: (a -> c) -> (b -> d) -> f a b -> f c d
    bimap g h = first g . second h
    first :: (a -> c) -> f a b -> f c b
    first g = bimap g id
    second :: (b -> d) -> f a b -> f a d
    second = bimap id
```

The type variable f represents the bifunctor. You can see that in all type signatures it's always applied to two type arguments. The first type signature defines `bimap`: a mapping of two functions at once. The result is a lifted function, (f a b -> f c d), operating on types generated by the bifunctor's type constructor. There is a default implementation of `bimap` in terms of `first` and `second`, which shows that it's enough to have functoriality in each argument separately to be able to define a bifunctor. (This is not true in general in category theory, because the two maps may not commute: `first g . second h` might not be the same as `second h . first g`.)

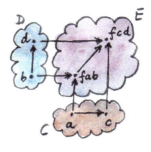

bimap

The two other type signatures, `first` and `second`, are the two `fmaps` witnessing the functoriality of `f` in the first and the second argument, respectively.

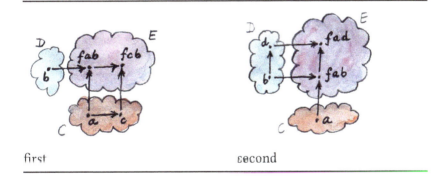

first                                            second

The typeclass definition provides default implementations for both of them in terms of `bimap`.

When declaring an instance of `Bifunctor`, you have a choice of either implementing `bimap` and accepting the defaults for `first` and `second`, or implementing both `first` and `second` and accepting the default for `bimap` (of course, you may implement all three of them, but then it's up to you to make sure they are related to each other in this manner).

## 8.2 Product and Coproduct Bifunctors

An important example of a bifunctor is the categorical product — a product of two objects that is defined by a universal construction. If the product exists for any pair of objects, the mapping from those objects to the product is bifunctorial. This is true in general, and in Haskell in particular. Here's the Bifunctor instance for a pair constructor — the simplest product type:

```
instance Bifunctor (,) where
    bimap f g (x, y) = (f x, g y)
```

There isn't much choice: bimap simply applies the first function to the first component, and the second function to the second component of a pair. The code pretty much writes itself, given the types:

```
bimap :: (a -> c) -> (b -> d) -> (a, b) -> (c, d)
```

The action of the bifunctor here is to make pairs of types, for instance:

```
(,) a b = (a, b)
```

By duality, a coproduct, if it's defined for every pair of objects in a category, is also a bifunctor. In Haskell, this is exemplified by the Either type constructor being an instance of Bifunctor:

```
instance Bifunctor Either where
    bimap f _ (Left x) = Left (f x)
    bimap _ g (Right y) = Right (g y)
```

This code also writes itself.

Now, remember when we talked about monoidal categories? A monoidal category defines a binary operator acting on objects, together with a unit object. I mentioned that **Set** is a monoidal category with respect to Cartesian product, with the singleton set as a unit. And it's also a monoidal category with respect to disjoint union, with the empty set as a unit. What I haven't mentioned is that one of the requirements for a monoidal category is that the binary operator be a bifunctor. This is a very important requirement — we want the monoidal product to be compatible with the structure of the category, which is defined by morphisms. We are now one step closer to the full definition of a monoidal category (we still need to learn about naturality, before we can get there).

## 8.3 Functorial Algebraic Data Types

We've seen several examples of parameterized data types that turned out to be functors — we were able to define fmap for them. Complex data types are constructed from simpler data types. In particular, algebraic data types (ADTs) are created using sums and products. We have just seen that sums and products are functorial. We also know that functors compose. So if we can show that the basic building blocks of ADTs are functorial, we'll know that parameterized ADTs are functorial too.

So what are the building blocks of parameterized algebraic data types? First, there are the items that have no dependency on the type parameter of the functor, like Nothing in Maybe, or Nil in List. They are equivalent to the Const functor. Remember, the Const functor ignores its type parameter (really, the *second* type parameter, which is the one of interest to us, the first one being kept constant).

Then there are the elements that simply encapsulate the type parameter itself, like Just in Maybe. They are equivalent to the identity functor. I mentioned the identity functor previously, as the identity morphism in *Cat*, but didn't give its definition in Haskell. Here it is:

```
data Identity a = Identity a

instance Functor Identity where
    fmap f (Identity x) = Identity (f x)
```

You can think of Identity as the simplest possible container that always stores just one (immutable) value of type a.

Everything else in algebraic data structures is constructed from these two primitives using products and sums.

With this new knowledge, let's have a fresh look at the Maybe type constructor:

```
data Maybe a = Nothing | Just a
```

It's a sum of two types, and we now know that the sum is functorial. The first part, Nothing can be represented as a Const () acting on a (the first type parameter of Const is set to unit — later we'll see more interesting uses of Const). The second part is just a different name for the identity functor. We could have defined Maybe, up to isomorphism, as:

```
type Maybe a = Either (Const () a) (Identity a)
```

So Maybe is the composition of the bifunctor Either with two functors, Const () and Identity. (Const is really a bifunctor, but here we always use it partially applied.)

We've already seen that a composition of functors is a functor — we can easily convince ourselves that the same is true of bifunctors. All we need is to figure out how a composition of a bifunctor with two functors works on morphisms. Given two morphisms, we simply lift one with one functor and the other with the other functor. We then lift the resulting pair of lifted morphisms with the bifunctor.

We can express this composition in Haskell. Let's define a data type that is parameterized by a bifunctor bf (it's a type variable that is a type constructor that takes two types as arguments), two functors fu and gu (type constructors that take one type variable each), and two regular types a and b. We apply fu to a and gu to b, and then apply bf to the resulting two types:

```
newtype BiComp bf fu gu a b = BiComp (bf (fu a) (gu b))
```

That's the composition on objects, or types. Notice how in Haskell we apply type constructors to types, just like we apply functions to arguments. The syntax is the same.

If you're getting a little lost, try applying BiComp to Either, Const (), Identity, a, and b, in this order. You will recover our bare-bone version of Maybe b (a is ignored).

The new data type BiComp is a bifunctor in a and b, but only if bf is itself a Bifunctor and fu and gu are Functors. The compiler must know that there will be a definition of bimap available for bf, and definitions of fmap for fu and gu. In Haskell, this is expressed as a precondition in the instance declaration: a set of class constraints followed by a double arrow:

```
instance (Bifunctor bf, Functor fu, Functor gu) =>
  Bifunctor (BiComp bf fu gu) where
    bimap f1 f2 (BiComp x) = BiComp ((bimap (fmap f1) (fmap f2))
    ↪  x)
```

The implementation of bimap for BiComp is given in terms of bimap for bf and the two fmaps for fu and gu. The compiler automatically infers all the types and picks the correct overloaded functions whenever BiComp is used.

The x in the definition of bimap has the type:

```
bf (fu a) (gu b)
```

which is quite a mouthful. The outer `bimap` breaks through the outer `bf` layer, and the two `fmaps` dig under `fu` and `gu`, respectively. If the types of `f1` and `f2` are:

```
f1 :: a -> a'
f2 :: b -> b'
```

then the final result is of the type `bf (fu a') (gu b')`:

```
bimap :: (fu a -> fu a') -> (gu b -> gu b')
  -> bf (fu a) (gu b) -> bf (fu a') (gu b')
```

If you like jigsaw puzzles, these kinds of type manipulations can provide hours of entertainment.

So it turns out that we didn't have to prove that `Maybe` was a functor — this fact followed from the way it was constructed as a sum of two functorial primitives.

A perceptive reader might ask the question: If the derivation of the `Functor` instance for algebraic data types is so mechanical, can't it be automated and performed by the compiler? Indeed, it can, and it is. You need to enable a particular Haskell extension by including this line at the top of your source file:

```
{-# LANGUAGE DeriveFunctor #-}
```

and then add `deriving Functor` to your data structure:

```
data Maybe a = Nothing | Just a deriving Functor
```

and the corresponding `fmap` will be implemented for you.

The regularity of algebraic data structures makes it possible to derive instances not only of `Functor` but of several other type classes, including the `Eq` type class I mentioned before. There is also the option of teaching the compiler to derive instances of your own typeclasses, but that's a bit more advanced. The idea though is the same: You provide the behavior for the basic building blocks and sums and products, and let the compiler figure out the rest.

## 8.4 Functors in C++

If you are a C++ programmer, you obviously are on your own as far as implementing functors goes. However, you should be able to recognize some types of algebraic data structures in C++. If such a data structure is made into a generic template, you should be able to quickly implement fmap for it.

Let's have a look at a tree data structure, which we would define in Haskell as a recursive sum type:

```
data Tree a = Leaf a | Node (Tree a) (Tree a)
    deriving Functor
```

As I mentioned before, one way of implementing sum types in C++ is through class hierarchies. It would be natural, in an object-oriented language, to implement fmap as a virtual function of the base class Functor and then override it in all subclasses. Unfortunately this is impossible because fmap is a template, parameterized not only by the type of the object it's acting upon (the this pointer) but also by the return type of the function that's been applied to it. Virtual functions cannot be templatized in C++. We'll implement fmap as a generic free function, and we'll replace pattern matching with dynamic_cast.

The base class must define at least one virtual function in order to support dynamic casting, so we'll make the destructor virtual (which is a good idea in any case):

```
template<class T>
struct Tree {
    virtual ~Tree() {};
};
```

The Leaf is just an Identity functor in disguise:

```
template<class T>
struct Leaf : public Tree<T> {
    T _label;
    Leaf(T l) : _label(l) {}
};
```

The Node is a product type:

```
template<class T>
struct Node : public Tree<T> {
    Tree<T> * _left;
    Tree<T> * _right;
    Node(Tree<T> * l, Tree<T> * r) : _left(l), _right(r) {}
};
```

When implementing fmap we take advantage of dynamic dispatching
on the type of the Tree. The Leaf case applies the Identity version of
fmap, and the Node case is treated like a bifunctor composed with two
copies of the Tree functor. As a C++ programmer, you're probably not
used to analyzing code in these terms, but it's a good exercise in categorical thinking.

```
template<class A, class B>
Tree<B> * fmap(std::function<B(A)> f, Tree<A> * t) {
    Leaf<A> * pl = dynamic_cast <Leaf<A>*>(t);
    if (pl)
        return new Leaf<B>(f (pl->_label));
    Node<A> * pn = dynamic_cast<Node<A>*>(t);
    if (pn)
        return new Node<B>( fmap<A>(f, pn->_left)
                          , fmap<A>(f, pn->_right));
    return nullptr;
}
```

For simplicity, I decided to ignore memory and resource management
issues, but in production code you would probably use smart pointers
(unique or shared, depending on your policy).

Compare it with the Haskell implementation of fmap:

```
instance Functor Tree where
    fmap f (Leaf a) = Leaf (f a)
    fmap f (Node t t') = Node (fmap f t) (fmap f t')
```

This implementation can also be automatically derived by the compiler.

## 8.5   The Writer Functor

I promised that I would come back to the Kleisli category I described
earlier. Morphisms in that category were represented as "embellished"
functions returning the Writer data structure.

```
type Writer a = (a, String)
```

I said that the embellishment was somehow related to endofunctors. And, indeed, the Writer type constructor is functorial in a. We don't even have to implement fmap for it, because it's just a simple product type.

But what's the relation between a Kleisli category and a functor — in general? A Kleisli category, being a category, defines composition and identity. Let me remind you that the composition is given by the fish operator:

```
(>=>) :: (a -> Writer b) -> (b -> Writer c) -> (a -> Writer c)
m1 >=> m2 = \x ->
    let (y, s1) = m1 x
        (z, s2) = m2 y
    in (z, s1 ++ s2)
```

and the identity morphism by a function called return:

```
return :: a -> Writer a
return x = (x, "")
```

It turns out that, if you look at the types of these two functions long enough (and I mean, *long* enough), you can find a way to combine them to produce a function with the right type signature to serve as fmap. Like this:

```
fmap f = id >=> (\x -> return (f x))
```

Here, the fish operator combines two functions: one of them is the familiar id, and the other is a lambda that applies return to the result of acting with f on the lambda's argument. The hardest part to wrap your brain around is probably the use of id. Isn't the argument to the fish operator supposed to be a function that takes a "normal" type and returns an embellished type? Well, not really. Nobody says that a in a -> Writer b must be a "normal" type. It's a type variable, so it can be anything, in particular it can be an embellished type, like Writer b.

So id will take Writer a and turn it into Writer a. The fish operator will fish out the value of a and pass it as x to the lambda. There, f will turn it into a b and return will embellish it, making it Writer b. Putting it all together, we end up with a function that takes Writer a and returns Writer b, exactly what fmap is supposed to produce.

Notice that this argument is very general: you can replace `Writer` with any type constructor. As long as it supports a fish operator and `return`, you can define `fmap` as well. So the embellishment in the Kleisli category is always a functor. (Not every functor, though, gives rise to a Kleisli category.)

You might wonder if the `fmap` we have just defined is the same `fmap` the compiler would have derived for us with `deriving Functor`. Interestingly enough, it is. This is due to the way Haskell implements polymorphic functions. It's called *parametric polymorphism*, and it's a source of so called *theorems for free*. One of those theorems says that, if there is an implementation of `fmap` for a given type constructor, one that preserves identity, then it must be unique.

## 8.6 Covariant and Contravariant Functors

Now that we've reviewed the writer functor, let's go back to the reader functor. It was based on the partially applied function-arrow type constructor:

```
(->) r
```

We can rewrite it as a type synonym:

```
type Reader r a = r -> a
```

for which the `Functor` instance, as we've seen before, reads:

```
instance Functor (Reader r) where
    fmap f g = f . g
```

But just like the pair type constructor, or the `Either` type constructor, the function type constructor takes two type arguments. The pair and `Either` were functorial in both arguments — they were bifunctors. Is the function constructor a bifunctor too?

Let's try to make it functorial in the first argument. We'll start with a type synonym — it's just like the `Reader` but with the arguments flipped:

```
type Op r a = a -> r
```

This time we fix the return type, r, and vary the argument type, a. Let's see if we can somehow match the types in order to implement `fmap`, which would have the following type signature:

99

```
fmap :: (a -> b) -> (a -> r) -> (b -> r)
```

With just two functions taking a and returning, respectively, b and r, there is simply no way to build a function taking b and returning r! It would be different if we could somehow invert the first function, so that it took b and returned a instead. We can't invert an arbitrary function, but we can go to the opposite category.

A short recap: For every category $C$ there is a dual category $C^{op}$. It's a category with the same objects as $C$, but with all the arrows reversed.

Consider a functor that goes between $C^{op}$ and some other category $D$:

$$F :: C^{op} \to D$$

Such a functor maps a morphism $f^{op} :: a \to b$ in $C^{op}$ to the morphism $F f^{op} :: Fa \to Fb$ in $D$. But the morphism $f^{op}$ secretly corresponds to some morphism $f :: b \to a$ in the original category $C$. Notice the inversion.

Now, $F$ is a regular functor, but there is another mapping we can define based on $F$, which is not a functor — let's call it $G$. It's a mapping from $C$ to $D$. It maps objects the same way $F$ does, but when it comes to mapping morphisms, it reverses them. It takes a morphism $f :: b \to a$ in $C$, maps it first to the opposite morphism $f^{op} :: a \to b$ and then uses the functor $F$ on it, to get $F f^{op} :: F a \to F b$.

Considering that $Fa$ is the same as $Ga$ and $Fb$ is the same as $Gb$, the whole trip can be described as: $Gf :: (b \to a) \to (Ga \to Gb)$ It's a "functor with a twist." A mapping of categories that inverts the direction of morphisms in this manner is called a *contravariant functor*. Notice that a contravariant functor is just a regular functor from the opposite category. The regular functors, by the way — the kind we've been studying thus far — are called *covariant* functors.

Here's the typeclass defining a contravariant functor (really, a contravariant *endo*functor) in Haskell:

```
class Contravariant f where
    contramap :: (b -> a) -> (f a -> f b)
```

Our type constructor Op is an instance of it:

```
instance Contravariant (Op r) where
    -- (b -> a) -> Op r a -> Op r b
    contramap f g = g . f
```

Notice that the function f inserts itself *before* (that is, to the right of) the contents of Op — the function g.

The definition of contramap for Op may be made even terser, if you notice that it's just the function composition operator with the arguments flipped. There is a special function for flipping arguments, called flip:

```
flip :: (a -> b -> c) -> (b -> a -> c)
flip f y x = f x y
```

With it, we get:

```
contramap = flip (.)
```

## 8.7   Profunctors

We've seen that the function-arrow operator is contravariant in its first argument and covariant in the second. Is there a name for such a beast? It turns out that, if the target category is **Set**, such a beast is called a *profunctor*. Because a contravariant functor is equivalent to a covariant functor from the opposite category, a profunctor is defined as:

$$C^{op} \times D \to \textbf{Set}$$

Since, to first approximation, Haskell types are sets, we apply the name Profunctor to a type constructor p of two arguments, which is contra-functorial in the first argument and functorial in the second. Here's the appropriate typeclass taken from the Data.Profunctor library:

```
class Profunctor p where
    dimap :: (a -> b) -> (c -> d) -> p b c -> p a d
    dimap f g = lmap f . rmap g
    lmap :: (a -> b) -> p b c -> p a c
    lmap f = dimap f id
    rmap :: (b -> c) -> p a b -> p a c
    rmap = dimap id
```

All three functions come with default implementations. Just like with
Bifunctor, when declaring an instance of Profunctor, you have a choice
of either implementing dimap and accepting the defaults for lmap and
rmap, or implementing both lmap and rmap and accepting the default for
dimap.

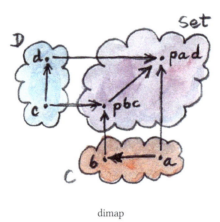

dimap

Now we can assert that the function-arrow operator is an instance of a
Profunctor:

```
instance Profunctor (->) where
    dimap ab cd bc = cd . bc . ab
    lmap = flip (.)
    rmap = (.)
```

Profunctors have their application in the Haskell lens library. We'll see
them again when we talk about ends and coends.

## 8.8  The Hom-Functor

The above examples are the reflection of a more general statement that
the mapping that takes a pair of objects *a* and *b* and assigns to it the

set of morphisms between them, the hom-set $C(a, b)$, is a functor. It is a functor from the product category $C^{op} \times C$ to the category of sets, **Set**.

Let's define its action on morphisms. A morphism in $C^{op} \times C$ is a pair of morphisms from **C**:

$$f :: a' \rightarrow a$$
$$g :: b \rightarrow b'$$

The lifting of this pair must be a morphism (a function) from the set $C(a, b)$ to the set $C(a', b')$. Just pick any element $h$ of $C(a, b)$ (it's a morphism from $a$ to $b$) and assign to it:

$$g \circ h \circ f$$

which is an element of $C(a', b')$.

As you can see, the hom-functor is a special case of a profunctor.

## 8.9  Challenges

1. Show that the data type:

   ```
   data Pair a b = Pair a b
   ```

   is a bifunctor. For additional credit implement all three methods of Bifunctor and use equational reasoning to show that these definitions are compatible with the default implementations whenever they can be applied.

2. Show the isomorphism between the standard definition of Maybe and this desugaring:

   ```
   type Maybe' a = Either (Const () a) (Identity a)
   ```

   Hint: Define two mappings between the two implementations. For additional credit, show that they are the inverse of each other using equational reasoning.

3. Let's try another data structure. I call it a PreList because it's a precursor to a List. It replaces recursion with a type parameter b.

   ```
   data PreList a b = Nil | Cons a b
   ```

   You could recover our earlier definition of a List by recursively applying PreList to itself (we'll see how it's done when we talk about fixed points).

   Show that PreList is an instance of Bifunctor.

4. Show that the following data types define bifunctors in a and b:

```
data K2 c a b = K2 c

data Fst a b = Fst a

data Snd a b = Snd b
```

For additional credit, check your solutions against Conor McBride's paper Clowns to the Left of me, Jokers to the Right[1].

5. Define a bifunctor in a language other than Haskell. Implement bimap for a generic pair in that language.

6. Should std::map be considered a bifunctor or a profunctor in the two template arguments Key and T? How would you redesign this data type to make it so?

---

[1] http://strictlypositive.org/CJ.pdf

# 9

# Function Types

S O FAR I've been glossing over the meaning of function types. A function type is different from other types.

Take `Integer`, for instance: It's just a set of integers. `Bool` is a two element set. But a function type $a \rightarrow b$ is more than that: it's a set of morphisms between objects $a$ and $b$. A set of morphisms between two objects in any category is called a hom-set. It just so happens that in the category **Set** every hom-set is itself an object in the same category —because it is, after all, a *set*.

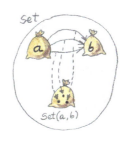

Hom-set in Set is just a set

The same is not true of other categories where hom-sets are external to a category. They are even called *external* hom-sets.

It's the self-referential nature of the category **Set** that makes function types special. But there is a way, at least in some categories, to construct objects that represent hom-sets. Such objects are called *internal* hom-sets.

## 9.1  Universal Construction

Let's forget for a moment that function types are sets and try to construct a function type, or more generally, an internal hom-set, from scratch. As usual, we'll take our cues from the **Set** category, but care-

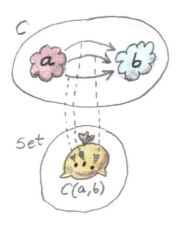

Hom-set in category C is an external set

fully avoid using any properties of sets, so that the construction will automatically work for other categories.

A function type may be considered a composite type because of its relationship to the argument type and the result type. We've already seen the constructions of composite types — those that involved relationships between objects. We used universal constructions to define a product type and a coproduct types. We can use the same trick to define a function type. We will need a pattern that involves three objects: the function type that we are constructing, the argument type, and the result type.

The obvious pattern that connects these three types is called *function application* or *evaluation*. Given a candidate for a function type, let's call it $z$ (notice that, if we are not in the category **Set**, this is just an object like any other object), and the argument type $a$ (an object), the application maps this pair to the result type $b$ (an object). We have three objects, two of them fixed (the ones representing the argument type and the result type).

We also have the application, which is a mapping. How do we incorporate this mapping into our pattern? If we were allowed to look inside objects, we could pair a function $f$ (an element of $z$) with an argument $x$ (an element of $a$) and map it to $fx$ (the application of $f$ to $x$, which is an element of $b$).

But instead of dealing with individual pairs $(f, x)$, we can as well talk about the whole *product* of the function type $z$ and the argument

In Set we can pick a function $f$ from a set of functions $z$ and we can pick an argument $x$ from the set (type) $a$. We get an element $fx$ in the set (type) $b$.

type $a$. The product $z \times a$ is an object, and we can pick, as our application morphism, an arrow $g$ from that object to $b$. In **Set**, $g$ would be the function that maps every pair $(f, x)$ to $fx$.

So that's the pattern: a product of two objects $z$ and $a$ connected to another object $b$ by a morphism $g$.

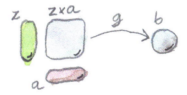

A pattern of objects and morphisms that is the starting point of the universal construction

Is this pattern specific enough to single out the function type using a universal construction? Not in every category. But in the categories of interest to us it is. And another question: Would it be possible to define a function object without first defining a product? There are categories in which there is no product, or there isn't a product for all pairs of objects. The answer is no: there is no function type, if there is no product type. We'll come back to this later when we talk about exponentials.

Let's review the universal construction. We start with a pattern of objects and morphisms. That's our imprecise query, and it usually yields lots and lots of hits. In particular, in **Set**, pretty much everything is connected to everything. We can take any object $z$, form its product with $a$, and there's going to be a function from it to $b$ (except when $b$ is an empty set).

That's when we apply our secret weapon: ranking. This is usually done by requiring that there be a unique mapping between candidate objects — a mapping that somehow factorizes our construction. In our case, we'll decree that $z$ together with the morphism $g$ from $z \times a$ to $b$ is *better* than some other $z'$ with its own application $g'$, if and only if there is a unique mapping $h$ from $z'$ to $z$ such that the application of $g'$ factors through the application of $g$. (Hint: Read this sentence while looking at the picture.)

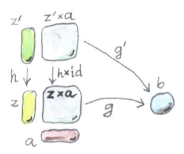

Establishing a ranking between candidates for the function object

Now here's the tricky part, and the main reason I postponed this particular universal construction till now. Given the morphism $h :: z' \rightarrow z$, we want to close the diagram that has both $z'$ and $z$ crossed with $a$. What we really need, given the mapping $h$ from $z'$ to $z$, is a mapping from $z' \times a$ to $z \times a$. And now, after discussing the functoriality of the product, we know how to do it. Because the product itself is a functor (more precisely an endo-bi-functor), it's possible to lift pairs of morphisms. In other words, we can define not only products of objects but also products of morphisms.

Since we are not touching the second component of the product $z' \times a$, we will lift the pair of morphisms $(h, \mathrm{id})$, where id is an identity on $a$.

So, here's how we can factor one application, $g$, out of another application $g'$:

$$g' = g \circ (h \times \mathrm{id})$$

The key here is the action of the product on morphisms.

The third part of the universal construction is selecting the object that is universally the best. Let's call this object $a \Rightarrow b$ (think of this as a symbolic name for one object, not to be confused with a Haskell typeclass constraint — I'll discuss different ways of naming it later). This object comes with its own application — a morphism from $(a \Rightarrow b) \times a$ to $b$ — which we will call *eval*. The object $a \Rightarrow b$ is the best if any other candidate for a function object can be uniquely mapped to it in such a way that its application morphism $g$ factorizes through *eval*. This object is better than any other object according to our ranking.

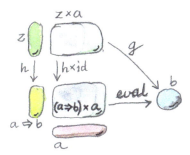

The definition of the universal function object. This is the same diagram as above, but now the object $a \Rightarrow b$ is *universal*.

Formally:

---

A *function object* from $a$ to $b$ is an object $a \Rightarrow b$ together with the morphism

$$eval :: ((a \Rightarrow b) \times a) \to b$$

such that for any other object $z$ with a morphism

$$g :: z \times a \to b$$

there is a unique morphism

$$h :: z \to (a \Rightarrow b)$$

that factors $g$ through *eval*:

$$g = eval \circ (h \times \text{id})$$

---

Of course, there is no guarantee that such an object $a \Rightarrow b$ exists for any pair of objects $a$ and $b$ in a given category. But it always does in **Set**. Moreover, in **Set**, this object is isomorphic to the hom-set $\text{Set}(a, b)$.

This is why, in Haskell, we interpret the function type `a -> b` as the categorical function object $a \Rightarrow b$.

## 9.2 Currying

Let's have a second look at all the candidates for the function object. This time, however, let's think of the morphism $g$ as a function of two variables, $z$ and $a$.

$$g :: z \times a \to b$$

Being a morphism from a product comes as close as it gets to being a function of two variables. In particular, in **Set**, $g$ is a function from pairs of values, one from the set $z$ and one from the set $a$.

On the other hand, the universal property tells us that for each such $g$ there is a unique morphism $h$ that maps $z$ to a function object $a \Rightarrow b$.

$$h :: z \to (a \Rightarrow b)$$

In **Set**, this just means that $h$ is a function that takes one variable of type $z$ and returns a function from $a$ to $b$. That makes $h$ a higher order function. Therefore the universal construction establishes a one-to-one correspondence between functions of two variables and functions of one variable returning functions. This correspondence is called *currying*, and $h$ is called the curried version of $g$.

This correspondence is one-to-one, because given any $g$ there is a unique $h$, and given any $h$ you can always recreate the two-argument function $g$ using the formula:

$$g = eval \circ (h \times \mathrm{id})$$

The function $g$ can be called the *uncurried* version of $h$.

Currying is essentially built into the syntax of Haskell. A function returning a function:

```
a -> (b -> c)
```

is often thought of as a function of two variables. That's how we read the un-parenthesized signature:

```
a -> b -> c
```

This interpretation is apparent in the way we define multi-argument functions. For instance:

```
catstr :: String -> String -> String
catstr s s' = s ++ s'
```

The same function can be written as a one-argument function returning a function — a lambda:

```
catstr' s = \s' -> s ++ s'
```

These two definitions are equivalent, and either can be partially applied to just one argument, producing a one-argument function, as in:

```
greet :: String -> String
greet = catstr "Hello "
```

Strictly speaking, a function of two variables is one that takes a pair (a product type):

```
(a, b) -> c
```

It's trivial to convert between the two representations, and the two (higher-order) functions that do it are called, unsurprisingly, curry and uncurry:

```
curry :: ((a, b) -> c) -> (a -> b -> c)
curry f a b = f (a, b)
```

and

```
uncurry :: (a -> b -> c) -> ((a, b) -> c)
uncurry f (a, b) = f a b
```

Notice that curry is the *factorizer* for the universal construction of the function object. This is especially apparent if it's rewritten in this form:

```
factorizer :: ((a, b) -> c) -> (a -> (b -> c))
factorizer g = \a -> (\b -> g (a, b))
```

(As a reminder: A factorizer produces the factorizing function from a candidate.)

In non-functional languages, like C++, currying is possible but non-trivial. You can think of multi-argument functions in C++ as corresponding to Haskell functions taking tuples (although, to confuse things even more, in C++ you can define functions that take an explicit std::tuple, as well as variadic functions, and functions taking initializer lists).

You can partially apply a C++ function using the template std::bind. For instance, given a function of two strings:

```
std::string catstr(std::string s1, std::string s2) {
    return s1 + s2;
}
```

you can define a function of one string:

```
using namespace std::placeholders;

auto greet = std::bind(catstr, "Hello ", _1);
std::cout << greet("Haskell Curry");
```

Scala, which is more functional than C++ or Java, falls somewhere in between. If you anticipate that the function you're defining will be partially applied, you define it with multiple argument lists:

```
def catstr(s1: String)(s2: String) = s1 + s2
```

Of course that requires some amount of foresight or prescience on the part of a library writer.

## 9.3 Exponentials

In mathematical literature, the function object, or the internal hom-object between two objects $a$ and $b$, is often called the *exponential* and denoted by $b^a$. Notice that the argument type is in the exponent. This notation might seem strange at first, but it makes perfect sense if you think of the relationship between functions and products. We've already seen that we have to use the product in the universal construction of the internal hom-object, but the connection goes deeper than that.

This is best seen when you consider functions between finite types — types that have a finite number of values, like Bool, Char, or even Int or Double. Such functions, at least in principle, can be fully memoized or turned into data structures to be looked up. And this is the essence of the equivalence between functions, which are morphisms, and function types, which are objects.

For instance a (pure) function from Bool is completely specified by a pair of values: one corresponding to False, and one corresponding to True. The set of all possible functions from Bool to, say, Int is the set of all pairs of Ints. This is the same as the product Int × Int or, being a little creative with notation, $Int^2$.

For another example, let's look at the C++ type `char`, which contains 256 values (Haskell `Char` is larger, because Haskell uses Unicode). There are several functions in the part of the C++ Standard Library that are usually implemented using lookups. Functions like `isupper` or `isspace` are implemented using tables, which are equivalent to tuples of 256 Boolean values. A tuple is a product type, so we are dealing with products of 256 Booleans: `bool` × `bool` × `bool` × ... × `bool`. We know from arithmetics that an iterated product defines a power. If you "multiply" `bool` by itself 256 (or `char`) times, you get `bool` to the power of `char`, or $bool^{char}$.

How many values are there in the type defined as 256-tuples of `bool`? Exactly $2^{256}$. This is also the number of different functions from `char` to `bool`, each function corresponding to a unique 256-tuple. You can similarly calculate that the number of functions from `bool` to `char` is $256^2$, and so on. The exponential notation for function types makes perfect sense in these cases.

We probably wouldn't want to fully memoize a function from `int` or `double`. But the equivalence between functions and data types, if not always practical, is there. There are also infinite types, for instance lists, strings, or trees. Eager memoization of functions from those types would require infinite storage. But Haskell is a lazy language, so the boundary between lazily evaluated (infinite) data structures and functions is fuzzy. This function vs. data duality explains the identification of Haskell's function type with the categorical exponential object — which corresponds more to our idea of *data*.

## 9.4  Cartesian Closed Categories

Although I will continue using the category of sets as a model for types and functions, it's worth mentioning that there is a larger family of categories that can be used for that purpose. These categories are called *Cartesian closed*, and **Set** is just one example of such a category.

A Cartesian closed category must contain:

1. The terminal object,
2. A product of any pair of objects, and
3. An exponential for any pair of objects.

If you consider an exponential as an iterated product (possibly infinitely many times), then you can think of a Cartesian closed category as one supporting products of an arbitrary arity. In particular, the terminal object can be thought of as a product of zero objects — or the zero-th power of an object.

What's interesting about Cartesian closed categories from the perspective of computer science is that they provide models for the simply typed lambda calculus, which forms the basis of all typed programming languages.

The terminal object and the product have their duals: the initial object and the coproduct. A Cartesian closed category that also supports those two, and in which product can be distributed over coproduct

$$a \times (b + c) = a \times b + a \times c$$
$$(b + c) \times a = b \times a + c \times a$$

is called a *bicartesian closed* category. We'll see in the next section that bicartesian closed categories, of which **Set** is a prime example, have some interesting properties.

## 9.5 Exponentials and Algebraic Data Types

The interpretation of function types as exponentials fits very well into the scheme of algebraic data types. It turns out that all the basic identities from high-school algebra relating numbers zero and one, sums, products, and exponentials hold pretty much unchanged in any bicartesian closed category theory for, respectively, initial and final objects, coproducts, products, and exponentials. We don't have the tools yet to prove them (such as adjunctions or the Yoneda lemma), but I'll list them here nevertheless as a source of valuable intuitions.

### 9.5.1 Zeroth Power

$$a^0 = 1$$

In the categorical interpretation, we replace 0 with the initial object, 1 with the final object, and equality with isomorphism. The exponential is the internal hom-object. This particular exponential represents the set of morphisms going from the initial object to an arbitrary object $a$. By the definition of the initial object, there is exactly one such morphism, so the hom-set $C(0, a)$ is a singleton set. A singleton set is the terminal object in **Set**, so this identity trivially works in **Set**. What we are saying is that it works in any bicartesian closed category.

In Haskell, we replace 0 with `Void`; 1 with the unit type `()`; and the exponential with function type. The claim is that the set of functions from `Void` to any type `a` is equivalent to the unit type — which is a singleton. In other words, there is only one function `Void -> a`. We've seen this function before: it's called `absurd`.

This is a little bit tricky, for two reasons. One is that in Haskell we don't really have uninhabited types — every type contains the "result of a never ending calculation," or the bottom. The second reason is that all implementations of `absurd` are equivalent because, no matter what they do, nobody can ever execute them. There is no value that can be passed to `absurd`. (And if you manage to pass it a never ending calculation, it will never return!)

### 9.5.2 Powers of One

$$1^a = 1$$

This identity, when interpreted in **Set**, restates the definition of the terminal object: There is a unique morphism from any object to the terminal object. In general, the internal hom-object from $a$ to the terminal object is isomorphic to the terminal object itself.

In Haskell, there is only one function from any type a to unit. We've seen this function before — it's called `unit`. You can also think of it as the function `const` partially applied to `()`.

### 9.5.3 First Power

$$a^1 = a$$

This is a restatement of the observation that morphisms from the terminal object can be used to pick "elements" of the object a. The set of such morphisms is isomorphic to the object itself. In **Set**, and in Haskell, the isomorphism is between elements of the set a and functions that pick those elements, `() -> a`.

### 9.5.4 Exponentials of Sums

$$a^{b+c} = a^b \times a^c$$

Categorically, this says that the exponential from a coproduct of two objects is isomorphic to a product of two exponentials. In Haskell, this algebraic identity has a very practical, interpretation. It tells us that a function from a sum of two types is equivalent to a pair of functions from individual types. This is just the case analysis that we use when defining functions on sums. Instead of writing one function definition with a `case` statement, we usually split it into two (or more) functions dealing with each type constructor separately. For instance, take a function from the sum type (`Either Int Double`):

```
f :: Either Int Double -> String
```

It may be defined as a pair of functions from, respectively, `Int` and `Double`:

```
f (Left n) = if n < 0 then "Negative int" else "Positive int"
f (Right x) = if x < 0.0 then "Negative double" else "Positive
↪   double"
```

Here, `n` is an `Int` and `x` is a `Double`.

### 9.5.5  Exponentials of Exponentials

$$(a^b)^c = a^{b \times c}$$

This is just a way of expressing currying purely in terms of exponential objects. A function returning a function is equivalent to a function from a product (a two-argument function).

### 9.5.6  Exponentials over Products

$$(a \times b)^c = a^c \times b^c$$

In Haskell: A function returning a pair is equivalent to a pair of functions, each producing one element of the pair.

It's pretty incredible how those simple high-school algebraic identities can be lifted to category theory and have practical application in functional programming.

## 9.6  Curry-Howard Isomorphism

I have already mentioned the correspondence between logic and algebraic data types. The `Void` type and the unit type `()` correspond to false and true. Product types and sum types correspond to logical conjunction $\wedge$ (AND) and disjunction $\vee$ (OR). In this scheme, the function type we have just defined corresponds to logical implication $\Rightarrow$. In other words, the type a -> b can be read as "if a then b."

According to the Curry-Howard isomorphism, every type can be interpreted as a proposition — a statement or a judgment that may be true or false. Such a proposition is considered true if the type is inhabited and false if it isn't. In particular, a logical implication is true if the function type corresponding to it is inhabited, which means that there exists a function of that type. An implementation of a function is therefore a proof of a theorem. Writing programs is equivalent to proving theorems. Let's see a few examples.

Let's take the function eval we have introduced in the definition of the function object. Its signature is:

```
eval :: ((a -> b), a) -> b
```

It takes a pair consisting of a function and its argument and produces a result of the appropriate type. It's the Haskell implementation of the morphism:

$$eval :: (a \Rightarrow b) \times a \to b$$

which defines the function type $a \Rightarrow b$ (or the exponential object $b^a$). Let's translate this signature to a logical predicate using the Curry-Howard isomorphism:

$$((a \Rightarrow b) \wedge a) \Rightarrow b$$

Here's how you can read this statement: If it's true that $b$ follows from $a$, and $a$ is true, then $b$ must be true. This makes perfect intuitive sense and has been known since antiquity as *modus ponens*. We can prove this theorem by implementing the function:

```
eval :: ((a -> b), a) -> b
eval (f, x) = f x
```

If you give me a pair consisting of a function f taking a and returning b, and a concrete value x of type a, I can produce a concrete value of type b by simply applying the function f to x. By implementing this function I have just shown that the type ((a -> b), a) -> b is inhabited. Therefore *modus ponens* is true in our logic.

How about a predicate that is blatantly false? For instance: if $a$ or $b$ is true then $a$ must be true.

117

$$a \vee b \Longrightarrow a$$

This is obviously wrong because you can chose an *a* that is false and a *b* that is true, and that's a counter-example.

Mapping this predicate into a function signature using the Curry-Howard isomorphism, we get:

```
Either a b -> a
```

Try as you may, you can't implement this function — you can't produce a value of type a if you are called with the Right value. (Remember, we are talking about *pure* functions.)

Finally, we come to the meaning of the absurd function:

```
absurd :: Void -> a
```

Considering that Void translates into false, we get:

$$false \Longrightarrow a$$

Anything follows from falsehood (*ex falso quodlibet*). Here's one possible proof (implementation) of this statement (function) in Haskell:

```
absurd (Void a) = absurd a
```

where Void is defined as:

```
newtype Void = Void Void
```

As always, the type Void is tricky. This definition makes it impossible to construct a value because in order to construct one, you would need to provide one. Therefore, the function absurd can never be called.

These are all interesting examples, but is there a practical side to Curry-Howard isomorphism? Probably not in everyday programming. But there are programming languages like Agda or Coq, which take advantage of the Curry-Howard isomorphism to prove theorems.

Computers are not only helping mathematicians do their work — they are revolutionizing the very foundations of mathematics. The latest hot research topic in that area is called Homotopy Type Theory, and is an outgrowth of type theory. It's full of Booleans, integers, products and coproducts, function types, and so on. And, as if to dispel any doubts, the theory is being formulated in Coq and Agda. Computers are revolutionizing the world in more than one way.

## 9.7  Bibliography

1. Ralph Hinze, Daniel W. H. James, Reason Isomorphically![1]. This paper contains proofs of all those high-school algebraic identities in category theory that I mentioned in this chapter.

---

[1]http://www.cs.ox.ac.uk/ralf.hinze/publications/WGP10.pdf

# 10

# Natural Transformations

W E TALKED ABOUT functors as mappings between categories that
preserve their structure.
A functor "embeds" one category in another. It may
collapse multiple things into
one, but it never breaks connections. One way of thinking about it is that with a
functor we are modeling one
category inside another. The
source category serves as a
model, a blueprint, for some
structure that's part of the
target category.

There may be many ways
of embedding one category in another. Sometimes they are equivalent,
sometimes very different. One may collapse the whole source category
into one object, another may map every object to a different object
and every morphism to a different morphism. The same blueprint may
be realized in many different ways. Natural transformations help us
compare these realizations. They are mappings of functors — special
mappings that preserve their functorial nature.

Consider two functors $F$ and $G$ between categories $\mathbf{C}$ and $\mathbf{D}$. If you
focus on just one object $a$ in $\mathbf{C}$, it is mapped to two objects: $Fa$ and $Ga$.
A mapping of functors should therefore map $Fa$ to $Ga$.

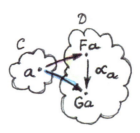

Notice that $Fa$ and $Ga$ are objects in the same category **D**. Mappings between objects in the same category should not go against the grain of the category. We don't want to make artificial connections between objects. So it's *natural* to use existing connections, namely morphisms. A natural transformation is a selection of morphisms: for every object $a$, it picks one morphism from $Fa$ to $Ga$. If we call the natural transformation $\alpha$, this morphism is called the *component* of $\alpha$ at $a$, or $\alpha_a$.

$$\alpha_a :: Fa \rightarrow Ga$$

Keep in mind that $a$ is an object in **C** while $\alpha_a$ is a morphism in **D**.

If, for some $a$, there is no morphism between $Fa$ and $Ga$ in **D**, there can be no natural transformation between $F$ and $G$.

Of course that's only half of the story, because functors not only map objects, they map morphisms as well. So what does a natural transformation do with those mappings? It turns out that the mapping of morphisms is fixed — under any natural transformation between $F$ and $G$, $Ff$ must be transformed into $Gf$. What's more, the mapping of morphisms by the two functors drastically restricts the choices we have in defining a natural transformation that's compatible with it. Consider a morphism $f$ between two objects $a$ and $b$ in **C**. It's mapped to two morphisms, $Ff$ and $Gf$ in **D**:

$$Ff :: Fa \rightarrow Fb$$
$$Gf :: Ga \rightarrow Gb$$

The natural transformation $\alpha$ provides two additional morphisms that complete the diagram in $D$:

$$\alpha_a :: Fa \rightarrow Ga$$
$$\alpha_b :: Fb \rightarrow Gb$$

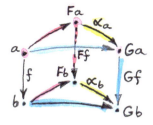

Now we have two ways of getting from $Fa$ to $Gb$. To make sure that they are equal, we must impose the *naturality condition* that holds for any $f$:

$$Gf \circ \alpha_a = \alpha_b \circ Ff$$

The naturality condition is a pretty stringent requirement. For instance, if the morphism $Ff$ is invertible, naturality determines $\alpha_b$ in terms of $\alpha_a$. It *transports* $\alpha_a$ along $f$:

$$\alpha_b = (Gf) \circ \alpha_a \circ (Ff)^{-1}$$

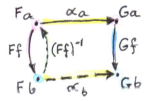

If there is more than one invertible morphism between two objects, all these transports have to agree. In general, though, morphisms are not invertible; but you can see that the existence of natural transformations between two functors is far from guaranteed. So the scarcity or the abundance of functors that are related by natural transformations may tell you a lot about the structure of categories between which they operate. We'll see some examples of that when we talk about limits and the Yoneda lemma.

Looking at a natural transformation component-wise, one may say that it maps objects to morphisms. Because of the naturality condition, one may also say that it maps morphisms to commuting squares — there is one commuting naturality square in **D** for every morphism in **C**.

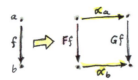

This property of natural transformations comes in very handy in a lot of categorical constructions, which often include commuting diagrams. With a judicious choice of functors, a lot of these commutativity conditions may be transformed into naturality conditions. We'll see examples of that when we get to limits, colimits, and adjunctions.

Finally, natural transformations may be used to define isomorphisms of functors. Saying that two functors are naturally isomorphic is almost like saying they are the same. *Natural isomorphism* is defined as a natural transformation whose components are all isomorphisms (invertible morphisms).

## 10.1  Polymorphic Functions

We talked about the role of functors (or, more specifically, endofunctors) in programming. They correspond to type constructors that map types to types. They also map functions to functions, and this mapping is implemented by a higher order function `fmap` (or `transform`, `then`, and the like in C++).

To construct a natural transformation we start with an object, here a type, a. One functor, F, maps it to the type $Fa$. Another functor, G, maps it to $Ga$. The component of a natural transformation `alpha` at a is a function from $Fa$ to $Ga$. In pseudo-Haskell:

```
alphaₐ :: F a -> G a
```

A natural transformation is a polymorphic function that is defined for all types a:

```
alpha :: forall a . F a -> G a
```

The `forall a` is optional in Haskell (and in fact requires turning on the language extension `ExplicitForAll`). Normally, you would write it like this:

```
alpha :: F a -> G a
```

Keep in mind that it's really a family of functions parameterized by a. This is another example of the terseness of the Haskell syntax. A similar construct in C++ would be slightly more verbose:

```
template<class A> G<A> alpha(F<A>);
```

There is a more profound difference between Haskell's polymorphic functions and C++ generic functions, and it's reflected in the way these functions are implemented and type-checked. In Haskell, a polymorphic function must be defined uniformly for all types. One formula must work across all types. This is called *parametric polymorphism.*

C++, on the other hand, supports by default *ad hoc polymorphism,* which means that a template doesn't have to be well-defined for all types. Whether a template will work for a given type is decided at instantiation time, where a concrete type is substituted for the type parameter. Type checking is deferred, which unfortunately often leads to incomprehensible error messages.

In C++, there is also a mechanism for function overloading and template specialization, which allows different definitions of the same function for different types. In Haskell this functionality is provided by type classes and type families.

Haskell's parametric polymorphism has an unexpected consequence: any polymorphic function of the type:

```
alpha :: F a -> G a
```

where F and G are functors, automatically satisfies the naturality condition. Here it is in categorical notation ($f$ is a function $f :: a \rightarrow b$):

$$Gf \circ \alpha_a = \alpha_b \circ Ff$$

In Haskell, the action of a functor G on a morphism f is implemented using fmap. I'll first write it in pseudo-Haskell, with explicit type annotations:

```
fmapG f . alphaa = alphab . fmapF f
```

Because of type inference, these annotations are not necessary, and the following equation holds:

```
fmap f . alpha = alpha . fmap f
```

125

This is still not real Haskell — function equality is not expressible in code — but it's an identity that can be used by the programmer in equational reasoning; or by the compiler, to implement optimizations.

The reason why the naturality condition is automatic in Haskell has to do with "theorems for free." Parametric polymorphism, which is used to define natural transformations in Haskell, imposes very strong limitations on the implementation — one formula for all types. These limitations translate into equational theorems about such functions. In the case of functions that transform functors, free theorems are the naturality conditions.[1]

One way of thinking about functors in Haskell that I mentioned earlier is to consider them generalized containers. We can continue this analogy and consider natural transformations to be recipes for repackaging the contents of one container into another container. We are not touching the items themselves: we don't modify them, and we don't create new ones. We are just copying (some of) them, sometimes multiple times, into a new container.

The naturality condition becomes the statement that it doesn't matter whether we modify the items first, through the application of fmap, and repackage later; or repackage first, and then modify the items in the new container, with its own implementation of fmap. These two actions, repackaging and fmapping, are orthogonal. "One moves the eggs, the other boils them."

Let's see a few examples of natural transformations in Haskell. The first is between the list functor, and the Maybe functor. It returns the head of the list, but only if the list is non-empty:

```
safeHead :: [a] -> Maybe a
safeHead [] = Nothing
safeHead (x:xs) = Just x
```

It's a function polymorphic in a. It works for any type a, with no limitations, so it is an example of parametric polymorphism. Therefore it is a natural transformation between the two functors. But just to convince ourselves, let's verify the naturality condition.

```
fmap f . safeHead = safeHead . fmap f
```

We have two cases to consider; an empty list:

---

[1] You may read more about free theorems in my blog Parametricity: Money for Nothing and Theorems for Free.

```
fmap f (safeHead []) = fmap f Nothing = Nothing
```

```
safeHead (fmap f []) = safeHead [] = Nothing
```

and a non-empty list:

```
fmap f (safeHead (x:xs)) = fmap f (Just x) = Just (f x)
```

```
safeHead (fmap f (x:xs)) = safeHead (f x : fmap f xs) = Just (f
↪   x)
```

I used the implementation of fmap for lists:

```
fmap f [] = []
fmap f (x:xs) = f x : fmap f xs
```

and for Maybe:

```
fmap f Nothing = Nothing
fmap f (Just x) = Just (f x)
```

An interesting case is when one of the functors is the trivial Const functor. A natural transformation from or to a Const functor looks just like a function that's either polymorphic in its return type or in its argument type.

For instance, length can be thought of as a natural transformation from the list functor to the Const Int functor:

```
length :: [a] -> Const Int a
length [] = Const 0
length (x:xs) = Const (1 + unConst (length xs))
```

Here, unConst is used to peel off the Const constructor:

```
unConst :: Const c a -> c
unConst (Const x) = x
```

Of course, in practice length is defined as:

```
length :: [a] -> Int
```

which effectively hides the fact that it's a natural transformation.

Finding a parametrically polymorphic function *from* a Const functor is a little harder, since it would require the creation of a value from nothing. The best we can do is:

```
scam :: Const Int a -> Maybe a
scam (Const x) = Nothing
```

Another common functor that we've seen already, and which will play an important role in the Yoneda lemma, is the `Reader` functor. I will rewrite its definition as a `newtype`:

```
newtype Reader e a = Reader (e -> a)
```

It is parameterized by two types, but is (covariantly) functorial only in the second one:

```
instance Functor (Reader e) where
    fmap f (Reader g) = Reader (\x -> f (g x))
```

For every type `e`, you can define a family of natural transformations from `Reader e` to any other functor `f`. We'll see later that the members of this family are always in one to one correspondence with the elements of `f e` (the Yoneda lemma).

For instance, consider the somewhat trivial unit type `()` with one element `()`. The functor `Reader ()` takes any type `a` and maps it into a function type `() -> a`. These are just all the functions that pick a single element from the set `a`. There are as many of these as there are elements in `a`. Now let's consider natural transformations from this functor to the `Maybe` functor:

```
alpha :: Reader () a -> Maybe a
```

There are only two of these, `dumb` and `obvious`:

```
dumb (Reader _) = Nothing
```

and

```
obvious (Reader g) = Just (g ())
```

(The only thing you can do with `g` is to apply it to the unit value `()`.)

And, indeed, as predicted by the Yoneda lemma, these correspond to the two elements of the `Maybe ()` type, which are `Nothing` and `Just ()`. We'll come back to the Yoneda lemma later — this was just a little teaser.

## 10.2  Beyond Naturality

A parametrically polymorphic function between two functors (including the edge case of the `Const` functor) is always a natural transformation. Since all standard algebraic data types are functors, any polymorphic function between such types is a natural transformation.

We also have function types at our disposal, and those are functorial in their return type. We can use them to build functors (like the `Reader` functor) and define natural transformations that are higher-order functions.

However, function types are not covariant in the argument type. They are *contravariant*. Of course contravariant functors are equivalent to covariant functors from the opposite category. Polymorphic functions between two contravariant functors are still natural transformations in the categorical sense, except that they work on functors from the opposite category to Haskell types.

You might remember the example of a contravariant functor we've looked at before:

```
newtype Op r a = Op (a -> r)
```

This functor is contravariant in a:

```
instance Contravariant (Op r) where
    contramap f (Op g) = Op (g . f)
```

We can write a polymorphic function from, say, `Op Bool` to `Op String`:

```
predToStr (Op f) = Op (\x -> if f x then "T" else "F")
```

But since the two functors are not covariant, this is not a natural transformation in Hask. However, because they are both contravariant, they satisfy the "opposite" naturality condition:

```
contramap f . predToStr = predToStr . contramap f
```

Notice that the function `f` must go in the opposite direction than what you'd use with `fmap`, because of the signature of `contramap`:

```
contramap :: (b -> a) -> (Op Bool a -> Op Bool b)
```

Are there any type constructors that are not functors, whether covariant or contravariant? Here's one example:

```
a -> a
```

This is not a functor because the same type a is used both in the negative (contravariant) and positive (covariant) position. You can't implement fmap or contramap for this type. Therefore a function of the signature:

```
(a -> a) -> f a
```

where f is an arbitrary functor, cannot be a natural transformation. Interestingly, there is a generalization of natural transformations, called dinatural transformations, that deals with such cases. We'll get to them when we discuss ends.

## 10.3 Functor Category

Now that we have mappings between functors — natural transformations — it's only natural to ask the question whether functors form a category. And indeed they do! There is one category of functors for each pair of categories, **C** and **D**. Objects in this category are functors from **C** to **D**, and morphisms are natural transformations between those functors.

We have to define composition of two natural transformations, but that's quite easy. The components of natural transformations are morphisms, and we know how to compose morphisms.

Indeed, let's take a natural transformation $\alpha$ from functor $F$ to $G$. Its component at object $a$ is some morphism:

$$\alpha_a :: Fa \rightarrow Ga$$

We'd like to compose $\alpha$ with $\beta$, which is a natural transformation from functor $G$ to $H$. The component of $\beta$ at $a$ is a morphism:

$$\beta_a :: Ga \rightarrow Ha$$

These morphisms are composable and their composition is another morphism:

$$\beta_a \circ \alpha_a :: Fa \rightarrow Ha$$

We will use this morphism as the component of the natural transformation $\beta \cdot \alpha$ — the composition of two natural transformations $\beta$ after $\alpha$:

$$(\beta \cdot \alpha)_a = \beta_a \circ \alpha_a$$

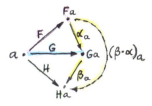

One (long) look at a diagram convinces us that the result of this composition is indeed a natural transformation from F to H:

$$Hf \circ (\beta \cdot \alpha)_a = (\beta \cdot \alpha)_b \circ Ff$$

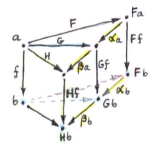

Composition of natural transformations is associative, because their components, which are regular morphisms, are associative with respect to their composition.

Finally, for each functor F there is an identity natural transformation $1_F$ whose components are the identity morphisms:

$$\mathrm{id}_{Fa} :: Fa \to Fa$$

So, indeed, functors form a category.

A word about notation. Following Saunders Mac Lane I use the dot for the kind of natural transformation composition I have just described. The problem is that there are two ways of composing natural transformations. This one is called the vertical composition, because the functors are usually stacked up vertically in the diagrams that describe it. Vertical composition is important in defining the functor category. I'll explain horizontal composition shortly.

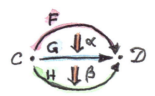

The functor category between categories **C** and **D** is written as **Fun**(**C**, **D**), or [**C**, **D**], or sometimes as **D**$^C$. This last notation suggests that a functor category itself might be considered a function object (an exponential) in some other category. Is this indeed the case?

Let's have a look at the hierarchy of abstractions that we've been building so far. We started with a category, which is a collection of objects and morphisms. Categories themselves (or, strictly speaking *small* categories, whose objects form sets) are themselves objects in a higher-level category **Cat**. Morphisms in that category are functors. A Hom-set in **Cat** is a set of functors. For instance **Cat**(**C**, **D**) is a set of functors between two categories **C** and **D**.

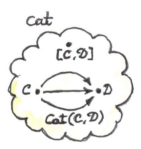

A functor category [**C**, **D**] is also a set of functors between two categories (plus natural transformations as morphisms). Its objects are the same as the members of **Cat**(**C**, **D**). Moreover, a functor category, being a category, must itself be an object of **Cat** (it so happens that the functor category between two small categories is itself small). We have a relationship between a Hom-set in a category and an object in the same category. The situation is exactly like the exponential object that we've seen in the last section. Let's see how we can construct the latter in **Cat**.

As you may remember, in order to construct an exponential, we need to first define a product. In **Cat**, this turns out to be relatively easy, because small categories are *sets* of objects, and we know how to define Cartesian products of sets. So an object in a product category $C \times D$ is just a pair of objects, $(c, d)$, one from $C$ and one from $D$. Similarly, a morphism between two such pairs, $(c, d)$ and $(c', d')$, is a pair of morphisms, $(f, g)$, where $f :: c \rightarrow c'$ and $g :: d \rightarrow d'$. These pairs of morphisms compose component-wise, and there is always an identity pair that is just a pair of identity morphisms. To make the long story short, $\mathbf{Cat}$ is a full-blown Cartesian closed category in which there is an exponential object $D^C$ for any pair of categories. And by "object" in $\mathbf{Cat}$ I mean a category, so $D^C$ is a category, which we can identify with the functor category between $C$ and $D$.

## 10.4  2-Categories

With that out of the way, let's have a closer look at $\mathbf{Cat}$. By definition, any Hom-set in $\mathbf{Cat}$ is a set of functors. But, as we have seen, functors between two objects have a richer structure than just a set. They form a category, with natural transformations acting as morphisms. Since functors are considered morphisms in $\mathbf{Cat}$, natural transformations are morphisms between morphisms.

This richer structure is an example of a 2-category, a generalization of a category where, besides objects and morphisms (which might be called 1-morphisms in this context), there are also 2-morphisms, which are morphisms between morphisms.

In the case of $\mathbf{Cat}$ seen as a 2-category we have:

- Objects: (Small) categories
- 1-morphisms: Functors between categories
- 2-morphisms: Natural transformations between functors.

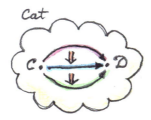

Instead of a Hom-set between two categories $C$ and $D$, we have a Hom-category — the functor category $D^C$. We have regular functor composition: a functor $F$ from $D^C$ composes with a functor $G$ from $E^D$ to give

$G \circ F$ from $\mathbf{E}^C$. But we also have composition inside each Hom-category — vertical composition of natural transformations, or 2-morphisms, between functors.

With two kinds of composition in a 2-category, the question arises: How do they interact with each other?

Let's pick two functors, or 1-morphisms, in **Cat**:

$$F :: \mathbf{C} \to \mathbf{D}$$
$$G :: \mathbf{D} \to \mathbf{E}$$

and their composition:

$$G \circ F :: \mathbf{C} \to \mathbf{E}$$

Suppose we have two natural transformations, $\alpha$ and $\beta$, that act, respectively, on functors $F$ and $G$:

$$\alpha :: F \to F'$$
$$\beta :: G \to G'$$

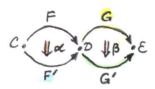

Notice that we cannot apply vertical composition to this pair, because the target of $\alpha$ is different from the source of $\beta$. In fact they are members of two different functor categories: $\mathbf{D}^C$ and $\mathbf{E}^D$. We can, however, apply composition to the functors $F'$ and $G'$, because the target of $F'$ is the source of $G'$ — it's the category $\mathbf{D}$. What's the relation between the functors $G' \circ F'$ and $G \circ F$?

Having $\alpha$ and $\beta$ at our disposal, can we define a natural transformation from $G \circ F$ to $G' \circ F'$? Let me sketch the construction.

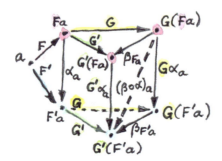

134

As usual, we start with an object $a$ in C. Its image splits into two objects in D: $Fa$ and $F'a$. There is also a morphism, a component of $\alpha$, connecting these two objects:

$$\alpha_a :: Fa \rightarrow F'a$$

When going from D to E, these two objects split further into four objects: $G(Fa)$, $G'(Fa)$, $G(F'a)$, $G'(F'a)$. We also have four morphisms forming a square. Two of these morphisms are the components of the natural transformation $\beta$:

$$\beta_{Fa} :: G(Fa) \rightarrow G'(Fa)$$
$$\beta_{F'a} :: G(F'a) \rightarrow G'(F'a)$$

The other two are the images of $\alpha_a$ under the two functors (functors map morphisms):

$$G\alpha_a :: G(Fa) \rightarrow G(F'a)$$
$$G'\alpha_a :: G'(Fa) \rightarrow G'(F'a)$$

That's a lot of morphisms. Our goal is to find a morphism that goes from $G(Fa)$ to $G'(F'a)$, a candidate for the component of a natural transformation connecting the two functors $G \circ F$ and $G' \circ F'$. In fact there's not one but two paths we can take from $G(Fa)$ to $G'(F'a)$:

$$G'\alpha_a \circ \beta_{Fa}$$
$$\beta_{F'a} \circ G\alpha_a$$

Luckily for us, they are equal, because the square we have formed turns out to be the naturality square for $\beta$.

We have just defined a component of a natural transformation from $G \circ F$ to $G' \circ F'$. The proof of naturality for this transformation is pretty straightforward, provided you have enough patience.

We call this natural transformation the *horizontal composition* of $\alpha$ and $\beta$:

$$\beta \circ \alpha :: G \circ F \rightarrow G' \circ F'$$

Again, following Mac Lane I use the small circle for horizontal composition, although you may also encounter star in its place.

Here's a categorical rule of thumb: Every time you have composition, you should look for a category. We have vertical composition of natural transformations, and it's part of the functor category. But what about the horizontal composition? What category does that live in?

The way to figure this out is to look at **Cat** sideways. Look at natural transformations not as arrows between functors but as arrows between categories. A natural transformation sits between two categories, the ones that are connected by the functors it transforms. We can think of it as connecting these two categories.

Let's focus on two objects of **Cat** — categories **C** and **D**. There is a set of natural transformations that go between functors that connect **C** to **D**. These natural transformations are our new arrows from **C** to **D**. By the same token, there are natural transformations going between functors that connect **D** to **E**, which we can treat as new arrows going from **D** to **E**. Horizontal composition is the composition of these arrows.

We also have an identity arrow going from **C** to **C**. It's the identity natural transformation that maps the identity functor on **C** to itself. Notice that the identity for horizontal composition is also the identity for vertical composition, but not vice versa.

Finally, the two compositions satisfy the interchange law:

$$(\beta' \cdot \alpha') \circ (\beta \cdot \alpha) = (\beta' \circ \beta) \cdot (\alpha' \circ \alpha)$$

I will quote Saunders Mac Lane here: The reader may enjoy writing down the evident diagrams needed to prove this fact.

There is one more piece of notation that might come in handy in the future. In this new sideways interpretation of **Cat** there are two ways of getting from object to object: using a functor or using a natural transformation. We can, however, re-interpret the functor arrow as a special kind of natural transformation: the identity natural transformation acting on this functor. So you'll often see this notation:

$$F \circ \alpha$$

where $F$ is a functor from **D** to **E**, and $\alpha$ is a natural transformation between two functors going from **C** to **D**. Since you can't compose a functor with a natural transformation, this is interpreted as a horizontal composition of the identity natural transformation $1_F$ after $\alpha$.

Similarly:

$$\alpha \circ F$$

is a horizontal composition of $\alpha$ after $1_F$.

## 10.5 Conclusion

This concludes the first part of the book. We've learned the basic vocabulary of category theory. You may think of objects and categories as nouns; and morphisms, functors, and natural transformations as verbs. Morphisms connect objects, functors connect categories, natural transformations connect functors.

But we've also seen that, what appears as an action at one level of abstraction, becomes an object at the next level. A set of morphisms turns into a function object. As an object, it can be a source or a target of another morphism. That's the idea behind higher order functions.

A functor maps objects to objects, so we can use it as a type constructor, or a parametric type. A functor also maps morphisms, so it is a higher order function — fmap. There are some simple functors, like Const, product, and coproduct, that can be used to generate a large variety of algebraic data types. Function types are also functorial, both covariant and contravariant, and can be used to extend algebraic data types.

Functors may be looked upon as objects in the functor category. As such, they become sources and targets of morphisms: natural transformations. A natural transformation is a special type of polymorphic function.

## 10.6 Challenges

1. Define a natural transformation from the Maybe functor to the list functor. Prove the naturality condition for it.
2. Define at least two different natural transformations between Reader () and the list functor. How many different lists of () are there?
3. Continue the previous exercise with Reader Bool and Maybe.
4. Show that horizontal composition of natural transformation satisfies the naturality condition (hint: use components). It's a good exercise in diagram chasing.

5. Write a short essay about how you may enjoy writing down the evident diagrams needed to prove the interchange law.
6. Create a few test cases for the opposite naturality condition of transformations between different Op functors. Here's one choice:

```
op :: Op Bool Int
op = Op (\x -> x > 0)
```

and

```
f :: String -> Int
f x = read x
```

# Part Two

# 11

# Declarative Programming

I N THE FIRST PART of the book I argued that both category theory and programming are about composability. In programming, you keep decomposing a problem until you reach the level of detail that you can deal with, solve each subproblem in turn, and re-compose the solutions bottom-up. There are, roughly speaking, two ways of doing it: by telling the computer what to do, or by telling it how to do it. One is called declarative and the other imperative.

You can see this even at the most basic level. Composition itself may be defined declaratively; as in, h is a composite of g after f:

```
h = g . f
```

or imperatively; as in, call f first, remember the result of that call, then call g with the result:

```
h x = let y = f x
      in g y
```

The imperative version of a program is usually described as a sequence of actions ordered in time. In particular, the call to g cannot happen before the execution of f completes. At least, that's the conceptual picture — in a lazy language, with *call-by-need* argument passing, the actual execution may proceed differently.

In fact, depending on the cleverness of the compiler, there may be little or no difference between how declarative and imperative code is executed. But the two methodologies differ, sometimes drastically, in the way we approach problem solving and in the maintainability and testability of the resulting code.

The main question is: when faced with a problem, do we always have the choice between a declarative and imperative approaches to solving it? And, if there is a declarative solution, can it always be translated into computer code? The answer to this question is far from obvious and, if we could find it, we would probably revolutionize our understanding of the universe.

Let me elaborate. There is a similar duality in physics, which either points at some deep underlying principle, or tells us something about how our minds work. Richard Feynman mentions this duality as an inspiration in his own work on quantum electrodynamics.

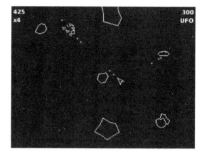

There are two forms of expressing most laws of physics. One uses local, or infinitesimal, considerations. We look at the state of a system around a small neighborhood, and predict how it will evolve within the next instant of time. This is usually expressed using differential equations that have to be integrated, or summed up, over a period of time.

Notice how this approach resembles imperative thinking: we reach the final solution by following a sequence of small steps, each depending on the result of the previous one. In fact, computer simulations of physical systems are routinely implemented by turning differential equations into difference equations and iterating them. This is how spaceships are animated in the asteroids game. At each time step, the position of a spaceship is changed by adding a small increment, which is calculated by multiplying its velocity by the time delta. The velocity, in turn, is changed by a small increment proportional to acceleration, which is given by force divided by mass.

These are the direct encodings of the differential equations corresponding to Newton's laws of motion:

$$F = m\frac{dv}{dt}$$
$$v = \frac{dx}{dt}$$

Similar methods may be applied to more complex problems, like the propagation of electromagnetic fields using Maxwell's equations, or even the behavior of quarks and gluons inside a proton using lattice QCD (quantum chromodynamics).

This local thinking combined with discretization of space and time that is encouraged by the use of digital computers found its extreme expression in the heroic attempt by Stephen Wolfram to reduce the complexity of the whole universe to a system of cellular automata.

The other approach is global. We look at the initial and the final state of the system, and calculate a trajectory that connects them by minimizing a certain functional. The simplest example is the Fermat's principle of least time. It states that light rays propagate along paths that minimize their flight time. In particular, in the absence of reflecting or refracting objects, a light ray from point $A$ to point $B$ will take the shortest path, which is a straight line. But light propagates slower in dense (transparent) materials, like water or glass. So if you pick the starting point in the air, and the ending point under water, it's more advantageous for light to travel longer in the air and then take a shortcut through water. The path of minimum time makes the ray refract at the boundary of air and water, resulting in Snell's law of refraction:

$$\frac{sin(\theta_1)}{sin(\theta_2)} = \frac{v_1}{v_2}$$

where $v_1$ is the speed of light in the air and $v_2$ is the speed of light in the water.

All of classical mechanics can be derived from the principle of least action. The action can be calculated for any trajectory by integrating the Lagrangian, which is the difference between kinetic and potential energy (notice: it's the difference, not the sum — the sum would be the total energy). When you fire a mortar to hit a given target, the projectile will first go up, where the potential energy due to gravity is higher, and spend some time there racking up negative contribution to the action. It will also slow down at the top of the parabola, to minimize kinetic energy. Then it will speed up to go quickly through the area of low potential energy.

Feynman's greatest contribution was to realize that the principle of least action can be generalized to quantum mechanics. There, again, the problem is formulated in terms of initial state and final state. The Feynman path integral between those states is used to calculate the probability of transition.

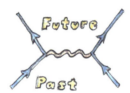

The point is that there is a curious unexplained duality in the way we can describe the laws of physics. We can use the local picture, in which things happen sequentially and in small increments. Or we can use the global picture, where we declare the initial and final conditions, and everything in between just follows.

The global approach can be also used in programming, for instance when implementing ray tracing. We declare the position of the eye and the positions of light sources, and figure out the paths that the light rays may take to connect them. We don't explicitly minimize the time of flight for each ray, but we do use Snell's law and the geometry of reflection to the same effect.

The biggest difference between the local and the global approach is in their treatment of space and, more importantly, time. The local approach embraces the immediate gratification of here and now, whereas the global approach takes a long-term static view, as if the future had been preordained, and we were only analyzing the properties of some eternal universe.

Nowhere is it better illustrated than in the Functional Reactive Programming (FRP) approach to user interaction. Instead of writing separate handlers for every possible user action, all having access to some shared mutable state, FRP treats external events as an infinite list, and applies a series of transformations to it. Conceptually, the list of all our future actions is there, available as the input data to our program. From a program's perspective there's no difference between the list of digits of $\pi$, a list of pseudo-random numbers, or a list of mouse positions coming through computer hardware. In each case, if you want to get the $n^{\text{th}}$ item, you have to first go through the first $n - 1$ items. When applied to temporal events, we call this property *causality*.

So what does it have to do with category theory? I will argue that category theory encourages a global approach and therefore supports declarative programming. First of all, unlike calculus, it has no built-in notion of distance, or neighborhood, or time. All we have is abstract objects and abstract connections between them. If you can get from $A$ to $B$ through a series of steps, you can also get there in one leap. Moreover, the major tool of category theory is the universal construction, which is the epitome of a global approach. We've seen it in action, for instance, in the definition of the categorical product. It was done by specifying its properties — a very declarative approach. It's an object equipped with two projections, and it's the best such object — it optimizes a certain property: the property of factorizing the projections of other such objects.

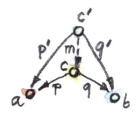

Compare this with Fermat's principle of minimum time, or the principle of least action.

Conversely, contrast this with the traditional definition of a Cartesian product, which is much more imperative. You describe how to create an element of the product by picking one element from one set and another element from another set. It's a recipe for creating a pair. And there's another for disassembling a pair.

In almost every programming language, including functional languages like Haskell, product types, coproduct types, and function types are built in, rather than being defined by universal constructions; although there have been attempts at creating categorical programming languages (see, e.g., Tatsuya Hagino's thesis[1]).

Whether used directly or not, categorical definitions justify pre-existing programming constructs, and give rise to new ones. Most importantly, category theory provides a meta-language for reasoning about computer programs at a declarative level. It also encourages reasoning about problem specification before it is cast into code.

---

[1]http://web.sfc.keio.ac.jp/~hagino/thesis.pdf

# 12

## Limits and Colimits

I T SEEMS LIKE IN CATEGORY THEORY everything is related to everything and everything can be viewed from many angles. Take for instance the universal construction of the product. Now that we know more about functors and natural transformations, can we simplify and, possibly, generalize it? Let us try.

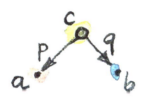

The construction of a product starts with the selection of two objects *a* and *b*, whose product we want to construct. But what does it mean to *select objects*? Can we rephrase this action in more categorical terms? Two objects form a pattern — a very simple pattern. We can abstract this pattern into a category — a very simple category, but a category nevertheless. It's a category that we'll call 2. It contains just two objects, 1 and 2, and no morphisms other than the two obligatory identities. Now we can rephrase the selection of two objects in C as the act of defining a functor *D* from the category 2 to C. A functor maps objects to objects, so its image is just two objects (or it could be one, if the functor collapses objects, which is fine too). It also maps morphisms — in this case it simply maps identity morphisms to identity morphisms.

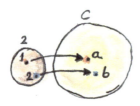

What's great about this approach is that it builds on categorical notions, eschewing the imprecise descriptions like "selecting objects", taken straight from the hunter-gatherer lexicon of our ancestors. And, incidentally, it is also easily generalized, because nothing can stop us from using categories more complex than 2 to define our patterns.

But let's continue. The next step in the definition of a product is the selection of the candidate object $c$. Here again, we could rephrase the selection in terms of a functor from a singleton category. And indeed, if we were using Kan extensions, that would be the right thing to do. But since we are not ready for Kan extensions yet, there is another trick we can use: a constant functor $\Delta$ from the same category 2 to C. The selection of $c$ in C can be done with $\Delta_c$. Remember, $\Delta_c$ maps all objects into $c$ and all morphisms into $id_c$.

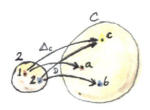

Now we have two functors, $\Delta_c$ and $D$ going between 2 and C so it's only natural to ask about natural transformations between them. Since there are only two objects in 2, a natural transformation will have two components. Object 1 in 2 is mapped to $c$ by $\Delta_c$ and to $a$ by $D$. So the component of a natural transformation between $\Delta_c$ and $D$ at 1 is a morphism from $c$ to $a$. We can call it $p$. Similarly, the second component is a morphism $q$ from $c$ to $b$ — the image of the object 2 in 2 under $D$. But these are exactly like the two projections we used in our original definition of the product. So instead of talking about selecting objects and projections, we can just talk about picking functors and natural transformations. It so happens that in this simple case the naturality condition for our transformation is trivially satisfied, because there are no morphisms (other than the identities) in 2.

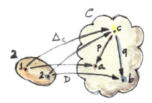

A generalization of this construction to categories other than 2 — ones that, for instance, contain non-trivial morphisms — will impose naturality conditions on the transformation between $\Delta_c$ and $D$. We call such transformation a *cone*, because the image of $\Delta$ is the apex of a cone/pyramid whose sides are formed by the components of the natural transformation. The image of $D$ forms the base of the cone.

In general, to build a cone, we start with a category $I$ that defines the pattern. It's a small, often finite category. We pick a functor $D$ from $I$ to $C$ and call it (or its image) a *diagram*. We pick some $c$ in $C$ as the apex of our cone. We use it to define the constant functor $\Delta_c$ from $I$ to $C$. A natural transformation from $\Delta_c$ to $D$ is then our cone. For a finite $I$ it's just a bunch of morphisms connecting $c$ to the diagram: the image of $I$ under $D$.

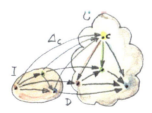

Naturality requires that all triangles (the walls of the pyramid) in this diagram commute. Indeed, take any morphism $f$ in $I$. The functor $D$ maps it to a morphism $Df$ in $C$, a morphism that forms the base of some triangle. The constant functor $\Delta_c$ maps $f$ to the identity morphism on $c$. $\Delta$ squishes the two ends of the morphism into one object, and the naturality square becomes a commuting triangle. The two arms of this triangle are the components of the natural transformation.

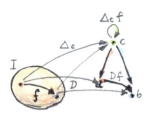

So that's one cone. What we are interested in is the *universal cone* — just like we picked a universal object for our definition of a product.

There are many ways to go about it. For instance, we may define a *category of cones* based on a given functor $D$. Objects in that category are cones. Not every object $c$ in $C$ can be an apex of a cone, though, because there may be no natural transformation between $\Delta_c$ and $D$.

To make it a category, we also have to define morphisms between cones. These would be fully determined by morphisms between their apexes. But not just any morphism will do. Remember that, in our construction of the product, we imposed the condition that the morphisms between candidate objects (the apexes) must be common factors for the projections. For instance:

```
p' = p . m
q' = q . m
```

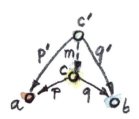

This condition translates, in the general case, to the condition that the triangles whose one side is the factorizing morphism all commute.

150

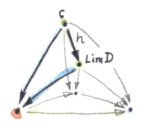

The commuting triangle connecting two cones, with the factorizing morphism $h$ (here, the lower cone is the universal one, with $\mathrm{Lim}D$ as its apex)

We'll take those factorizing morphisms as the morphisms in our category of cones. It's easy to check that those morphisms indeed compose, and that the identity morphism is a factorizing morphism as well. Cones therefore form a category.

Now we can define the universal cone as the *terminal object* in the category of cones. The definition of the terminal object states that there is a unique morphism from any other object to that object. In our case it means that there is a unique factorizing morphism from the apex of any other cone to the apex of the universal cone. We call this universal cone the *limit* of the diagram $D$, $\mathrm{Lim}D$ (in the literature, you'll often see a left arrow pointing towards $I$ under the Lim sign). Often, as a shorthand, we call the apex of this cone the limit (or the limit object).

The intuition is that the limit embodies the properties of the whole diagram in a single object. For instance, the limit of our two-object diagram is the product of two objects. The product (together with the two projections) contains the information about both objects. And being universal means that it has no extraneous junk.

## 12.1   Limit as a Natural Isomorphism

There is still something unsatisfying about this definition of a limit. I mean, it's workable, but we still have this commutativity condition for the triangles that are linking any two cones. It would be so much more elegant if we could replace it with some naturality condition. But how?

We are no longer dealing with one cone but with a whole collection (in fact, a category) of cones. If the limit exists (and — let's make it clear — there's no guarantee of that), one of those cones is the universal cone. For every other cone we have a unique factorizing morphism that maps its apex, let's call it $c$, to the apex of the universal cone, which we named $\text{Lim}D$. (In fact, I can skip the word "other", because the identity morphism maps the universal cone to itself and it trivially factorizes through itself.) Let me repeat the important part: given any cone, there is a unique morphism of a special kind. We have a mapping of cones to special morphisms, and it's a one-to-one mapping.

This special morphism is a member of the hom-set $C(c, \text{Lim}D)$. The other members of this hom-set are less fortunate, in the sense that they don't factorize the mapping of cones. What we want is to be able to pick, for each $c$, one morphism from the set $C(c, \text{Lim}D)$ — a morphism that satisfies the particular commutativity condition. Does that sound like defining a natural transformation? It most certainly does!

But what are the functors that are related by this transformation?

One functor is the mapping of $c$ to the set $C(c, \text{Lim}D)$. It's a functor from C to **Set** — it maps objects to sets. In fact it's a contravariant functor. Here's how we define its action on morphisms: Let's take a morphism $f$ from $c'$ to $c$:

$$f :: c' \to c$$

Our functor maps $c'$ to the set $C(c', \text{Lim}D)$. To define the action of this functor on $f$ (in other words, to lift $f$), we have to define the corresponding mapping between $C(c, \text{Lim}D)$ and $C(c', \text{Lim}D)$. So let's pick one element $u$ of $C(c, \text{Lim}D)$ and see if we can map it to some element of $C(c', \text{Lim}D)$. An element of a hom-set is a morphism, so we have:

$$u :: c \to \text{Lim}D$$

We can precompose $u$ with $f$ to get:

$$u.f :: c' \to \text{Lim}D$$

And that's an element of $C(c', \text{Lim}D)$— so indeed, we have found a mapping of morphisms:

```
contramap :: (c' -> c) -> (c -> LimD) -> (c' -> LimD)
contramap f u = u . f
```

Notice the inversion in the order of $c$ and $c'$ characteristic of a *contravariant* functor.

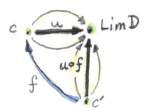

To define a natural transformation, we need another functor that's also a mapping from **C** to **Set**. But this time we'll consider a set of cones. Cones are just natural transformations, so we are looking at the set of natural transformations $Nat(\Delta_c, D)$. The mapping from c to this particular set of natural transformations is a (contravariant) functor. How can we show that? Again, let's define its action on a morphism:

$$f :: c' \rightarrow c$$

The lifting of $f$ should be a mapping of natural transformations between two functors that go from **I** to **C**:

$$Nat(\Delta_c, D) \rightarrow Nat(\Delta_{c'}, D)$$

How do we map natural transformations? Every natural transformation is a selection of morphisms — its components — one morphism per element of **I**. A component of some $\alpha$ (a member of $Nat(\Delta_c, D)$) at $a$ (an object in **I**) is a morphism:

$$\alpha_u \ :: \ \Delta_\iota a \longrightarrow Da$$

or, using the definition of the constant functor $\Delta$,

$$\alpha_a :: c \rightarrow Da$$

Given $f$ and $\alpha$, we have to construct a $\beta$, a member of $Nat(\Delta_{c'}, D)$. Its component at $a$ should be a morphism:

$$\beta_a :: c' \rightarrow Da$$

We can easily get the latter ($\beta_a$) from the former ($\alpha_a$) by precomposing it with $f$:

$$\beta_a = \alpha_a \cdot f$$

It's relatively easy to show that those components indeed add up to a natural transformation.

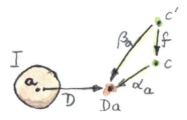

Given our morphism $f$, we have thus built a mapping between two natural transformations, component-wise. This mapping defines contramap for the functor:

$$c \rightarrow Nat(\Delta_c, D)$$

What I have just done is to show you that we have two (contravariant) functors from **C** to **Set**. I haven't made any assumptions — these functors always exist.

Incidentally, the first of these functors plays an important role in category theory, and we'll see it again when we talk about Yoneda's lemma. There is a name for contravariant functors from any category **C** to **Set**: they are called "presheaves". This one is called a *representable presheaf*. The second functor is also a presheaf.

Now that we have two functors, we can talk about natural transformations between them. So without further ado, here's the conclusion: A functor $D$ from **I** to **C** has a limit $\mathrm{Lim}D$ if and only if there is a natural isomorphism between the two functors I have just defined:

$$\mathbf{C}(c, \mathrm{Lim}D) \simeq Nat(\Delta_c, D)$$

Let me remind you what a natural isomorphism is. It's a natural transformation whose every component is an isomorphism, that is to say an invertible morphism.

I'm not going to go through the proof of this statement. The procedure is pretty straightforward if not tedious. When dealing with natural transformations, you usually focus on components, which are morphisms. In this case, since the target of both functors is **Set**, the components of the natural isomorphism will be functions. These are higher order functions, because they go from the hom-set to the set of natural transformations. Again, you can analyze a function by considering what it does to its argument: here the argument will be a morphism — a member of $\mathbf{C}(c, \mathrm{Lim}D)$ — and the result will be a natural transformation — a member of $Nat(\Delta_c, D)$, or what we have called a cone.

This natural transformation, in turn, has its own components, which are morphisms. So it's morphisms all the way down, and if you can keep track of them, you can prove the statement.

The most important result is that the naturality condition for this isomorphism is exactly the commutativity condition for the mapping of cones.

As a preview of coming attractions, let me mention that the set $Nat(\Delta_c, D)$ can be thought of as a hom-set in the functor category; so our natural isomorphism relates two hom-sets, which points at an even more general relationship called an adjunction.

## 12.2   Examples of Limits

We've seen that the categorical product is a limit of a diagram generated by a simple category we called 2.

There is an even simpler example of a limit: the terminal object. The first impulse would be to think of a singleton category as leading to a terminal object, but the truth is even starker than that: the terminal object is a limit generated by an empty category. A functor from an empty category selects no object, so a cone shrinks to just the apex. The universal cone is the lone apex that has a unique morphism coming to it from any other apex. You will recognize this as the definition of the terminal object.

The next interesting limit is called the *equalizer*. It's a limit generated by a two-element category with two parallel morphisms going between them (and, as always, the identity morphisms). This category selects a diagram in C consisting of two objects, *a* and *b*, and two morphisms:

```
f :: a -> b
g :: a -> b
```

To build a cone over this diagram, we have to add the apex, *c* and two projections:

```
p :: c -> a
q :: c -> b
```

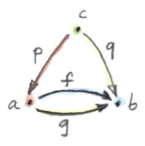

We have two triangles that must commute:

```
q = f . p
q = g . p
```

This tells us that $q$ is uniquely determined by one of these equations, say, $q = f . p$, and we can omit it from the picture. So we are left with just one condition:

```
f . p = g . p
```

The way to think about it is that, if we restrict our attention to **Set**, the image of the function $p$ selects a subset of $a$. When restricted to this subset, the functions $f$ and $g$ are equal.

For instance, take $a$ to be the two-dimensional plane parameterized by coordinates $x$ and $y$. Take $b$ to be the real line, and take:

```
f (x, y) = 2 * y + x
g (x, y) = y - x
```

The equalizer for these two functions is the set of real numbers (the apex, $c$) and the function:

```
p t = (t, (-2) * t)
```

Notice that $(p\ t)$ defines a straight line in the two-dimensional plane. Along this line, the two functions are equal.

Of course, there are other sets $c'$ and functions $p'$ that may lead to the equality:

```
f . p' = g . p'
```

but they all uniquely factor out through $p$. For instance, we can take the singleton set () as $c'$ and the function:

```
p'() = (0, 0)
```

It's a good cone, because $f(0,0) = g(0,0)$. But it's not universal, because of the unique factorization through $h$:

```
p' = p . h
```

with

```
h () = 0
```

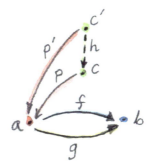

An equalizer can thus be used to solve equations of the type $f\ x = g\ x$. But it's much more general, because it's defined in terms of objects and morphisms rather than algebraically.

An even more general idea of solving an equation is embodied in another limit — the pullback. Here, we still have two morphisms that we want to equate, but this time their domains are different. We start with a three-object category of the shape: $1 \rightarrow 2 \leftarrow 3$. The diagram corresponding to this category consists of three objects, $a$, $b$, and $c$, and two morphisms:

```
f :: a -> b
g :: c -> b
```

This diagram is often called a *cospan*.

A cone built on top of this diagram consists of the apex, $d$, and three morphisms:

```
p :: d -> a
q :: d -> c
r :: d -> b
```

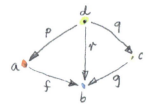

Commutativity conditions tell us that $r$ is completely determined by the other morphisms, and can be omitted from the picture. So we are only left with the following condition:

```
g . q = f . p
```

A pullback is a universal cone of this shape.

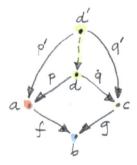

Again, if you narrow your focus down to sets, you can think of the object $d$ as consisting of pairs of elements from $a$ and $c$ for which $f$ acting on the first component is equal to $g$ acting on the second component. If this is still too general, consider the special case in which $g$ is a constant function, say $g\_ = 1.23$ (assuming that $b$ is a set of real numbers). Then you are really solving the equation:

```
f x = 1.23
```

In this case, the choice of $c$ is irrelevant (as long as it's not an empty set), so we can take it to be a singleton set. The set $a$ could, for instance, be the set of three-dimensional vectors, and $f$ the vector length. Then the pullback is the set of pairs $(v, ())$, where $v$ is a vector of length 1.23 (a solution to the equation $\sqrt{(x^2 + y^2 + z^2)} = 1.23$), and $()$ is the dummy element of the singleton set.

But pullbacks have more general applications, also in programming. For instance, consider C++ classes as a category in which morphism are arrows that connect subclasses to superclasses. We'll consider inheritance a transitive property, so if C inherits from B and B inherits from A then we'll say that C inherits from A (after all, you can pass a pointer to C where a pointer to A is expected). Also, we'll assume that C inherits from C, so we have the identity arrow for every class. This way subclassing is aligned with subtyping. C++ also supports multiple inheritance, so you can construct a diamond inheritance diagram with two classes B and C inheriting from A, and a fourth class D multiply inheriting from B and C. Normally, D would get two copies of A, which is rarely desirable; but you can use virtual inheritance to have just one copy of A in D.

What would it mean to have D be a pullback in this diagram? It would mean that any class E that multiply inherits from B and C is also a subclass of D. This is not directly expressible in C++, where subtyping is nominal (the C++ compiler wouldn't infer this kind of class relationship — it would require "duck typing"). But we could go outside of the subtyping relationship and instead ask whether a cast from E to D would be safe or not. This cast would be safe if D were the bare-bone combination of B and C, with no additional data and no overriding of methods. And, of course, there would be no pullback if there is a name conflict between some methods of B and C.

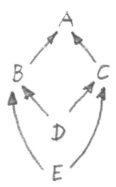

There's also a more advanced use of a pullback in type inference. There is often a need to *unify* types of two expressions. For instance, suppose that the compiler wants to infer the type of a function:

```
twice f x = f (f x)
```

It will assign preliminary types to all variables and sub-expressions. In particular, it will assign:

```
f         :: t0
x         :: t1
f x       :: t2
f (f x)   :: t3
```

from which it will deduce that:

```
twice :: t0 -> t1 -> t3
```

It will also come up with a set of constraints resulting from the rules of function application:

```
t0 = t1 -> t2 -- because f is applied to x
t0 = t2 -> t3 -- because f is applied to (f x)
```

These constraints have to be unified by finding a set of types (or type variables) that, when substituted for the unknown types in both expressions, produce the same type. One such substitution is:

```
t1 = t2 = t3 = Int
twice :: (Int -> Int) -> Int -> Int
```

but, obviously, it's not the most general one. The most general substitution is obtained using a pullback. I won't go into the details, because they are beyond the scope of this book, but you can convince yourself that the result should be:

```
twice :: (t -> t) -> t -> t
```

with t a free type variable.

## 12.3 Colimits

Just like all constructions in category theory, limits have their dual image in opposite categories. When you invert the direction of all arrows in a cone, you get a co-cone, and the universal one of those is called a colimit. Notice that the inversion also affects the factorizing morphism, which now flows from the universal co-cone to any other co-cone.

160

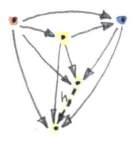

Cocone with a factorizing morphism $h$ connecting two apexes.

A typical example of a colimit is a coproduct, which corresponds to the diagram generated by 2, the category we've used in the definition of the product.

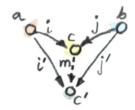

Both the product and the coproduct embody the essence of a pair of objects, each in a different way.

Just like the terminal object was a limit, so the initial object is a colimit corresponding to the diagram based on an empty category.

The dual of the pullback is called the *pushout*. It's based on a diagram called a span, generated by the category $1 \leftarrow 2 \rightarrow 3$.

## 12.4 Continuity

I said previously that functors come close to the idea of continuous mappings of categories, in the sense that they never break existing connections (morphisms). The actual definition of a *continuous functor F* from a category **C** to **C'** includes the requirement that the functor preserve limits. Every diagram $D$ in **C** can be mapped to a diagram $F \circ D$ in **C'** by simply composing two functors. The continuity condition for $F$ states that, if the diagram $D$ has a limit $\mathrm{Lim}D$, then the diagram $F \circ D$ also has a limit, and it is equal to $F(\mathrm{Lim}D)$.

Notice that, because functors map morphisms to morphisms, and compositions to compositions, an image of a cone is always a cone. A commuting triangle is always mapped to a commuting triangle (functors preserve composition). The same is true for the factorizing morphisms: the image of a factorizing morphism is also a factorizing morphism. So every functor is *almost* continuous. What may go wrong is the uniqueness condition. The factorizing morphism in **C′** might not be unique. There may also be other "better cones" in **C′** that were not available in **C**.

A hom-functor is an example of a continuous functor. Recall that the hom-functor, $C(a, b)$, is contravariant in the first variable and covariant in the second. In other words, it's a functor:

$$C^{op} \times C \to \mathbf{Set}$$

When its second argument is fixed, the hom-set functor (which becomes the representable presheaf) maps colimits in **C** to limits in **Set**; and when its first argument is fixed, it maps limits to limits.

In Haskell, a hom-functor is the mapping of any two types to a function type, so it's just a parameterized function type. When we fix the second parameter, let's say to String, we get the contravariant functor:

```
newtype ToString a = ToString (a -> String)
instance Contravariant ToString where
    contramap f (ToString g) = ToString (g . f)
```

Continuity means that when ToString is applied to a colimit, for instance a coproduct Either b c, it will produce a limit; in this case a product of two function types:

```
ToString (Either b c) ~ (b -> String, c -> String)
```

Indeed, any function of Either b c is implemented as a case statement with the two cases being serviced by a pair of functions.

Similarly, when we fix the first argument of the hom-set, we get the familiar reader functor. Its continuity means that, for instance, any function returning a product is equivalent to a product of functions; in particular:

```
r -> (a, b) ~ (r -> a, r -> b)
```

I know what you're thinking: You don't need category theory to figure these things out. And you're right! Still, I find it amazing that such results can be derived from first principles with no recourse to bits and bytes, processor architectures, compiler technologies, or even lambda calculus.

If you're curious where the names "limit" and "continuity" come from, they are a generalization of the corresponding notions from calculus. In calculus limits and continuity are defined in terms of open neighborhoods. Open sets, which define topology, form a category (a poset).

## 12.5  Challenges

1. How would you describe a pushout in the category of C++ classes?
2. Show that the limit of the identity functor Id :: C → C is the initial object.
3. Subsets of a given set form a category. A morphism in that category is defined to be an arrow connecting two sets if the first is the subset of the second. What is a pullback of two sets in such a category? What's a pushout? What are the initial and terminal objects?
4. Can you guess what a coequalizer is?
5. Show that, in a category with a terminal object, a pullback towards the terminal object is a product.
6. Similarly, show that a pushout from an initial object (if one exists) is the coproduct.

# 13
# Free Monoids

M ONOIDS ARE AN IMPORTANT concept in both category theory and in programming. Categories correspond to strongly typed langua- ges, monoids to untyped languages. That's because in a monoid you can compose any two arrows, just as in an untyped language you can compose any two functions (of course, you may end up with a runtime error when you execute your program).

We've seen that a monoid may be described as a category with a single object, where all logic is encoded in the rules of morphism com- position. This categorical model is fully equivalent to the more tradi- tional set-theoretical definition of a monoid, where we "multiply" two elements of a set to get a third element. This process of "multiplication" can be further dissected into first forming a pair of elements and then identifying this pair with an existing element — their "product."

What happens when we forgo the second part of multiplication — the identification of pairs with existing elements? We can, for in- stance, start with an arbitrary set, form all possible pairs of elements, and call them new elements. Then we'll pair these new elements with all possible elements, and so on. This is a chain reaction — we'll keep adding new elements forever. The result, an infinite set, will be *almost* a monoid. But a monoid also needs a unit element and the law of asso- ciativity. No problem, we can add a special unit element and identify some of the pairs — just enough to support the unit and associativity laws.

Let's see how this works in a simple example. Let's start with a set of two elements, $\{a, b\}$. We'll call them the generators of the free monoid. First, we'll add a special element $e$ to serve as the unit. Next we'll add all the pairs of elements and call them "products". The product of $a$ and $b$ will be the pair $(a, b)$. The product of $b$ and $a$ will be the pair $(b, a)$, the product of $a$ with $a$ will be $(a, a)$, the product of $b$ with $b$ will be $(b, b)$. We can also form pairs with $e$, like $(a, e)$, $(e, b)$, etc., but we'll identify them with $a$, $b$, etc. So in this round we'll only add $(a, a)$, $(a, b)$ and $(b, a)$ and $(b, b)$, and end up with the set $\{e, a, b, (a, a), (a, b), (b, a), (b, b)\}$.

In the next round we'll keep adding elements like: $(a, (a, b))$, $((a, b), a)$, etc. At this point we'll have to make sure that associativity holds, so we'll identify $(a, (b, a))$ with $((a, b), a)$, etc. In other words, we won't be needing internal parentheses.

You can guess what the final result of this process will be: we'll create all possible lists of $a$s and $b$s. In fact, if we represent $e$ as an empty list, we can see that our "multiplication" is nothing but list concatenation.

This kind of construction, in which you keep generating all possible combinations of elements, and perform the minimum number of identifications — just enough to uphold the laws — is called a free construction. What we have just done is to construct a *free monoid* from the set of generators $\{a, b\}$.

## 13.1 Free Monoid in Haskell

A two-element set in Haskell is equivalent to the type `Bool`, and the free monoid generated by this set is equivalent to the type `[Bool]` (list of `Bool`). (I am deliberately ignoring problems with infinite lists.)

A monoid in Haskell is defined by the type class:

166

```
class Monoid m where
    mempty :: m
    mappend :: m -> m -> m
```

This just says that every `Monoid` must have a neutral element, which is called `mempty`, and a binary function (multiplication) called `mappend`. The unit and associativity laws cannot be expressed in Haskell and must be verified by the programmer every time a monoid is instantiated.

The fact that a list of any type forms a monoid is described by this instance definition:

```
instance Monoid [a] where
    mempty = []
    mappend = (++)
```

It states that an empty list `[]` is the unit element, and list concatenation (++) is the binary operation.

As we have seen, a list of type a corresponds to a free monoid with the set a serving as generators. The set of natural numbers with multiplication is not a free monoid, because we identify lots of products. Compare for instance:

```
2 * 3 = 6
[2] ++ [3] = [2, 3] // not the same as [6]
```

That was easy, but the question is, can we perform this free construction in category theory, where we are not allowed to look inside objects? We'll use our workhorse: the universal construction.

The second interesting question is, can any monoid be obtained from some free monoid by identifying more than the minimum number of elements required by the laws? I'll show you that this follows directly from the universal construction.

## 13.2  Free Monoid Universal Construction

If you recall our previous experiences with universal constructions, you might notice that it's not so much about constructing something as about selecting an object that best fits a given pattern. So if we want to use the universal construction to "construct" a free monoid, we have to consider a whole bunch of monoids from which to pick one. We need

167

a whole category of monoids to chose from. But do monoids form a category?

Let's first look at monoids as sets equipped with additional structure defined by unit and multiplication. We'll pick as morphisms those functions that preserve the monoidal structure. Such structure-preserving functions are called *homomorphisms*. A monoid homomorphism must map the product of two elements to the product of the mapping of the two elements:

```
h (a * b) = h a * h b
```

and it must map unit to unit.

For instance, consider a homomorphism from lists of integers to integers. If we map [2] to 2 and [3] to 3, we have to map [2, 3] to 6, because concatenation

```
[2] ++ [3] = [2, 3]
```

becomes multiplication

```
2 * 3 = 6
```

Now let's forget about the internal structure of individual monoids, and only look at them as objects with corresponding morphisms. You get a category **Mon** of monoids.

Okay, maybe before we forget about internal structure, let us notice an important property. Every object of **Mon** can be trivially mapped to a set. It's just the set of its elements. This set is called the *underlying* set. In fact, not only can we map objects of **Mon** to sets, but we can also map morphisms of **Mon** (homomorphisms) to functions. Again, this seems sort of trivial, but it will become useful soon. This mapping of objects and morphisms from **Mon** to **Set** is in fact a functor. Since this functor "forgets" the monoidal structure — once we are inside a plain set, we no longer distinguish the unit element or care about multiplication — it's called a *forgetful functor*. Forgetful functors come up regularly in category theory.

We now have two different views of **Mon**. We can treat it just like any other category with objects and morphisms. In that view, we don't see the internal structure of monoids. All we can say about a particular object in **Mon** is that it connects to itself and to other objects through morphisms. The "multiplication" table of morphisms — the composition rules — are derived from the other view: monoids-as-sets. By going to category theory we haven't lost this view completely — we can still access it through our forgetful functor.

To apply the universal construction, we need to define a special property that would let us search through the category of monoids and pick the best candidate for a free monoid. But a free monoid is defined by its generators. Different choices of generators produce different free monoids (a list of Bool is not the same as a list of Int). Our construction must start with a set of generators. So we're back to sets!

That's where the forgetful functor comes into play. We can use it to X-ray our monoids. We can identify the generators in the X-ray images of those blobs. Here's how it works:

We start with a set of generators, *x*. That's a set in **Set**.

The pattern we are going to match consists of a monoid *m* — an object of **Mon** — and a function *p* in **Set**:

```
p :: x -> U m
```

where *U* is our forgetful functor from **Mon** to **Set**. This is a weird heterogeneous pattern — half in **Mon** and half in **Set**.

The idea is that the function *p* will identify the set of generators inside the X-ray image of *m*. It doesn't matter that functions may be lousy at identifying points inside sets (they may collapse them). It will all be sorted out by the universal construction, which will pick the best representative of this pattern.

We also have to define the ranking among candidates. Suppose we have another candidate: a monoid *n* and a function that identifies the generators in its X-ray image:

```
q :: x -> U n
```

We'll say that *m* is better than *n* if there is a morphism of monoids (that's a structure-preserving homomorphism):

```
h :: m -> n
```

whose image under $U$ (remember, $U$ is a functor, so it maps morphisms to functions) factorizes through $p$:

```
q = U h . p
```

If you think of $p$ as selecting the generators in $m$; and $q$ as selecting "the same" generators in $n$; then you can think of $h$ as mapping these generators between the two monoids. Remember that $h$, by definition, preserves the monoidal structure. It means that a product of two generators in one monoid will be mapped to a product of the corresponding two generators in the second monoid, and so on.

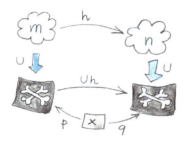

This ranking may be used to find the best candidate — the free monoid. Here's the definition:

> We'll say that $m$ (together with the function $p$) is the **free monoid** with the generators $x$ if and only if there is a *unique* morphism $h$ from $m$ to any other monoid $n$ (together with the function $q$) that satisfies the above factorization property.

Incidentally, this answers our second question. The function $Uh$ is the one that has the power to collapse multiple elements of $Um$ to a single element of $Un$. This collapse corresponds to identifying some elements of the free monoid. Therefore any monoid with generators $x$ can be obtained from the free monoid based on $x$ by identifying some of the elements. The free monoid is the one where only the bare minimum of identifications have been made.

We'll come back to free monoids when we talk about adjunctions.

## 13.3 Challenges

1. You might think (as I did, originally) that the requirement that a homomorphism of monoids preserve the unit is redundant. After all, we know that for all $a$

   ```
   h a * h e = h (a * e) = h a
   ```

   So *he* acts like a right unit (and, by analogy, as a left unit). The problem is that *ha*, for all $a$ might only cover a sub-monoid of the target monoid. There may be a "true" unit outside of the image of *h*. Show that an isomorphism between monoids that preserves multiplication must automatically preserve unit.

2. Consider a monoid homomorphism from lists of integers with concatenation to integers with multiplication. What is the image of the empty list []? Assume that all singleton lists are mapped to the integers they contain, that is [3] is mapped to 3, etc. What's the image of [1, 2, 3, 4]? How many different lists map to the integer 12? Is there any other homomorphism between the two monoids?

3. What is the free monoid generated by a one-element set? Can you see what it's isomorphic to?

# 14

# Representable Functors

IT'S ABOUT TIME we had a little talk about sets. Mathematicians have a love/hate relationship with set theory. It's the assembly language of mathematics — at least it used to be. Category theory tries to step away from set theory, to some extent. For instance, it's a known fact that the set of all sets doesn't exist, but the category of all sets, **Set**, does. So that's good. On the other hand, we assume that morphisms between any two objects in a category form a set. We even called it a hom-set. To be fair, there is a branch of category theory where morphisms don't form sets. Instead they are objects in another category. Those categories that use hom-objects rather than hom-sets, are called *enriched* categories. In what follows, though, we'll stick to categories with good old-fashioned hom-sets.

A set is the closest thing to a featureless blob you can get outside of categorical objects. A set has elements, but you can't say much about these elements. If you have a finite set, you can count the elements. You can kind of count the elements of an infinite set using cardinal numbers. The set of natural numbers, for instance, is smaller than the set of real numbers, even though both are infinite. But, maybe surprisingly, a set of rational numbers is the same size as the set of natural numbers.

Other than that, all the information about sets can be encoded in functions between them — especially the invertible ones called isomorphisms. For all intents and purposes isomorphic sets are identical. Before I summon the wrath of foundational mathematicians, let me explain that the distinction between equality and isomorphism is of fundamental importance. In fact it is one of the main concerns of the latest branch of mathematics, the Homotopy Type Theory (HoTT). I'm mentioning HoTT because it's a pure mathematical theory that takes inspiration from computation, and one of its main proponents, Vladimir Voevodsky, had a major epiphany while studying the Coq theorem prover. The interaction between mathematics and programming goes both ways.

The important lesson about sets is that it's okay to compare sets of unlike elements. For instance, we can say that a given set of natural transformations is isomorphic to some set of morphisms, because a set is just a set. Isomorphism in this case just means that for every natural transformation from one set there is a unique morphism from the other set and vice versa. They can be paired against each other. You can't compare apples with oranges, if they are objects from different categories, but you can compare sets of apples against sets of oranges. Often transforming a categorical problem into a set-theoretical problem gives us the necessary insight or even lets us prove valuable theorems.

## 14.1  The Hom Functor

Every category comes equipped with a canonical family of mappings to **Set**. Those mappings are in fact functors, so they preserve the structure of the category. Let's build one such mapping.

Let's fix one object $a$ in C and pick another object $x$ also in C. The hom-set $C(a, x)$ is a set, an object in **Set**. When we vary $x$, keeping $a$ fixed, $C(a, x)$ will also vary in **Set**. Thus we have a mapping from $x$ to **Set**.

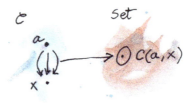

If we want to stress the fact that we are considering the hom-set as a mapping in its second argument, we use the notation $C(a, -)$ with the dash serving as the placeholder for the argument.

This mapping of objects is easily extended to the mapping of morphisms. Let's take a morphism $f$ in C between two arbitrary objects

$x$ and $y$. The object $x$ is mapped to the set $C(a, x)$, and the object $y$ is mapped to $C(a, y)$, under the mapping we have just defined. If this mapping is to be a functor, $f$ must be mapped to a function between the two sets: $C(a, x) \to C(a, y)$

Let's define this function point-wise, that is for each argument separately. For the argument we should pick an arbitrary element of $C(a, x)$ — let's call it $h$. Morphisms are composable, if they match end to end. It so happens that the target of $h$ matches the source of $f$, so their composition:

$$f \circ h :: a \to y$$

is a morphism going from $a$ to $y$. It is therefore a member of $C(a, y)$.

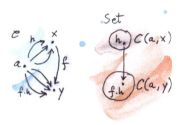

We have just found our function from $C(a, x)$ to $C(a, y)$, which can serve as the image of $f$. If there is no danger of confusion, we'll write this lifted function as: $C(a, f)$ and its action on a morphism $h$ as:

$$C(a, f)h = f \circ h$$

Since this construction works in any category, it must also work in the category of Haskell types. In Haskell, the hom-functor is better known as the Reader functor:

```
type Reader a x = a -> x
```

```
instance Functor (Reader a) where
    fmap f h = f . h
```

Now let's consider what happens if, instead of fixing the source of the hom-set, we fix the target. In other words, we're asking the question if the mapping $C(-, a)$ is also a functor. It is, but instead of being co-variant, it's contravariant. That's because the same kind of matching of morphisms end to end results in postcomposition by $f$; rather than precomposition, as was the case with $C(a, -)$.

We have already seen this contravariant functor in Haskell. We called it Op:

```
type Op a x = x -> a

instance Contravariant (Op a) where
    contramap f h = h . f
```

Finally, if we let both objects vary, we get a profunctor $C(-,=)$, which is contravariant in the first argument and covariant in the second (to underline the fact that the two arguments may vary independently, we use a double dash as the second placeholder). We have seen this profunctor before, when we talked about functoriality:

```
instance Profunctor (->) where
    dimap ab cd bc = cd . bc . ab
    lmap = flip (.)
    rmap = (.)
```

The important lesson is that this observation holds in any category: the mapping of objects to hom-sets is functorial. Since contravariance is equivalent to a mapping from the opposite category, we can state this fact succinctly as:

$$C(-,=) :: C^{op} \times C \to \text{Set}$$

## 14.2 Representable Functors

We've seen that, for every choice of an object $a$ in C, we get a functor from C to **Set**. This kind of structure-preserving mapping to **Set** is often called a *representation*. We are representing objects and morphisms of C as sets and functions in **Set**.

The functor $C(a,-)$ itself is sometimes called representable. More generally, any functor $F$ that is naturally isomorphic to the hom-functor, for some choice of $a$, is called *representable*. Such functor must necessarily be **Set**-valued, since $C(a,-)$ is.

I said before that we often think of isomorphic sets as identical. More generally, we think of isomorphic *objects* in a category as identical. That's because objects have no structure other than their relation to other objects (and themselves) through morphisms.

For instance, we've previously talked about the category of monoids, **Mon**, that was initially modeled with sets. But we were careful to pick as morphisms only those functions that preserved the monoidal structure of those sets. So if two objects in **Mon** are isomorphic, meaning there is an invertible morphism between them, they have exactly the same structure. If we peeked at the sets and functions that they were based upon, we'd see that the unit element of one monoid was mapped to the unit element of another, and that a product of two elements was mapped to the product of their mappings.

The same reasoning can be applied to functors. Functors between two categories form a category in which natural transformations play the role of morphisms. So two functors are isomorphic, and can be thought of as identical, if there is an invertible natural transformation between them.

Let's analyze the definition of the representable functor from this perspective. For $F$ to be representable we require that: There be an object $a$ in C; one natural transformation $\alpha$ from $C(a, -)$ to $F$; another natural transformation, $\beta$, in the opposite direction; and that their composition be the identity natural transformation.

Let's look at the component of $\alpha$ at some object $x$. It's a function in **Set**:

$$\alpha_x :: C(a, x) \rightarrow Fx$$

The naturality condition for this transformation tells us that, for any morphism $f$ from $x$ to $y$, the following diagram commutes:

$$Ff \circ \alpha_x = \alpha_y \circ C(a, f)$$

In Haskell, we would replace natural transformations with polymorphic functions:

```
alpha :: forall x. (a -> x) -> F x
```

with the optional `forall` quantifier. The naturality condition

```
fmap f . alpha = alpha . fmap f
```

is automatically satisfied due to parametricity (it's one of those theorems for free I mentioned earlier), with the understanding that `fmap` on the left is defined by the functor $F$, whereas the one on the right is defined by the reader functor. Since `fmap` for reader is just function precomposition, we can be even more explicit. Acting on $h$, an element of $C(a, x)$, the naturality condition simplifies to:

```
fmap f (alpha h) = alpha (f . h)
```

The other transformation, beta, goes the opposite way:

```
beta :: forall x. F x -> (a -> x)
```

It must respect naturality conditions, and it must be the inverse of alpha:

```
alpha . beta = id = beta . alpha
```

We will see later that a natural transformation from $C(a, -)$ to any **Set**-valued functor always exists (Yoneda's lemma) but it is not necessarily invertible.

Let me give you an example in Haskell with the list functor and Int as a. Here's a natural transformation that does the job:

```
alpha :: forall x. (Int -> x) -> [x]
alpha h = map h [12]
```

I have arbitrarily picked the number 12 and created a singleton list with it. I can then fmap the function h over this list and get a list of the type returned by h. (There are actually as many such transformations as there are list of integers.)

The naturality condition is equivalent to the composability of map (the list version of fmap):

```
map f (map h [12]) = map (f . h) [12]
```

But if we tried to find the inverse transformation, we would have to go from a list of arbitrary type x to a function returning x:

```
beta :: forall x. [x] -> (Int -> x)
```

You might think of retrieving an x from the list, e.g., using head, but that won't work for an empty list. Notice that there is no choice for the type a (in place of Int) that would work here. So the list functor is not representable.

Remember when we talked about Haskell (endo-) functors being a little like containers? In the same vein we can think of representable functors as containers for storing memoized results of function calls (the members of hom-sets in Haskell are just functions). The representing object, the type $a$ in $C(a, -)$, is thought of as the key type, with which we can access the tabulated values of a function. The transformation we called alpha is called tabulate, and its inverse, beta, is called index. Here's a (slightly simplified) Representable class definition:

```
class Representable f where
    type Rep f :: *
    tabulate :: (Rep f -> x) -> f x
    index    :: f x -> Rep f -> x
```

Notice that the representing type, our *a*, which is called Rep f here, is part of the definition of Representable. The star just means that Rep f is a type (as opposed to a type constructor, or other more exotic kinds).

Infinite lists, or streams, which cannot be empty, are representable.

```
data Stream x = Cons x (Stream x)
```

You can think of them as memoized values of a function taking an Integer as an argument. (Strictly speaking, I should be using non-negative natural numbers, but I didn't want to complicate the code.)

To tabulate such a function, you create an infinite stream of values. Of course, this is only possible because Haskell is lazy. The values are evaluated on demand. You access the memoized values using index:

```
instance Representable Stream where
    type Rep Stream = Integer
    tabulate f = Cons (f 0) (tabulate (f . (+1)))
    index (Cons b bs) n = if n == 0 then b else index bs (n - 1)
```

It's interesting that you can implement a single memoization scheme to cover a whole family of functions with arbitrary return types.

Representability for contravariant functors is similarly defined, except that we keep the second argument of $C(-, a)$ fixed. Or, equivalently, we may consider functors from $C^{op}$ to **Set**, because $C^{op}(a, -)$ is the same as $C(-, a)$.

There is an interesting twist to representability. Remember that hom-sets can internally be treated as exponential objects, in Cartesian closed categories. The hom-set $C(a, x)$ is equivalent to $x^a$, and for a representable functor $F$ we can write: $-^a = F$.

Let's take the logarithm of both sides, just for kicks: $a = \log F$

Of course, this is a purely formal transformation, but if you know some of the properties of logarithms, it is quite helpful. In particular, it turns out that functors that are based on product types can be represented with sum types, and that sum-type functors are not in general representable (example: the list functor).

Finally, notice that a representable functor gives us two different implementations of the same thing — one a function, one a data structure. They have exactly the same content — the same values are retrieved using the same keys. That's the sense of "sameness" I was talking about. Two naturally isomorphic functors are identical as far as their contents are involved. On the other hand, the two representations are often implemented differently and may have different performance characteristics. Memoization is used as a performance enhancement and may lead to substantially reduced run times. Being able to generate different representations of the same underlying computation is very valuable in practice. So, surprisingly, even though it's not concerned with performance at all, category theory provides ample opportunities to explore alternative implementations that have practical value.

## 14.3 Challenges

1. Show that the hom-functors map identity morphisms in $C$ to corresponding identity functions in **Set**.
2. Show that Maybe is not representable.
3. Is the Reader functor representable?
4. Using Stream representation, memoize a function that squares its argument.
5. Show that tabulate and index for Stream are indeed the inverse of each other. (Hint: use induction.)
6. The functor:

   ```
   Pair a = Pair a a
   ```

   is representable. Can you guess the type that represents it? Implement tabulate and index.

## 14.4 Bibliography

1. The Catsters video about representable functors[1].

---

# 15

# The Yoneda Lemma

MOST CONSTRUCTIONS IN category theory are generalizations of results from other more specific areas of mathematics. Things like products, coproducts, monoids, exponentials, etc., have been known long before category theory. They might have been known under different names in different branches of mathematics. A Cartesian product in set theory, a meet in order theory, a conjunction in logic — they are all specific examples of the abstract idea of a categorical product.

The Yoneda lemma stands out in this respect as a sweeping statement about categories in general with little or no precedent in other branches of mathematics. Some say that its closest analog is Cayley's theorem in group theory (every group is isomorphic to a permutation group of some set).

The setting for the Yoneda lemma is an arbitrary category $C$ together with a functor $F$ from $C$ to **Set**. We've seen in the previous section that some **Set**-valued functors are representable, that is isomorphic to a hom-functor. The Yoneda lemma tells us that all **Set**-valued functors can be obtained from hom-functors through natural transformations, and it explicitly enumerates all such transformations.

When I talked about natural transformations, I mentioned that the naturality condition can be quite restrictive. When you define a component of a natural transformation at one object, naturality may be strong enough to "transport" this component to another object that is connected to it through a morphism. The more arrows between objects in the source and the target categories there are, the more constraints you have for transporting the components of natural transformations. **Set** happens to be a very arrow-rich category.

The Yoneda lemma tells us that a natural transformation between a hom-functor and any other functor $F$ is completely determined by specifying the value of its single component at just one point! The rest of the natural transformation just follows from naturality conditions.

So let's review the naturality condition between the two functors involved in the Yoneda lemma. The first functor is the hom-functor. It maps any object $x$ in **C** to the set of morphisms $C(a, x)$ — for $a$ a fixed object in **C**. We've also seen that it maps any morphism $f$ from $x \rightarrow y$ to $C(a, f)$.

The second functor is an arbitrary **Set**-valued functor $F$.

Let's call the natural transformation between these two functors $\alpha$. Because we are operating in **Set**, the components of the natural transformation, like $\alpha_x$ or $\alpha_y$, are just regular functions between sets:

$$\alpha_x :: C(a, x) \rightarrow Fx$$
$$\alpha_y :: C(a, y) \rightarrow Fy$$

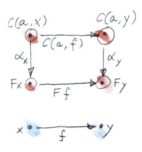

And because these are just functions, we can look at their values at specific points. But what's a point in the set $C(a, x)$? Here's the key observation: Every point in the set $C(a, x)$ is also a morphism $h$ from $a$ to $x$.

So the naturality square for $\alpha$:

$$\alpha_y \circ C(a, f) = Ff \circ \alpha_x$$

becomes, point-wise, when acting on $h$:

$$\alpha_y(C(a, f)h) = (Ff)(\alpha_x h)$$

You might recall from the previous section that the action of the hom-functor $C(a, -)$ on a morphism $f$ was defined as precomposition:

$$C(a, f)h = f \circ h$$

which leads to:

$$\alpha_y(f \circ h) = (Ff)(\alpha_x h)$$

Just how strong this condition is can be seen by specializing it to the case of $x = a$.

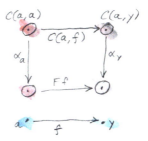

In that case $h$ becomes a morphism from $a$ to $a$. We know that there is at least one such morphism, $h = \mathrm{id}_a$. Let's plug it in:

$$\alpha_y f = (Ff)(\alpha_a \mathrm{id}_a)$$

Notice what has just happened: The left hand side is the action of $\alpha_y$ on an arbitrary element $f$ of $C(a, y)$. And it is totally determined by the single value of $\alpha_a$ at $\mathrm{id}_a$. We can pick any such value and it will generate a natural transformation. Since the values of $\alpha_a$ are in the set $Fa$, any point in $Fa$ will define some $\alpha$.

Conversely, given any natural transformation $\alpha$ from $C(a, -)$ to $F$, you can evaluate it at $\mathrm{id}_a$ to get a point in $Fa$.

We have just proven the Yoneda lemma:

> There is a one-to-one correspondence between natural trans-formations from $C(a, -)$ to $F$ and elements of $Fa$.

in other words,

$$\mathrm{Nat}(C(a, -), F) \cong Fa$$

Or, if we use the notation $[C, \mathbf{Set}]$ for the functor category between C and **Set**, the set of natural transformation is just a hom-set in that category, and we can write:

$$[C, \mathbf{Set}](C(a, -), F) \cong Fa$$

I'll explain later how this correspondence is in fact a natural isomorphism.

Now let's try to get some intuition about this result. The most amazing thing is that the whole natural transformation crystallizes from just one nucleation site: the value we assign to it at $id_a$. It spreads from that point following the naturality condition. It floods the image of C in **Set**. So let's first consider what the image of C is under $C(a, -)$.

Let's start with the image of $a$ itself. Under the hom-functor $C(a, -)$, $a$ is mapped to the set $C(a, a)$. Under the functor $F$, on the other hand, it is mapped to the set $Fa$. The component of the natural transformation $\alpha_a$ is some function from $C(a, a)$ to $Fa$. Let's focus on just one point in the set $C(a, a)$, the point corresponding to the morphism $id_a$. To emphasize the fact that it's just a point in a set, let's call it $p$. The component $\alpha_a$ should map $p$ to some point $q$ in $Fa$. I'll show you that any choice of $q$ leads to a unique natural transformation.

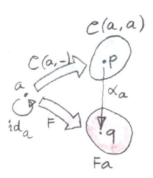

The first claim is that the choice of one point $q$ uniquely determines the rest of the function $\alpha_a$. Indeed, let's pick any other point, $p'$ in $C(a, a)$, corresponding to some morphism $g$ from $a$ to $a$. And here's where the magic of the Yoneda lemma happens: $g$ can be viewed as a point $p'$ in the set $C(a, a)$. At the same time, it selects two *functions* between sets. Indeed, under the hom-functor, the morphism $g$ is mapped to a function $C(a, g)$; and under $F$ it's mapped to $Fg$.

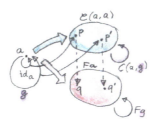

Now let's consider the action of $C(a, g)$ on our original $p$ which, as you remember, corresponds to $\mathrm{id}_a$. It is defined as precomposition, $g \circ \mathrm{id}_a$, which is equal to $g$, which corresponds to our point $p'$. So the morphism $g$ is mapped to a function that, when acting on $p$ produces $p'$, which is $g$. We have come full circle!

Now consider the action of $Fg$ on $q$. It is some $q'$, a point in $Fa$. To complete the naturality square, $p'$ must be mapped to $q'$ under $\alpha_a$. We picked an arbitrary $p'$ (an arbitrary $g$) and derived its mapping under $\alpha_a$. The function $\alpha_a$ is thus completely determined.

The second claim is that $\alpha_x$ is uniquely determined for any object $x$ in C that is connected to $a$. The reasoning is analogous, except that now we have two more sets, $C(a, x)$ and $Fx$, and the morphism $g$ from $a$ to $x$ is mapped, under the hom-functor, to:

$$C(a, g) :: C(a, a) \rightarrow C(a, x)$$

and under $F$ to:

$$Fg :: Fa \rightarrow Fx$$

Again, $C(a, g)$ acting on our $p$ is given by the precomposition: $g \circ \mathrm{id}_a$, which corresponds to a point $p'$ in $C(a, x)$. Naturality determines the value of $\alpha_x$ acting on $p'$ to be:

$$q' = (Fg)q$$

Since $p'$ was arbitrary, the whole function $\alpha_x$ is thus determined.

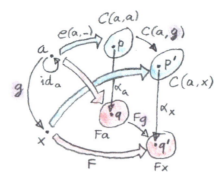

What if there are objects in **C** that have no connection to $a$? They are all mapped under $C(a, -)$ to a single set — the empty set. Recall that the empty set is the initial object in the category of sets. It means that there is a unique function from this set to any other set. We called this function absurd. So here, again, we have no choice for the component of the natural transformation: it can only be absurd.

One way of understanding the Yoneda lemma is to realize that natural transformations between **Set**-valued functors are just families of functions, and functions are in general lossy. A function may collapse information and it may cover only parts of its codomain. The only functions that are not lossy are the ones that are invertible — the isomorphisms. It follows then that the best structure-preserving **Set**-valued functors are the representable ones. They are either the hom-functors or the functors that are naturally isomorphic to hom-functors. Any other functor $F$ is obtained from a hom-functor through a lossy transformation. Such a transformation may not only lose information, but it may also cover only a small part of the image of the functor $F$ in **Set**.

## 15.1  Yoneda in Haskell

We have already encountered the hom-functor in Haskell under the guise of the reader functor:

```
type Reader a x = a -> x
```

The reader maps morphisms (here, functions) by precomposition:

```
instance Functor (Reader a) where
    fmap f h = f . h
```

186

The Yoneda lemma tells us that the reader functor can be naturally mapped to any other functor.

A natural transformation is a polymorphic function. So given a functor F, we have a mapping to it from the reader functor:

```
alpha :: forall x . (a -> x) -> F x
```

As usual, forall is optional, but I like to write it explicitly to emphasize parametric polymorphism of natural transformations.

The Yoneda lemma tells us that these natural transformations are in one-to-one correspondence with the elements of F a:

```
forall x . (a -> x) -> F x ≅ F a
```

The right hand side of this identity is what we would normally consider a data structure. Remember the interpretation of functors as generalized containers? F a is a container of a. But the left hand side is a polymorphic function that takes a function as an argument. The Yoneda lemma tells us that the two representations are equivalent — they contain the same information.

Another way of saying this is: Give me a polymorphic function of the type:

```
alpha :: forall x . (a -> x) -> F x
```

and I'll produce a container of a. The trick is the one we used in the proof of the Yoneda lemma: we call this function with id to get an element of F a:

```
alpha id :: F a
```

The converse is also true: Given a value of the type F a:

```
fa :: F a
```

one can define a polymorphic function:

```
alpha h = fmap h fa
```

of the correct type. You can easily go back and forth between the two representations.

The advantage of having multiple representations is that one might be easier to compose than the other, or that one might be more efficient in some applications than the other.

The simplest illustration of this principle is the code transformation that is often used in compiler construction: the continuation passing style or CPS. It's the simplest application of the Yoneda lemma to the identity functor. Replacing F with identity produces:

```
forall r . (a -> r) -> r ≅ a
```

The interpretation of this formula is that any type a can be replaced by a function that takes a "handler" for a. A handler is a function accepting a and performing the rest of the computation — the continuation. (The type r usually encapsulates some kind of status code.)

This style of programming is very common in UIs, in asynchronous systems, and in concurrent programming. The drawback of CPS is that it involves inversion of control. The code is split between producers and consumers (handlers), and is not easily composable. Anybody who's done any amount of nontrivial web programming is familiar with the nightmare of spaghetti code from interacting stateful handlers. As we'll see later, judicious use of functors and monads can restore some compositional properties of CPS.

## 15.2  Co-Yoneda

As usual, we get a bonus construction by inverting the direction of arrows. The Yoneda lemma can be applied to the opposite category $C^{op}$ to give us a mapping between contravariant functors.

Equivalently, we can derive the co-Yoneda lemma by fixing the target object of our hom-functors instead of the source. We get the contravariant hom-functor from C to **Set**: $C(-, a)$. The contravariant version of the Yoneda lemma establishes one-to-one correspondence between natural transformations from this functor to any other contravariant functor $F$ and the elements of the set $Fa$:

$$\mathbf{Nat}(C(-, a), F) \cong Fa$$

Here's the Haskell version of the co-Yoneda lemma:

```
forall x . (x -> a) -> F x ≅ F a
```

Notice that in some literature it's the contravariant version that's called the Yoneda lemma.

## 15.3 Challenges

1. Show that the two functions `phi` and `psi` that form the Yoneda isomorphism in Haskell are inverses of each other.

   ```
   phi :: (forall x . (a -> x) -> F x) -> F a
   phi alpha = alpha id

   psi :: F a -> (forall x . (a -> x) -> F x)
   psi fa h = fmap h fa
   ```

2. A discrete category is one that has objects but no morphisms other than identity morphisms. How does the Yoneda lemma work for functors from such a category?
3. A list of units `[()]` contains no other information but its length. So, as a data type, it can be considered an encoding of integers. An empty list encodes zero, a singleton `[()]` (a value, not a type) encodes one, and so on. Construct another representation of this data type using the Yoneda lemma for the list functor.

## 15.4 Bibliography

1. Catsters[1] video.

---

[1]https://www.youtube.com/watch?v=TLMxHB19khE

# 16

## Yoneda Embedding

WE'VE SEEN PREVIOUSLY that, when we fix an object $a$ in the category C, the mapping $C(a, -)$ is a (covariant) functor from C to Set.

$$x \rightarrow C(a, x)$$

(The codomain is **Set** because the hom-set $C(a, x)$ is a *set*.) We call this mapping a hom-functor — we have previously defined its action on morphisms as well.

Now let's vary $a$ in this mapping. We get a new mapping that assigns the hom-*functor* $C(a, -)$ to any $a$.

$$a \rightarrow C(a, -)$$

It's a mapping of objects from category C to functors, which are *objects* in the functor category (see the section about functor categories in Natural Transformations). Let's use the notation [C, Set] for the functor category from C to Set. You may also recall that hom-functors are the prototypical representable functors.

Every time we have a mapping of objects between two categories, it's natural to ask if such a mapping is also a functor. In other words whether we can lift a morphism from one category to a morphism in the other category. A morphism in C is just an element of $C(a, b)$, but a morphism in the functor category [C, Set] is a natural transformation. So we are looking for a mapping of morphisms to natural transformations.

Let's see if we can find a natural transformation corresponding to a morphism $f :: a \to b$. First, lets see what $a$ and $b$ are mapped to. They are mapped to two functors: $C(a, -)$ and $C(b, -)$. We need a natural transformation between those two functors.

And here's the trick: we use the Yoneda lemma:

$$[\mathbf{C}, \mathbf{Set}](C(a, -), F) \cong Fa$$

and replace the generic $F$ with the hom-functor $C(b, -)$. We get:

$$[\mathbf{C}, \mathbf{Set}](C(a, -), C(b, -)) \cong C(b, a)$$

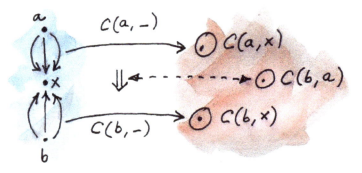

This is exactly the natural transformation between the two hom-functors we were looking for, but with a little twist: We have a mapping between a natural transformation and a morphism — an element of $C(b, a)$ — that goes in the "wrong" direction. But that's okay; it only means that the functor we are looking at is contravariant.

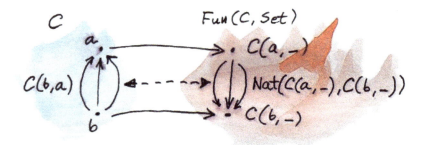

Actually, we've got even more than we bargained for. The mapping from $\mathbf{C}$ to $[\mathbf{C}, \mathbf{Set}]$ is not only a contravariant functor — it is a *fully*

*faithful* functor. Fullness and faithfulness are properties of functors that describe how they map hom-sets.

A *faithful* functor is *injective* on hom-sets, meaning that it maps distinct morphisms to distinct morphisms. In other words, it doesn't coalesce them.

A *full* functor is *surjective* on hom-sets, meaning that it maps one hom-set *onto* the other hom-set, fully covering the latter.

A fully faithful functor $F$ is a *bijection* on hom-sets — a one to one matching of all elements of both sets. For every pair of objects $a$ and $b$ in the source category $C$ there is a bijection between $C(a, b)$ and $D(Fa, Fb)$, where $D$ is the target category of $F$ (in our case, the functor category, $[C, Set]$). Notice that this doesn't mean that $F$ is a bijection on *objects*. There may be objects in $D$ that are not in the image of $F$, and we can't say anything about hom-sets for those objects.

## 16.1 The Embedding

The (contravariant) functor we have just described, the functor that maps objects in $C$ to functors in $[C, Set]$:

$$a \rightarrow C(a, -)$$

defines the *Yoneda embedding*. It *embeds* a category $C$ (strictly speaking, the category $C^{op}$, because of contravariance) inside the functor category $[C, Set]$. It not only maps objects in $C$ to functors, but also faithfully preserves all connections between them.

This is a very useful result because mathematicians know a lot about the category of functors, especially functors whose codomain is **Set**. We can get a lot of insight about an arbitrary category $C$ by embedding it in the functor category.

Of course there is a dual version of the Yoneda embedding, sometimes called the co-Yoneda embedding. Observe that we could have started by fixing the target object (rather than the source object) of each hom-set, $C(-, a)$. That would give us a contravariant hom-functor. Contravariant functors from $C$ to **Set** are our familiar presheaves (see, for instance, Limits and Colimits). The co-Yoneda embedding defines the embedding of a category $C$ in the category of presheaves. Its action on morphisms is given by:

$$[C, Set](C(-, a), C(-, b)) \cong C(a, b)$$

Again, mathematicians know a lot about the category of presheaves, so being able to embed an arbitrary category in it is a big win.

## 16.2 Application to Haskell

In Haskell, the Yoneda embedding can be represented as the isomorphism between natural transformations amongst reader functors on the one hand, and functions (going in the opposite direction) on the other hand:

```
forall x. (a -> x) -> (b -> x) ≅ b -> a
```

(Remember, the reader functor is equivalent to `((->) a)`.)

The left hand side of this identity is a polymorphic function that, given a function from a to x and a value of type b, can produce a value of type x (I'm uncurrying — dropping the parentheses around — the function b -> x). The only way this can be done for all x is if our function knows how to convert a b to an a. It has to secretly have access to a function b -> a.

Given such a converter, `btoa`, one can define the left hand side, call itfromY, as:

```
fromY :: (a -> x) -> b -> x
fromY f b = f (btoa b)
```

Conversely, given a function `fromY` we can recover the converter by calling `fromY` with the identity:

```
fromY id :: b -> a
```

This establishes the bijection between functions of the type `fromY` and `btoa`.

An alternative way of looking at this isomorphism is that it's a CPS encoding of a function from b to a. The argument a -> x is a continuation (the handler). The result is a function from b to x which, when called with a value of type b, will execute the continuation precomposed with the function being encoded.

The Yoneda embedding also explains some of the alternative representations of data structures in Haskell. In particular, it provides a very useful representation[1] of lenses from the `Control.Lens` library.

---

[1] https://bartoszmilewski.com/2015/07/13/from-lenses-to-yoneda-embedding/

## 16.3  Preorder Example

This example was suggested by Robert Harper. It's the application of the Yoneda embedding to a category defined by a preorder. A preorder is a set with an ordering relation between its elements that's traditionally written as ⩽ (less than or equal). The "pre" in preorder is there because we're only requiring the relation to be transitive and reflexive but not necessarily antisymmetric (so it's possible to have cycles).

A set with the preorder relation gives rise to a category. The objects are the elements of this set. A morphism from object $a$ to $b$ either doesn't exist, if the objects cannot be compared or if it's not true that $a ⩽ b$; or it exists if $a ⩽ b$, and it points from $a$ to $b$. There is never more than one morphism from one object to another. Therefore any hom-set in such a category is either an empty set or a one-element set. Such a category is called *thin*.

It's easy to convince yourself that this construction is indeed a category: The arrows are composable because, if $a ⩽ b$ and $b ⩽ c$ then $a ⩽ c$; and the composition is associative. We also have the identity arrows because every element is (less than or) equal to itself (reflexivity of the underlying relation).

We can now apply the co-Yoneda embedding to a preorder category. In particular, we're interested in its action on morphisms:

$$[C, Set](C(-, a), C(-, b)) \cong C(a, b)$$

The hom-set on the right hand side is non empty if and only if $a ⩽ b$ — in which case it's a one-element set. Consequently, if $a ⩽ b$, there exists a single natural transformation on the left. Otherwise there is no natural transformation.

So what's a natural transformation between hom-functors in a preorder? It should be a family of functions between sets $C(-, a)$ and $C(-, b)$. In a preorder, each of these sets can either be empty or a singleton. Let's see what kind of functions are there at our disposal.

There is a function from an empty set to itself (the identity acting on an empty set), a function absurd from an empty set to a singleton set (it does nothing, since it only needs to be defined for elements of an empty set, of which there are none), and a function from a singleton to itself (the identity acting on a one-element set). The only combination that is forbidden is the mapping from a singleton to an empty set (what would the value of such a function be when acting on the single element?).

So our natural transformation will never connect a singleton hom-set to an empty hom-set. In other words, if $x \leqslant a$ (singleton hom-set $C(x, a)$) then $C(x, b)$ cannot be empty. A non-empty $C(x, b)$ means that $x$ is less or equal to $b$. So the existence of the natural transformation in question requires that, for every $x$, if $x \leqslant a$ then $x \leqslant b$.

$$\text{for all } x, x \leqslant a \Rightarrow x \leqslant b$$

On the other hand, co-Yoneda tells us that the existence of this natural transformation is equivalent to $C(a, b)$ being non-empty, or to $a \leqslant b$. Together, we get:

$$a \leqslant b \text{ if and only if for all } x, x \leqslant a \Rightarrow x \leqslant b$$

We could have arrived at this result directly. The intuition is that, if $a \leqslant b$ then all elements that are below $a$ must also be below $b$. Conversely, when you substitute $a$ for $x$ on the right hand side, it follows that $a \leqslant b$. But you must admit that arriving at this result through the Yoneda embedding is much more exciting.

## 16.4  Naturality

The Yoneda lemma establishes the isomorphism between the set of natural transformations and an object in **Set**. Natural transformations are morphisms in the functor category $[C, Set]$. The set of natural transformation between any two functors is a hom-set in that category. The Yoneda lemma is the isomorphism:

$$[C, Set](C(a, -), F) \cong F a$$

This isomorphism turns out to be natural in both $F$ and $a$. In other words, it's natural in $(F, a)$, a pair taken from the product category $[C, Set] \times C$. Notice that we are now treating $F$ as an *object* in the functor category.

Let's think for a moment what this means. A natural isomorphism is an invertible *natural transformation* between two functors. And indeed, the right hand side of our isomorphism is a functor. It's a functor from $[C, Set] \times C$ to **Set**. Its action on a pair $(F, a)$ is a set — the result of evaluating the functor $F$ at the object $a$. This is called the evaluation functor.

The left hand side is also a functor that takes $(F, a)$ to a set of natural transformations $[\mathbf{C}, \mathbf{Set}](\mathbf{C}(a, -), F)$.

To show that these are really functors, we should also define their action on morphisms. But what's a morphism between a pair $(F, a)$ and $(G, b)$? It's a pair of morphisms, $(\Phi, f)$; the first being a morphism between functors — a natural transformation — the second being a regular morphism in $\mathbf{C}$.

The evaluation functor takes this pair $(\Phi, f)$ and maps it to a function between two sets, $Fa$ and $Gb$. We can easily construct such a function from the component of $\Phi$ at $a$ (which maps $Fa$ to $Ga$) and the morphism $f$ lifted by $G$:

$$(Gf) \circ \Phi_a$$

Notice that, because of naturality of $\Phi$, this is the same as:

$$\Phi_b \circ (Ff)$$

I'm not going to prove the naturality of the whole isomorphism — after you've established what the functors are, the proof is pretty mechanical. It follows from the fact that our isomorphism is built up from functors and natural transformations. There is simply no way for it to go wrong.

## 16.5 Challenges

1. Express the co-Yoneda embedding in Haskell.
2. Show that the bijection we established between fromY and btoa is an isomorphism (the two mappings are the inverse of each other).
3. Work out the Yoneda embedding for a monoid. What functor corresponds to the monoid's single object? What natural transformations correspond to monoid morphisms?
4. What is the application of the *covariant* Yoneda embedding to preorders? (Question suggested by Gershom Bazerman.)
5. Yoneda embedding can be used to embed an arbitrary functor category $[\mathbf{C}, \mathbf{D}]$ in the functor category $[[\mathbf{C}, \mathbf{D}], \mathbf{Set}]$. Figure out how it works on morphisms (which in this case are natural transformations).

# Part Three

# 17

# It's All About Morphisms

IF I HAVEN'T convinced you yet that category theory is all about morphisms then I haven't done my job properly. Since the next topic is
adjunctions, which are defined in terms of isomorphisms of hom-sets, it
makes sense to review our intuitions about the building blocks of hom-
sets. Also, you'll see that adjunctions provide a more general language
to describe a lot of constructions we've studied before, so it might help
to review them too.

## 17.1  Functors

To begin with, you should really think of functors as mappings of morphisms — the view that's emphasized in the Haskell definition of the
`Functor` typeclass, which revolves around `fmap`. Of course, functors also
map objects — the endpoints of morphisms — otherwise we wouldn't be
able to talk about preserving composition. Objects tell us which pairs
of morphisms are composable. The target of one morphism must be
equal to the source of the other — if they are to be composed. So if
we want the composition of morphisms to be mapped to the composition of *lifted* morphisms, the mapping of their endpoints is pretty much
determined.

## 17.2 Commuting Diagrams

A lot of properties of morphisms are expressed in terms of commuting diagrams. If a particular morphism can be described as a composition of other morphisms in more than one way, then we have a commuting diagram.

In particular, commuting diagrams form the basis of almost all universal constructions (with the notable exceptions of the initial and terminal objects). We've seen this in the definitions of products, coproducts, various other (co-)limits, exponential objects, free monoids, etc.

The product is a simple example of a universal construction. We pick two objects $a$ and $b$ and see if there exists an object $c$, together with a pair of morphisms $p$ and $q$, that has the universal property of being their product.

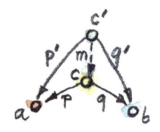

A product is a special case of a limit. A limit is defined in terms of cones. A general cone is built from commuting diagrams. Commutativity of those diagrams may be replaced with a suitable naturality condition for the mapping of functors. This way commutativity is reduced to the role of the assembly language for the higher level language of natural transformations.

## 17.3 Natural Transformations

In general, natural transformations are very convenient whenever we need a mapping from morphisms to commuting squares. Two opposing sides of a naturality square are the mappings of some morphism $f$ under two functors $F$ and $G$. The other sides are the components of the natural transformation (which are also morphisms).

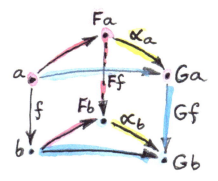

Naturality means that when you move to the "neighboring" component (by neighboring I mean connected by a morphism), you're not going against the structure of either the category or the functors. It doesn't matter whether you first use a component of the natural transformation to bridge the gap between objects, and then jump to its neighbor using the functor; or the other way around. The two directions are orthogonal. A natural transformation moves you left and right, and the functors move you up and down or back and forth — so to speak. You can visualize the *image* of a functor as a sheet in the target category. A natural transformation maps one such sheet corresponding to F, to another, corresponding to G.

We've seen examples of this orthogonality in Haskell. There the action of a functor modifies the content of a container without changing its shape, while a natural transformation repackages the untouched contents into a different container. The order of these operations doesn't matter.

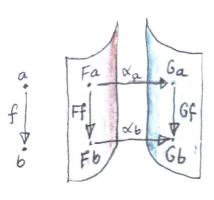

We've seen the cones in the definition of a limit replaced by natural transformations. Naturality ensures that the sides of every cone commute. Still, a limit is defined in terms of mappings *between* cones. These mappings must also satisfy commutativity conditions. (For instance, the triangles in the definition of the product must commute.)

These conditions, too, may be replaced by naturality. You may recall that the *universal* cone, or the limit, is defined as a natural transformation between the (contravariant) hom-functor:

$$F :: c \rightarrow \mathbf{C}(c, \mathrm{Lim}D)$$

and the (also contravariant) functor that maps objects in $C$ to cones, which themselves are natural transformations:

$$G :: c \rightarrow \mathrm{Nat}(\Delta_c, D)$$

Here, $\Delta_c$ is the constant functor, and $D$ is the functor that defines the diagram in C. Both functors $F$ and $G$ have well defined actions on morphisms in C. It so happens that this particular natural transformation between $F$ and $G$ is an *isomorphism*.

## 17.4  Natural Isomorphisms

A natural isomorphism — which is a natural transformation whose every component is reversible — is category theory's way of saying that "two things are the same." A component of such a transformation must be an isomorphism between objects — a morphism that has the inverse. If you visualize functor images as sheets, a natural isomorphism is a one-to-one invertible mapping between those sheets.

## 17.5  Hom-Sets

But what are morphisms? They do have more structure than objects: unlike objects, morphisms have two ends. But if you fix the source and the target objects, the morphisms between the two form a boring set (at least for locally small categories). We can give elements of this set names like $f$ or $g$, to distinguish one from another — but what is it, really, that makes them different?

The essential difference between morphisms in a given hom-set lies in the way they compose with other morphisms (from abutting hom-sets). If there is a morphism $h$ whose composition (either pre- or post-) with $f$ is different than that with $g$, for instance:

$$h \circ f \neq h \circ g$$

then we can directly "observe" the difference between $f$ and $g$. But even if the difference is not directly observable, we might use functors to zoom in on the hom-set. A functor $F$ may map the two morphisms to distinct morphisms:

$$Ff \neq Fg$$

in a richer category, where the abutting hom-sets provide more resolution, e.g.,

$$h' \circ Ff \neq h' \circ Fg$$

where $h'$ is not in the image of $F$.

## 17.6  Hom-Set Isomorphisms

A lot of categorical constructions rely on isomorphisms between hom-sets. But since hom-sets are just sets, a plain isomorphism between them doesn't tell you much. For finite sets, an isomorphism just says that they have the same number of elements. If the sets are infinite, their cardinality must be the same. But any meaningful isomorphism of hom-sets must take into account composition. And composition involves more than one hom-set. We need to define isomorphisms that span whole collections of hom-sets, and we need to impose some compatibility conditions that interoperate with composition. And a *natural* isomorphism fits the bill exactly.

But what's a natural isomorphism of hom-sets? Naturality is a property of mappings between functors, not sets. So we are really talking about a natural isomorphism between hom-set-valued functors. These functors are more than just set-valued functors. Their action on morphisms is induced by the appropriate hom-functors. Morphisms are canonically mapped by hom-functors using either pre- or post-composition (depending on the covariance of the functor).

The Yoneda embedding is one example of such an isomorphism. It maps hom-sets in C to hom-sets in the functor category; and it's natural. One functor in the Yoneda embedding is the hom-functor in C and the other maps objects to sets of natural transformations between hom-sets.

The definition of a limit is also a natural isomorphism between hom-sets (the second one, again, in the functor category):

$$\mathbf{C}(c, \mathrm{Lim}D) \simeq \mathbf{Nat}(\Delta_c, D)$$

It turns out that our construction of an exponential object, or that of a free monoid, can also be rewritten as a natural isomorphism between hom-sets.

This is no coincidence — we'll see next that these are just different examples of adjunctions, which are defined as natural isomorphisms of hom-sets.

## 17.7 Asymmetry of Hom-Sets

There is one more observation that will help us understand adjunctions. Hom-sets are, in general, not symmetric. A hom-set $C(a, b)$ is often very different from the hom-set $C(b, a)$. The ultimate demonstration of this asymmetry is a partial order viewed as a category. In a partial order, a morphism from $a$ to $b$ exists if and only if $a$ is less than or equal to $b$. If $a$ and $b$ are different, then there can be no morphism going the other way, from $b$ to $a$. So if the hom-set $C(a, b)$ is non-empty, which in this case means it's a singleton set, then $C(b, a)$ must be empty, unless $a = b$. The arrows in this category have a definite flow in one direction.

A preorder, which is based on a relation that's not necessarily antisymmetric, is also "mostly" directional, except for occasional cycles. It's convenient to think of an arbitrary category as a generalization of a preoder.

A preorder is a thin category — all hom-sets are either singletons or empty. We can visualize a general category as a "thick" preorder.

## 17.8 Challenges

1. Consider some degenerate cases of a naturality condition and draw the appropriate diagrams. For instance, what happens if either functor $F$ or $G$ map both objects $a$ and $b$ (the ends of $f :: a \to b$) to the same object, e.g., $Fa = Fb$ or $Ga = Gb$? (Notice that you get a cone or a co-cone this way.) Then consider cases where either $Fa = Ga$ or $Fb = Gb$. Finally, what if you start with a morphism that loops on itself — $f :: a \to a$?

# 18

# Adjunctions

IN MATHEMATICS WE HAVE various ways of saying that one thing is like another. The strictest is equality. Two things are equal if there is no way to distinguish one from another. One can be substituted for the other in every imaginable context. For instance, did you notice that we used *equality* of morphisms every time we talked about commuting diagrams? That's because morphisms form a set (hom-set) and set elements can be compared for equality.

But equality is often too strong. There are many examples of things being the same for all intents and purposes, without actually being equal. For instance, the pair type (Bool, Char) is not strictly equal to (Char, Bool), but we understand that they contain the same informa tion. This concept is best captured by an *isomorphism* between two types — a morphism that's invertible. Since it's a morphism, it preserves the structure; and being "iso" means that it's part of a round trip that lands you in the same spot, no matter on which side you start. In the case of pairs, this isomorphism is called swap:

```
swap :: (a,b) -> (b,a)
swap (a,b) = (b,a)
```

swap happens to be its own inverse.

## 18.1  Adjunction and Unit/Counit Pair

When we talk about categories being isomorphic, we express this in terms of mappings between categories, a.k.a. functors. We would like to be able to say that two categories C and D are isomorphic if there exists a functor $R$ ("right") from C to D, which is invertible. In other words, there exists another functor $L$ ("left") from **D** back to **C** which, when composed with $R$, is equal to the identity functor $I$. There are two possible compositions, $R \circ L$ and $L \circ R$; and two possible identity functors: one in **C** and another in **D**.

But here's the tricky part: What does it mean for two functors to be *equal*? What do we mean by this equality:

$$R \circ L = I_{\mathbf{D}}$$

or this one:

$$L \circ R = I_{\mathbf{C}}$$

It would be reasonable to define functor equality in terms of equality of objects. Two functors, when acting on equal objects, should produce equal objects. But we don't, in general, have the notion of object equality in an arbitrary category. It's just not part of the definition. (Going deeper into this rabbit hole of "what equality really is," we would end up in Homotopy Type Theory.)

You might argue that functors *are* morphisms in the category of categories, so they should be equality-comparable. And indeed, as long as we are talking about small categories, where objects form a set, we can indeed use the equality of elements of a set to equality-compare objects.

But, remember, **Cat** is really a 2-category. Hom-sets in a 2-category have additional structure — there are 2-morphisms acting between 1-morphisms. In **Cat**, 1-morphisms are functors, and 2-morphisms are natural transformations. So it's more natural (can't avoid this pun!) to consider natural isomorphisms as substitutes for equality when talking about functors.

So, instead of isomorphism of categories, it makes sense to consider a more general notion of *equivalence*. Two categories **C** and **D** are *equivalent* if we can find two functors going back and forth between them, whose composition (either way) is *naturally isomorphic* to the identity functor. In other words, there is a two-way natural transformation between the composition $R \circ L$ and the identity functor $I_D$, and another between $L \circ R$ and the identity functor $I_C$.

Adjunction is even weaker than equivalence, because it doesn't require that the composition of the two functors be *isomorphic* to the identity functor. Instead it stipulates the existence of a *one way* natural transformation from $I_D$ to $R \circ L$, and another from $L \circ R$ to $I_C$. Here are the signatures of these two natural transformations:

$$\eta :: I_D \to R \circ L$$
$$\varepsilon :: L \circ R \to I_C$$

$\eta$ is called the unit, and $\varepsilon$ the counit of the adjunction.

Notice the asymmetry between these two definitions. In general, we don't have the two remaining mappings:

$$R \circ L \to I_D \qquad \text{not necessarily}$$
$$I_C \to L \circ R \qquad \text{not necessarily}$$

Because of this asymmetry, the functor $L$ is called the *left adjoint* to the functor $R$, while the functor $R$ is the right adjoint to $L$. (Of course, left and right make sense only if you draw your diagrams one particular way.)

The compact notation for the adjunction is:

$$L \dashv R$$

To better understand the adjunction, let's analyze the unit and the counit in more detail.

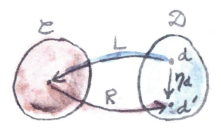

Let's start with the unit. It's a natural transformation, so it's a family of morphisms. Given an object $d$ in **D**, the component of $\eta$ is a morphism between $Id$, which is equal to $d$, and $(R \circ L)d$; which, in the picture, is called $d'$:

$$\eta_d :: d \rightarrow (R \circ L)d$$

Notice that the composition $R \circ L$ is an endofunctor in **D**.

This equation tells us that we can pick any object $d$ in **D** as our starting point, and use the round trip functor $R \circ L$ to pick our target object $d'$. Then we shoot an arrow — the morphism $\eta_d$ — to our target.

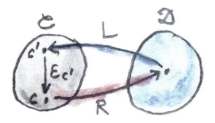

By the same token, the component of the counit $\varepsilon$ can be described as:

$$\varepsilon_{c'} :: (L \circ R)c \rightarrow c$$

where $c'$ is $(L \circ R)c$. It tells us that we can pick any object $c$ in **C** as our target, and use the round trip functor $L \circ R$ to pick the source $c'$. Then we shoot the arrow — the morphism $\varepsilon_{c'}$ — from the source to the target.

Another way of looking at unit and counit is that unit lets us *introduce* the composition $R \circ L$ anywhere we could insert an identity functor on **D**; and counit lets us *eliminate* the composition $L \circ R$, replacing it with the identity on **C**. That leads to some "obvious" consistency conditions, which make sure that introduction followed by elimination doesn't change anything:

$$L = L \circ I_D \longrightarrow L \circ R \circ L \longrightarrow I_C \circ L = L$$
$$R = I_D \circ R \longrightarrow R \circ L \circ R \longrightarrow R \circ I_C = R$$

These are called triangular identities because they make the following diagrams commute:

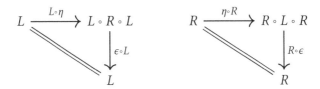

These are diagrams in the functor category: the arrows are natural transformations, and their composition is the horizontal composition of natural transformations. In components, these identities become:

$$\varepsilon_{Ld} \circ L\eta_d = \mathrm{id}_{Ld}$$
$$R\varepsilon_c \circ \eta_{Rc} = \mathrm{id}_{Rc}$$

We often see unit and counit in Haskell under different names. Unit is known as return (or pure, in the definition of Applicative):

```
return :: d -> m d
```

and counint as extract:

```
extract :: w c -> c
```

Here, m is the (endo-) functor corresponding to $R \circ L$, and w is the (endo-) functor corresponding to $L \circ R$. As we'll see later, they are part of the definition of a monad and a comonad, respectively.

If you think of an endofunctor as a container, the unit (or return) is a polymorphic function that creates a default box around a value of arbitrary type. The counit (or extract) does the reverse: it retrieves or produces a single value from a container.

We'll see later that every pair of adjoint functors defines a monad and a comonad. Conversely, every monad or comonad may be factorized into a pair of adjoint functors — this factorization is not unique, though.

In Haskell, we use monads a lot, but only rarely factorize them into pairs of adjoint functors, primarily because those functors would normally take us out of Hask.

We can however define adjunctions of *endofunctors* in Haskell. Here's part of the definition taken from `Data.Functor.Adjunction`:

```
class (Functor f, Representable u) =>
    Adjunction f u | f -> u, u -> f where
  unit :: a -> u (f a)
  counit :: f (u a) -> a
```

This definition requires some explanation. First of all, it describes a multi-parameter type class — the two parameters being f and u. It establishes a relation called `Adjunction` between these two type constructors.

Additional conditions, after the vertical bar, specify functional dependencies. For instance, f -> u means that u is determined by f (the relation between f and u is a function, here on type constructors). Conversely, u -> f means that, if we know u, then f is uniquely determined.

I'll explain in a moment why, in Haskell, we can impose the condition that the right adjoint u be a *representable* functor.

## 18.2  Adjunctions and Hom-Sets

There is an equivalent definition of the adjunction in terms of natural isomorphisms of hom-sets. This definition ties nicely with universal constructions we've been studying so far. Every time you hear the statement that there is some unique morphism, which factorizes some construction, you should think of it as a mapping of some set to a hom-set. That's the meaning of "picking a unique morphism."

Furthermore, factorization can be often described in terms of natural transformations. Factorization involves commuting diagrams — some morphism being equal to a composition of two morphisms (factors). A natural transformation maps morphisms to commuting diagrams. So, in a universal construction, we go from a morphism to a commuting diagram, and then to a unique morphism. We end up with a mapping from morphism to morphism, or from one hom-set to another (usually in different categories). If this mapping is invertible, and if it can be naturally extended across all hom-sets, we have an adjunction.

The main difference between universal constructions and adjunctions is that the latter are defined globally — for all hom-sets. For instance, using a universal construction you can define a product of two select objects, even if it doesn't exist for any other pair of objects in that category. As we'll see soon, if the product of *any pair* of objects exists in a category, it can be also defined through an adjunction.

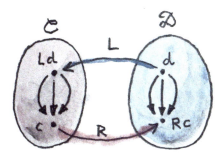

Here's the alternative definition of the adjunction using hom-sets. As before, we have two functors $L :: \mathbf{D} \to \mathbf{C}$ and $R :: \mathbf{C} \to \mathbf{D}$. We pick two arbitrary objects: the source object $d$ in $\mathbf{D}$, and the target object $c$ in $\mathbf{C}$. We can map the source object $d$ to $\mathbf{C}$ using $L$. Now we have two objects in $\mathbf{C}$, $Ld$ and $c$. They define a hom-set:

$$\mathbf{C}(Ld, c)$$

Similarly, we can map the target object $c$ using $R$. Now we have two objects in $\mathbf{D}$, $d$ and $Rc$. They, too, define a hom-set:

$$\mathbf{D}(d, Rc)$$

We say that $L$ is left adjoint to $R$ iff there is an isomorphism of hom-sets:

$$\mathbf{C}(Ld, c) \cong \mathbf{D}(d, Rc)$$

that is natural both in $d$ and $c$. Naturality means that the source $d$ can be varied smoothly across $\mathbf{D}$; and the target $c$, across $\mathbf{C}$. More precisely, we have a natural transformation $\varphi$ between the following two (covariant) functors from $\mathbf{C}$ to **Set**. Here's the action of these functors on objects:

$$c \to \mathbf{C}(Ld, c)$$
$$c \to \mathbf{D}(d, Rc)$$

213

The other natural transformation, $\psi$, acts between the following (contravariant) functors:

$$d \to \mathbf{C}(Ld, c)$$
$$d \to \mathbf{D}(d, Rc)$$

Both natural transformations must be invertible.

It's easy to show that the two definitions of the adjunction are equivalent. For instance, let's derive the unit transformation starting from the isomorphism of hom-sets:

$$\mathbf{C}(Ld, c) \cong \mathbf{D}(d, Rc)$$

Since this isomorphism works for any object $c$, it must also work for $c = Ld$:

$$\mathbf{C}(Ld, Ld) \cong \mathbf{D}(d, (R \circ L)d)$$

We know that the left hand side must contain at least one morphism, the identity. The natural transformation will map this morphism to an element of $\mathbf{D}(d, (R \circ L)d)$ or, inserting the identity functor $I$, a morphism in:

$$\mathbf{D}(Id, (R \circ L)d)$$

We get a family of morphisms parameterized by $d$. They form a natural transformation between the functor $I$ and the functor $R \circ L$ (the naturality condition is easy to verify). This is exactly our unit, $\eta$.

Conversely, starting from the existence of the unit and co-unit, we can define the transformations between hom-sets. For instance, let's pick an arbitrary morphism $f$ in the hom-set $\mathbf{C}(Ld, c)$. We want to define a $\varphi$ that, acting on $f$, produces a morphism in $\mathbf{D}(d, Rc)$.

There isn't really much choice. One thing we can try is to lift $f$ using $R$. That will produce a morphism $Rf$ from $R(Ld)$ to $Rc$ — a morphism that's an element of $\mathbf{D}((R \circ L)d, Rc)$.

What we need for a component of $\varphi$, is a morphism from $d$ to $Rc$. That's not a problem, since we can use a component of $\eta_d$ to get from $d$ to $(R \circ L)d$. We get:

$$\varphi_f = Rf \circ \eta_d$$

The other direction is analogous, and so is the derivation of $\psi$.

Going back to the Haskell definition of Adjunction, the natural transformations $\varphi$ and $\psi$ are replaced by polymorphic (in a and b) functions leftAdjunct and rightAdjunct, respectively. The functors $L$ and $R$ are called f and u:

```
class (Functor f, Representable u) =>
  Adjunction f u | f -> u, u -> f where
    leftAdjunct  :: (f a -> b) -> (a -> u b)
    rightAdjunct :: (a -> u b) -> (f a -> b)
```

The equivalence between the unit/counit formulation and the
leftAdjunct/rightAdjunct formulation is witnessed by these mappings:

```
unit            = leftAdjunct id
counit          = rightAdjunct id
leftAdjunct f   = fmap f . unit
rightAdjunct f = counit . fmap f
```

It's very instructive to follow the translation from the categorical de-
scription of the adjunction to Haskell code. I highly encourage this as
an exercise.

　　We are now ready to explain why, in Haskell, the right adjoint is
automatically a representable functor. The reason for this is that, to the
first approximation, we can treat the category of Haskell types as the
category of sets.

　　When the right category $D$ is Set, the right adjoint $R$ is a functor
from $C$ to Set. Such a functor is representable if we can find an object
$rep$ in $C$ such that the hom-functor $C(rep, \_)$ is naturally isomorphic
to $R$. It turns out that, if $R$ is the right adjoint of some functor $L$ from
Set to $C$, such an object always exists — it's the image of the singleton
set () under $L$:

$$rep = L()$$

Indeed, the adjunction tells us that the following two hom-sets are naturally isomorphic:

$$C(L(), c) \cong \mathbf{Set}((), Rc)$$

For a given $c$, the right hand side is the set of functions from the singleton set () to $Rc$. We've seen earlier that each such function picks one
element from the set $R$ $c$. The set of such functions is isomorphic to the
set $Rc$. So we have:

$$C(L(), -) \cong R$$

which shows that $R$ is indeed representable.
```
```

## 18.3  Product from Adjunction

We have previously introduced several concepts using universal constructions. Many of those concepts, when defined globally, are easier to express using adjunctions. The simplest non-trivial example is that of the product. The gist of the universal construction of the product is the ability to factorize any product-like candidate through the universal product.

More precisely, the product of two objects $a$ and $b$ is the object $(a \times b)$ (or (a, b) in the Haskell notation) equipped with two morphisms $fst$ and $snd$ such that, for any other candidate $c$ equipped with two morphisms $p :: c \to a$ and $q :: c \to b$, there exists a unique morphism $m :: c \to (a, b)$ that factorizes $p$ and $q$ through $fst$ and $snd$.

As we've seen earlier, in Haskell, we can implement a `factorizer` that generates this morphism from the two projections:

```
factorizer :: (c -> a) -> (c -> b) -> (c -> (a, b))
factorizer p q = \x -> (p x, q x)
```

It's easy to verify that the factorization conditions hold:

```
fst . factorizer p q = p
snd . factorizer p q = q
```

We have a mapping that takes a pair of morphisms p and q and produces another morphism m = `factorizer` p q.

How can we translate this into a mapping between two hom-sets that we need to define an adjunction? The trick is to go outside of Hask and treat the pair of morphisms as a single morphism in the product category.

Let me remind you what a product category is. Take two arbitrary categories $C$ and $D$. The objects in the product category $C \times D$ are pairs of objects, one from $C$ and one from $D$. The morphisms are pairs of morphisms, one from $C$ and one from $D$.

To define a product in some category $C$, we should start with the product category $C \times C$. Pairs of morphism from $C$ are single morphisms in the product category $C \times C$.

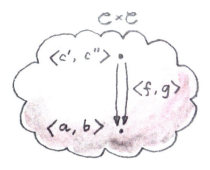

It might be a little confusing at first that we are using a product category to define a product. These are, however, very different products. We don't need a universal construction to define a product category. All we need is the notion of a pair of objects and a pair of morphisms.

However, a pair of objects from C is *not* an object in C. It's an object in a different category, C × C. We can write the pair formally as $\langle a, b \rangle$, where $a$ and $b$ are objects of C. The universal construction, on the other hand, is necessary in order to define the object $a \times b$ (or (a, b) in Haskell), which is an object in *the same* category C. This object is supposed to represent the pair $\langle a, b \rangle$ in a way specified by the universal construction. It doesn't always exist and, even if it exists for some, might not exist for other pairs of objects in C.

Let's now look at the factorizer as a mapping of hom-sets. The first hom-set is in the product category C × C, and the second is in C. A general morphism in C × C would be a pair of morphisms $\langle f, g \rangle$:

$$f :: c' \to a$$
$$g :: c'' \to b$$

with $c''$ potentially different from $c'$. But to define a product, we are interested in a special morphism in C × C, the pair $p$ and $q$ that share the same source object $c$. That's okay: In the definition of an adjunction, the source of the left hom-set is not an arbitrary object — it's the result of the left functor $L$ acting on some object from the right category. The functor that fits the bill is easy to guess — it's the diagonal functor $\Delta$ from C to C × C, whose action on objects is:

$$\Delta c = \langle c, c \rangle$$

The left-hand side hom-set in our adjunction should thus be:

$$(\mathbf{C} \times \mathbf{C})(\Delta c, \langle a, b \rangle)$$

It's a hom-set in the product category. Its elements are pairs of morphisms that we recognize as the arguments to our `factorizer`:

$$(c \rightarrow a) \rightarrow (c \rightarrow b) \dots$$

The right-hand side hom-set lives in C, and it goes between the source object $c$ and the result of some functor $R$ acting on the target object in C × C. That's the functor that maps the pair $\langle a, b \rangle$ to our product object, $a \times b$. We recognize this element of the hom-set as the *result* of the `factorizer`:

$$\dots \rightarrow (c \rightarrow (a, b))$$

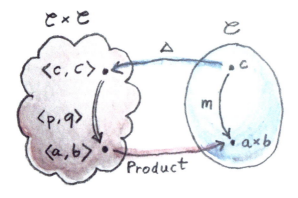

We still don't have a full adjunction. For that we first need our `factorizer` to be invertible — we are building an *isomorphism* between hom-sets. The inverse of the `factorizer` should start from a morphism $m$ — a morphism from some object $c$ to the product object $a \times b$. In other words, $m$ should be an element of:

$$C(c, a \times b)$$

The inverse factorizer should map $m$ to a morphism $\langle p, q \rangle$ in C × C that goes from $\langle c, c \rangle$ to $\langle a, b \rangle$; in other words, a morphism that's an element of:

$$(\text{C} \times \text{C})(\Delta\, c, \langle a, b \rangle)$$

If that mapping exists, we conclude that there exists the right adjoint to the diagonal functor. That functor defines a product.

In Haskell, we can always construct the inverse of the `factorizer` by composing m with, respectively, `fst` and `snd`.

```
p = fst . m
q = snd . m
```

To complete the proof of the equivalence of the two ways of defining a product we also need to show that the mapping between hom-sets is natural in $a$, $b$, and $c$. I will leave this as an exercise for the dedicated reader.

To summarize what we have done: A categorical product may be defined globally as the *right adjoint* of the diagonal functor:

$$(\mathbf{C} \times \mathbf{C})(\Delta c, \langle a, b \rangle) \cong \mathbf{C}(c, a \times b)$$

Here, $a \times b$ is the result of the action of our right adjoint functor *Product* on the pair $\langle a, b \rangle$. Notice that any functor from $\mathbf{C} \times \mathbf{C}$ is a bifunctor, so *Product* is a bifunctor. In Haskell, the *Product* bifunctor is written simply as $(,)$. You can apply it to two types and get their product type, for instance:

```
(,) Int Bool ~ (Int, Bool)
```

## 18.4  Exponential from Adjunction

The exponential $b^a$, or the function object $a \Rightarrow b$, can be defined using a universal construction. This construction, if it exists for all pairs of objects, can be seen as an adjunction. Again, the trick is to concentrate on the statement:

> For any other object $z$ with a morphism $g :: z \times a \to b$
> there is a unique morphism $h :: z \to (a \Rightarrow b)$

This statement establishes a mapping between hom-sets.

In this case, we are dealing with objects in the same category, so the two adjoint functors are endofunctors. The left (endo-)functor $L$, when acting on object $z$, produces $z \times a$. It's a functor that corresponds to taking a product with some fixed $a$.

The right (endo-)functor $R$, when acting on $b$ produces the function object $a \Rightarrow b$ (or $b^a$). Again, $a$ is fixed. The adjunction between these two functors is often written as:

$$- \times a \dashv (-)^a$$

The mapping of hom-sets that underlies this adjunction is best seen by redrawing the diagram that we used in the universal construction.

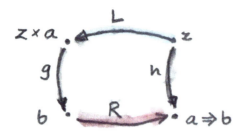

Notice that the *eval* morphism[1] is nothing else but the counit of this adjunction:

$$(a \Rightarrow b) \times a \to b$$

where:

$$(a \Rightarrow b) \times a = (L \circ R)b$$

I have previously mentioned that a universal construction defines a unique object, up to isomorphism. That's why we have "the" product and "the" exponential. This property translates to adjunctions as well: if a functor has an adjoint, this adjoint is unique up to isomorphism.

## 18.5 Challenges

1. Derive the naturality square for $\psi$, the transformation between the two (contravariant) functors:

$$a \to C(La, b)$$
$$a \to D(a, Rb)$$

2. Derive the counit $\varepsilon$ starting from the hom-sets isomorphism in the second definition of the adjunction.
3. Complete the proof of equivalence of the two definitions of the adjunction.
4. Show that the coproduct can be defined by an adjunction. Start with the definition of the factorizer for a coproduct.
5. Show that the coproduct is the left adjoint of the diagonal functor.
6. Define the adjunction between a product and a function object in Haskell.

---

[1]See ch.9 on universal construction.

# 19

# Free/Forgetful Adjunctions

FREE CONSTRUCTIONS ARE a powerful application of adjunctions. A *free functor* is defined as the left adjoint to a *forgetful functor*. A forgetful functor is usually a pretty simple functor that forgets some structure. For instance, lots of interesting categories are built on top of sets. But categorical objects, which abstract those sets, have no internal structure — they have no elements. Still, those objects often carry the memory of sets, in the sense that there is a mapping — a functor — from a given category C to **Set**. A set corresponding to some object in C is called its *underlying set*.

Monoids are such objects that have underlying sets — sets of elements. There is a forgetful functor $U$ from the category of monoids **Mon** to the category of sets, which maps monoids to their underlying sets. It also maps monoid morphisms (homomorphisms) to functions between sets.

I like to think of **Mon** as having split personality. On the one hand, it's a bunch of sets with multiplication and unit elements. On the other hand, it's a category with featureless objects whose only structure is encoded in morphisms that go between them. Every set-function that preserves multiplication and unit gives rise to a morphism in **Mon**.

Things to keep in mind:

- There may be many monoids that map to the same set, and
- There are fewer (or at most as many as) monoid morphisms than there are functions between their underlying sets.

221

Monoids $m_1$ and $m_2$ have the same underlying set. There are more functions between the underlying sets of $m_2$ and $m_3$ than there are morphisms between them.

The functor $F$ that's the left adjoint to the forgetful functor $U$ is the free functor that builds free monoids from their generator sets. The adjunction follows from the free monoid universal construction we've discussed before.[1]

In terms of hom-sets, we can write this adjunction as:

$$\mathbf{arg}(Fx, m) \cong \mathbf{Set}(x, Um)$$

This (natural in $x$ and $m$) isomorphism tells us that:

- For every monoid homomorphism between the free monoid $Fx$ generated by $x$ and an arbitrary monoid $m$ there is a unique function that embeds the set of generators $x$ in the underlying set of $m$. It's a function in $\mathbf{Set}(x, Um)$.
- For every function that embeds $x$ in the underlying set of some $m$ there is a unique monoid morphism between the free monoid generated by $x$ and the monoid $m$. (This is the morphism we called $h$ in our universal construction.)

---

[1]See ch.13 on free monoids.

The intuition is that $Fx$ is the "maximum" monoid that can be built on the basis of $x$. If we could look inside monoids, we would see that any morphism that belongs to $\mathbf{Mon}(Fx, m)$ *embeds* this free monoid in some other monoid $m$. It does it by possibly identifying some elements. In particular, it embeds the generators of $Fx$ (i.e., the elements of $x$) in $m$. The adjunction shows that the embedding of $x$, which is given by a function from $\mathbf{Set}(x, Um)$ on the right, uniquely determines the embedding of monoids on the left, and vice versa.

In Haskell, the list data structure is a free monoid (with some caveats: see Dan Doel's blog post[2]). A list type [a] is a free monoid with the type a representing the set of generators. For instance, the type [Char] contains the unit element — the empty list [] — and the singletons like ['a'], ['b'] — the generators of the free monoid. The rest is generated by applying the "product." Here, the product of two lists simply appends one to another. Appending is associative and unital (that is, there is a neutral element — here, the empty list). A free monoid generated by Char is nothing but the set of all strings of characters from Char. It's called String in Haskell:

```
type String = [Char]
```

(type defines a type synonym — a different name for an existing type).

Another interesting example is a free monoid built from just one generator. It's the type of the list of units, [()]. Its elements are [], [()], [(), ()], etc. Every such list can be described by one natural number — its length. There is no more information encoded in the list of units. Appending two such lists produces a new list whose length is the sum of the lengths of its constituents. It's easy to see that the type [()] is isomorphic to the additive monoid of natural numbers (with zero). Here

[2]http://comonad.com/reader/2015/free-monoids-in-haskell/

are the two functions that are the inverse of each other, witnessing this isomorphism:

```
toNat :: [()] -> Int
toNat = length

toLst :: Int -> [()]
toLst n = replicate n ()
```

For simplicity I used the type Int rather than Natural, but the idea is the same. The function replicate creates a list of length n pre-filled with a given value — here, the unit.

## 19.1  Some Intuitions

What follows are some hand-waving arguments. Those kind of arguments are far from rigorous, but they help in forming intuitions.

To get some intuition about the free/forgetful adjunctions it helps to keep in mind that functors and functions are lossy in nature. Functors may collapse multiple objects and morphisms, functions may bunch together multiple elements of a set. Also, their image may cover only part of their codomain.

An "average" hom-set in **Set** will contain a whole spectrum of functions starting with the ones that are least lossy (e.g., injections or, possibly, isomorphisms) and ending with constant functions that collapse the whole domain to a single element (if there is one).

I tend to think of morphisms in an arbitrary category as being lossy too. It's just a mental model, but it's a useful one, especially when thinking of adjunctions — in particular those in which one of the categories is **Set**.

Formally, we can only speak of morphisms that are invertible (isomorphisms) or non-invertible. It's that latter kind that may be thought of as lossy. There is also a notion of mono- and epi- morphisms that generalize the idea of injective (non-collapsing) and surjective (covering the whole codomain) functions, but it's possible to have a morphism that is both mono and epi, and which is still non-invertible.

In the Free ⊣ Forgetful adjunction, we have the more constrained category **C** on the left, and a less constrained category **D** on the right. Morphisms in **C** are "fewer" because they have to preserve some additional structure. In the case of **Mon**, they have to preserve multiplication and unit. Morphisms in **D** don't have to preserve as much structure, so there are "more" of them.

When we apply a forgetful functor $U$ to an object $c$ in **C**, we think of it as revealing the "internal structure" of $c$. In fact, if **D** is **Set** we think of $U$ as *defining* the internal structure of $c$ — its underlying set. (In an arbitrary category, we can't talk about the internals of an object other than through its connections to other objects, but here we are just hand-waving.)

If we map two objects $c'$ and $c$ using $U$, we expect that, in general, the mapping of the hom-set $\mathbf{C}(c', c)$ will cover only a subset of $\mathbf{D}(Uc', Uc)$. That's because morphisms in $\mathbf{C}(c', c)$ have to preserve the additional structure, whereas the ones in $\mathbf{D}(Uc', Uc)$ don't.

But since an adjunction is defined as an *isomporphism* of particular hom-sets, we have to be very picky with our selection of $c'$. In the adjunction, $c'$ is picked not from just anywhere in **C**, but from the (presumably smaller) image of the free functor $F$:

$$\mathbf{C}(Fd, c) \cong \mathbf{D}(d, Uc)$$

The image of $F$ must therefore consist of objects that have lots of morphisms going to an arbitrary $c$. In fact, there has to be as many structure-preserving morphisms from $Fd$ to $c$ as there are non-structure preserving morphisms from $d$ to $Uc$. It means that the image of $F$ must consist of essentially structure-free objects (so that there is no structure to preserve by morphisms). Such "structure-free" objects are called free objects.

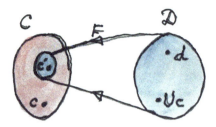

In the monoid example, a free monoid has no structure other than what's generated by unit and associativity laws. Other than that, all multiplications produce brand new elements.

In a free monoid, $2*3$ is not 6 — it's a new element $[2, 3]$. Since there is no identification of $[2, 3]$ and 6, a morphism from this free monoid to any other monoid $m$ is allowed to map them separately. But it's also okay for it to map both $[2, 3]$ and 6 (their product) to the same element of $m$. Or to identify $[2, 3]$ and 5 (their sum) in an additive monoid, and so on. Different identifications give you different monoids.

This leads to another interesting intuition: Free monoids, instead of performing the monoidal operation, accumulate the arguments that were passed to it. Instead of multiplying 2 and 3 they remember 2 and 3 in a list. The advantage of this scheme is that we don't have to specify what monoidal operation we will use. We can keep accumulating arguments, and only at the end apply an operator to the result. And it's then that we can chose what operator to apply. We can add the numbers, or multiply them, or perform addition modulo 2, and so on. A free monoid separates the creation of an expression from its evaluation. We'll see this idea again when we talk about algebras.

This intuition generalizes to other, more elaborate free constructions. For instance, we can accumulate whole expression trees before evaluating them. The advantage of this approach is that we can transform such trees to make the evaluation faster or less memory consuming. This is, for instance, done in implementing matrix calculus, where eager evaluation would lead to lots of allocations of temporary arrays to store intermediate results.

## 19.2 Challenges

1. Consider a free monoid built from a singleton set as its generator. Show that there is a one-to-one correspondence between

morphisms from this free monoid to any monoid $m$, and functions from the singleton set to the underlying set of $m$.

# 20

# Monads: Programmer's Definition

P ROGRAMMERS HAVE DEVELOPED a whole mythology around monads. It's supposed to be one of the most abstract and difficult concepts in programming. There are people who "get it" and those who don't. For many, the moment when they understand the concept of the monad is like a mystical experience. The monad abstracts the essence of so many diverse constructions that we simply don't have a good analogy for it in everyday life. We are reduced to groping in the dark, like those blind men touching different parts of the elephant end exclaiming triumphantly: "It's a rope," "It's a tree trunk," or "It's a burrito!"

Let me set the record straight: The whole mysticism around the monad is the result of a misunderstanding. The monad is a very simple concept. It's the diversity of applications of the monad that causes the confusion.

As part of research for this post I looked up duct tape (a.k.a., duck tape) and its applications. Here's a little sample of things that you can do with it:

- sealing ducts
- fixing $CO_2$ scrubbers on board Apollo 13
- wart treatment
- fixing Apple's iPhone 4 dropped call issue
- making a prom dress
- building a suspension bridge

Now imagine that you didn't know what duct tape was and you were trying to figure it out based on this list. Good luck!

So I'd like to add one more item to the collection of "the monad is like..." clichés: The monad is like duct tape. Its applications are widely diverse, but its principle is very simple: it glues things together. More precisely, it composes things.

This partially explains the difficulties a lot of programmers, especially those coming from the imperative background, have with understanding the monad. The problem is that we are not used to thinking of programming in terms of function composition. This is understandable. We often give names to intermediate values rather than pass them directly from function to function. We also inline short segments of glue code rather than abstract them into helper functions. Here's an imperative-style implementation of the vector-length function in C:

```
double vlen(double * v) {
    double d = 0.0;
    int n;
    for (n = 0; n < 3; ++n)
        d += v[n] * v[n];
    return sqrt(d);
}
```

Compare this with the (stylized) Haskell version that makes function composition explicit:

```
vlen = sqrt . sum . fmap (flip (^) 2)
```

(Here, to make things even more cryptic, I partially applied the exponentiation operator (^) by setting its second argument to 2.)

I'm not arguing that Haskell's point-free style is always better, just that function composition is at the bottom of everything we do in programming. And even though we are effectively composing functions, Haskell does go to great lengths to provide imperative-style syntax called the do notation for monadic composition. We'll see its use later. But first, let me explain why we need monadic composition in the first place.

## 20.1 The Kleisli Category

We have previously arrived at the writer monad by embellishing regular functions. The particular embellishment was done by pairing their return values with strings or, more generally, with elements of a monoid. We can now recognize that such embellishment is a functor:

```
newtype Writer w a = Writer (a, w)

instance Functor (Writer w) where
    fmap f (Writer (a, w)) = Writer (f a, w)
```

We have subsequently found a way of composing embellished functions, or Kleisli arrows, which are functions of the form:

```
a -> Writer w b
```

It was inside the composition that we implemented the accumulation of the log.

We are now ready for a more general definition of the Kleisli category. We start with a category C and an endofunctor m. The corresponding Kleisli category K has the same objects as C, but its morphisms are different. A morphism between two objects a and b in K is implemented as a morphism:

$$a \rightarrow m\ b$$

in the original category C. It's important to keep in mind that we treat a Kleisli arrow in K as a morphism between a and b, and not between a and m b.

In our example, m was specialized to Writer w, for some fixed monoid w.

Kleisli arrows form a category only if we can define proper composition for them. If there is a composition, which is associative and has an identity arrow for every object, then the functor m is called a *monad*, and the resulting category is called the Kleisli category.

In Haskell, Kleisli composition is defined using the fish operator >=>, and the identity arrow is a polymorphic function called return. Here's the definition of a monad using Kleisli composition:

```
class Monad m where
    (>=>) :: (a -> m b) -> (b -> m c) -> (a -> m c)
    return :: a -> m a
```

Keep in mind that there are many equivalent ways of defining a monad, and that this is not the primary one in the Haskell ecosystem. I like it for its conceptual simplicity and the intuition it provides, but there are other definitions that are more convenient when programming. We'll talk about them momentarily.

In this formulation, monad laws are very easy to express. They cannot be enforced in Haskell, but they can be used for equational reasoning. They are simply the standard composition laws for the Kleisli category:

```
(f >=> g) >=> h = f >=> (g >=> h) -- associativity
return >=> f = f                  -- left unit
f >=> return = f                  -- right unit
```

This kind of a definition also expresses what a monad really is: it's a way of composing embellished functions. It's not about side effects or state. It's about composition. As we'll see later, embellished functions may be used to express a variety of effects or state, but that's not what the monad is for. The monad is the sticky duct tape that ties one end of an embellished function to the other end of an embellished function.

Going back to our `Writer` example: The logging functions (the Kleisli arrows for the `Writer` functor) form a category because `Writer` is a monad:

```
instance Monoid w => Monad (Writer w) where
    f >=> g = \a ->
        let Writer (b, s) = f a
            Writer (c, s') = g b
        in Writer (c, s `mappend` s')
    return a = Writer (a, mempty)
```

Monad laws for `Writer` w are satisfied as long as monoid laws for w are satisfied (they can't be enforced in Haskell either).

There's a useful Kleisli arrow defined for the `Writer` monad called `tell`. It's sole purpose is to add its argument to the log:

```
tell :: w -> Writer w ()
tell s = Writer ((), s)
```

We'll use it later as a building block for other monadic functions.

## 20.2 Fish Anatomy

When implementing the fish operator for different monads you quickly realize that a lot of code is repeated and can be easily factored out. To begin with, the Kleisli composition of two functions must return a function, so its implementation may as well start with a lambda taking an argument of type a:

```
(>=>) :: (a -> m b) -> (b -> m c) -> (a -> m c)
f >=> g = \a -> ...
```

The only thing we can do with this argument is to pass it to `f`:

```
f >=> g = \a -> let mb = f a
                in ...
```

At this point we have to produce the result of type `m c`, having at our disposal an object of type `m b` and a function `g :: b -> m c`. Let's define a function that does that for us. This function is called *bind* and is usually written in the form of an infix operator:

```
(>>=) :: m a -> (a -> m b) -> m b
```

For every monad, instead of defining the fish operator, we may instead define bind. In fact the standard Haskell definition of a monad uses bind:

```
class Monad m where
    (>>=) :: m a -> (a -> m b) -> m b
    return :: a -> m a
```

Here's the definition of bind for the `Writer` monad:

```
(Writer (a, w)) >>= f = let Writer (b, w') = f a
                        in Writer (b, w `mappend` w')
```

It is indeed shorter than the definition of the fish operator.

It's possible to further dissect bind, taking advantage of the fact that `m` is a functor. We can use `fmap` to apply the function `a -> m b` to the contents of `m a`. This will turn a into `m b`. The result of the application is therefore of type `m (m b)`. This is not exactly what we want — we need the result of type `m b` — but we're close. All we need is a function that collapses or flattens the double application of `m`. Such function is called `join`:

```
join :: m (m a) -> m a
```

Using `join`, we can rewrite bind as:

```
ma >>= f = join (fmap f ma)
```

That leads us to the third option for defining a monad:

```
class Functor m => Monad m where
    join :: m (m a) -> m a
    return :: a -> m a
```

Here we have explicitly requested that m be a Functor. We didn't have to do that in the previous two definitions of the monad. That's because any type constructor m that either supports the fish or bind operator is automatically a functor. For instance, it's possible to define fmap in terms of bind and return:

```
fmap f ma = ma >>= \a -> return (f a)
```

For completeness, here's join for the Writer monad:

```
join :: Monoid w => Writer w (Writer w a) -> Writer w a
join (Writer ((Writer (a, w')), w)) = Writer (a, w `mappend` w')
```

## 20.3  The do Notation

One way of writing code using monads is to work with Kleisli arrows — composing them using the fish operator. This mode of programming is the generalization of the point-free style. Point-free code is compact and often quite elegant. In general, though, it can be hard to understand, bordering on cryptic. That's why most programmers prefer to give names to function arguments and intermediate values.

When dealing with monads it means favoring the bind operator over the fish operator. Bind takes a monadic value and returns a monadic value. The programmer may chose to give names to those values. But that's hardly an improvement. What we really want is to pretend that we are dealing with regular values, not the monadic containers that encapsulate them. That's how imperative code works — side effects, such as updating a global log, are mostly hidden from view. And that's what the do notation emulates in Haskell.

You might be wondering then, why use monads at all? If we want to make side effects invisible, why not stick to an imperative language? The answer is that the monad gives us much better control over side effects. For instance, the log in the Writer monad is passed from function to function and is never exposed globally. There is no possibility of garbling the log or creating a data race. Also, monadic code is clearly demarcated and cordoned off from the rest of the program.

The do notation is just syntactic sugar for monadic composition. On the surface, it looks a lot like imperative code, but it translates directly to a sequence of binds and lambda expressions.

For instance, take the example we used previously to illustrate the composition of Kleisli arrows in the Writer monad. Using our current definitions, it could be rewritten as:

```
process :: String -> Writer String [String]
process = upCase >=> toWords
```

This function turns all characters in the input string to upper case and splits it into words, all the while producing a log of its actions.

In the do notation it would look like this:

```
process s = do
    upStr <- upCase s
    toWords upStr
```

Here, upStr is just a String, even though upCase produces a Writer:

```
upCase :: String -> Writer String String
upCase s = Writer (map toUpper s, "upCase ")
```

This is because the do block is desugared by the compiler to:

```
process s =
    upCase s >>= \upStr ->
        toWords upStr
```

The monadic result of upCase is bound to a lambda that takes a String. It's the name of this string that shows up in the do block. When reading the line:

```
upStr <- upCase s
```

we say that upStr *gets* the result of upCase s.

The pseudo-imperative style is even more pronounced when we inline toWords. We replace it with the call to tell, which logs the string "toWords ", followed by the call to return with the result of splitting the string upStr using words. Notice that words is a regular function working on strings.

```
process s = do
    upStr <- upCase s
    tell "toWords "
    return (words upStr)
```

Here, each line in the do block introduces a new nested bind in the desugared code:

```
process s =
    upCase s >>= \upStr ->
        tell "toWords " >>= \() ->
            return (words upStr)
```

Notice that `tell` produces a unit value, so it doesn't have to be passed to the following lambda. Ignoring the contents of a monadic result (but not its effect — here, the contribution to the log) is quite common, so there is a special operator to replace bind in that case:

```
(>>) :: m a -> m b -> m b
m >> k = m >>= (\_ -> k)
```

The actual desugaring of our code looks like this:

```
process s =
  upCase s >>= \upStr ->
    tell "toWords " >>
      return (words upStr)
```

In general, do blocks consist of lines (or sub-blocks) that either use the left arrow to introduce new names that are then available in the rest of the code, or are executed purely for side-effects. Bind operators are implicit between the lines of code. Incidentally, it is possible, in Haskell, to replace the formatting in the do blocks with braces and semicolons. This provides the justification for describing the monad as a way of overloading the semicolon.

Notice that the nesting of lambdas and bind operators when desugaring the do notation has the effect of influencing the execution of the rest of the do block based on the result of each line. This property can be used to introduce complex control structures, for instance to simulate exceptions.

Interestingly, the equivalent of the do notation has found its application in imperative languages, C++ in particular. I'm talking about resumable functions or coroutines. It's not a secret that C++ futures form a monad[1]. It's an example of the continuation monad, which we'll discuss shortly. The problem with continuations is that they are very hard to compose. In Haskell, we use the do notation to turn the spaghetti of "my handler will call your handler" into something that looks very much like sequential code. Resumable functions make the same transformation possible in C++. And the same mechanism can be applied to turn the spaghetti of nested loops[2] into list comprehensions or "generators," which are essentially the do notation for the list monad. Without the unifying abstraction of the monad, each of these problems is typically addressed by providing custom extensions to the language. In Haskell, this is all dealt with through libraries.

---

[1]https://bartoszmilewski.com/2014/02/26/c17-i-see-a-monad-in-your-future/
[2]https://bartoszmilewski.com/2014/04/21/getting-lazy-with-c/

# 21

# Monads and Effects

Now that we know what the monad is for — it lets us compose embellished functions — the really interesting question is why embellished functions are so important in functional programming. We've already seen one example, the `Writer` monad, where embellishment let us create and accumulate a log across multiple function calls. A problem that would otherwise be solved using impure functions (e.g., by accessing and modifying some global state) was solved with pure functions.

## 21.1 The Problem

Here is a short list of similar problems, copied from Eugenio Moggi's seminal paper[1], all of which are traditionally solved by abandoning the purity of functions.

- Partiality: Computations that may not terminate
- Nondeterminism: Computations that may return many results
- Side effects: Computations that access/modify state
  - Read-only state, or the environment
  - Write-only state, or a log
  - Read/write state

- Exceptions: Partial functions that may fail
- Continuations: Ability to save state of the program and then restore it on demand

---

[1] https://core.ac.uk/download/pdf/21173011.pdf

- Interactive Input
- Interactive Output

What really is mind blowing is that all these problems may be solved using the same clever trick: turning to embellished functions. Of course, the embellishment will be totally different in each case.

You have to realize that, at this stage, there is no requirement that the embellishment be monadic. It's only when we insist on composition — being able to decompose a single embellished function into smaller embellished functions — that we need a monad. Again, since each of the embellishments is different, monadic composition will be implemented differently, but the overall pattern is the same. It's a very simple pattern: composition that is associative and equipped with identity.

The next section is heavy on Haskell examples. Feel free to skim or even skip it if you're eager to get back to category theory or if you're already familiar with Haskell's implementation of monads.

## 21.2 The Solution

First, let's analyze the way we used the `Writer` monad. We started with a pure function that performed a certain task — given arguments, it produced a certain output. We replaced this function with another function that embellished the original output by pairing it with a string. That was our solution to the logging problem.

We couldn't stop there because, in general, we don't want to deal with monolithic solutions. We needed to be able to decompose one log-producing function into smaller log-producing functions. It's the composition of those smaller functions that led us to the concept of a monad.

What's really amazing is that the same pattern of embellishing the function return types works for a large variety of problems that normally would require abandoning purity. Let's go through our list and identify the embellishment that applies to each problem in turn.

### 21.2.1 Partiality

We modify the return type of every function that may not terminate by turning it into a "lifted" type — a type that contains all values of the original type plus the special "bottom" value $\perp$. For instance, the `Bool` type, as a set, would contain two elements: `True` and `False`. The lifted

Bool contains three elements. Functions that return the lifted Bool may produce True or False, or execute forever.

The funny thing is that, in a lazy language like Haskell, a never-ending function may actually return a value, and this value may be passed to the next function. We call this special value the bottom. As long as this value is not explicitly needed (for instance, to be pattern matched, or produced as output), it may be passed around without stalling the execution of the program. Because every Haskell function may be potentially non-terminating, all types in Haskell are assumed to be lifted. This is why we often talk about the category Hask of Haskell (lifted) types and functions rather than the simpler **Set**. It is not clear, though, that Hask is a real category (see this Andrej Bauer post[2]).

### 21.2.2 Nondeterminism

If a function can return many different results, it may as well return them all at once. Semantically, a non-deterministic function is equivalent to a function that returns a list of results. This makes a lot of sense in a lazy garbage-collected language. For instance, if all you need is one value, you can just take the head of the list, and the tail will never be evaluated. If you need a random value, use a random number generator to pick the n-th element of the list. Laziness even allows you to return an infinite list of results.

In the list monad — Haskell's implementation of nondeterministic computations — join is implemented as concat. Remember that join is supposed to flatten a container of containers — concat concatenates a list of lists into a single list. return creates a singleton list:

```
instance Monad [] where
    join = concat
    return x = [x]
```

The bind operator for the list monad is given by the general formula: fmap followed by join which, in this case gives:

```
as >>= k = concat (fmap k as)
```

Here, the function k, which itself produces a list, is applied to every element of the list as. The result is a list of lists, which is flattened using concat.

---

[2]http://math.andrej.com/2016/08/06/hask-is-not-a-category/

From the programmer's point of view, working with a list is easier than, for instance, calling a non-deterministic function in a loop, or implementing a function that returns an iterator (although, in modern C++[3], returning a lazy range would be almost equivalent to returning a list in Haskell).

A good example of using non-determinism creatively is in game programming. For instance, when a computer plays chess against a human, it can't predict the opponent's next move. It can, however, generate a list of all possible moves and analyze them one by one. Similarly, a non-deterministic parser may generate a list of all possible parses for a given expression.

Even though we may interpret functions returning lists as non-deterministic, the applications of the list monad are much wider. That's because stitching together computations that produce lists is a perfect functional substitute for iterative constructs — loops — that are used in imperative programming. A single loop can be often rewritten using fmap that applies the body of the loop to each element of the list. The do notation in the list monad can be used to replace complex nested loops.

My favorite example is the program that generates Pythagorean triples — triples of positive integers that can form sides of right triangles.

```
triples = do
    z <- [1..]
    x <- [1..z]
    y <- [x..z]
    guard (x^2 + y^2 == z^2)
    return (x, y, z)
```

The first line tells us that z gets an element from an infinite list of positive numbers [1..]. Then x gets an element from the (finite) list [1..z] of numbers between 1 and z. Finally y gets an element from the list of numbers between x and z. We have three numbers $1 \leqslant x \leqslant y \leqslant z$ at our disposal. The function guard takes a Bool expression and returns a list of units:

```
guard :: Bool -> [()]
guard True = [()]
guard False = []
```

---

[3]http://ericniebler.com/2014/04/27/range-comprehensions/

This function (which is a member of a larger class called `MonadPlus`) is used here to filter out non-Pythagorean triples. Indeed, if you look at the implementation of bind (or the related operator `>>`), you'll notice that, when given an empty list, it produces an empty list. On the other hand, when given a non-empty list (here, the singleton list containing unit `[()]`), bind will call the continuation, here `return (x, y, z)`, which produces a singleton list with a verified Pythagorean triple. All those singleton lists will be concatenated by the enclosing binds to produce the final (infinite) result. Of course, the caller of `triples` will never be able to consume the whole list, but that doesn't matter, because Haskell is lazy.

The problem that normally would require a set of three nested loops has been dramatically simplified with the help of the list monad and the do notation. As if that weren't enough, Haskell let's you simplify this code even further using list comprehension:

```
triples = [(x, y, z) | z <- [1..]
                     , x <- [1..z]
                     , y <- [x..z]
                     , x^2 + y^2 == z^2]
```

This is just further syntactic sugar for the list monad (strictly speaking, `MonadPlus`).

You might see similar constructs in other functional or imperative languages under the guise of generators and coroutines.

### 21.2.3 Read-Only State

A function that has read-only access to some external state, or environment, can be always replaced by a function that takes that environment as an additional argument. A pure function `(a, e) -> b` (where e is the type of the environment) doesn't look, at first sight, like a Kleisli arrow. But as soon as we curry it to `a -> (e -> b)` we recognize the embellishment as our old friend the reader functor:

```
newtype Reader e a = Reader (e -> a)
```

You may interpret a function returning a `Reader` as producing a mini-executable: an action that given an environment produces the desired result. There is a helper function `runReader` to execute such an action:

```
runReader :: Reader e a -> e -> a
runReader (Reader f) e = f e
```

It may produce different results for different values of the environment.

Notice that both the function returning a `Reader`, and the `Reader` action itself are pure.

To implement bind for the `Reader` monad, first notice that you have to produce a function that takes the environment `e` and produces a b:

```
ra >>= k = Reader (\e -> ...)
```

Inside the lambda, we can execute the action `ra` to produce an a:

```
ra >>= k = Reader (\e -> let a = runReader ra e
                         in ...)
```

We can then pass the `a` to the continuation `k` to get a new action `rb`:

```
ra >>= k = Reader (\e -> let a  = runReader ra e
                             rb = k a
                         in ...)
```

Finally, we can run the action `rb` with the environment `e`:

```
ra >>= k = Reader (\e -> let a = runReader ra e
                             rb = k a
                         in runReader rb e)
```

To implement `return` we create an action that ignores the environment and returns the unchanged value.

Putting it all together, after a few simplifications, we get the following definition:

```
instance Monad (Reader e) where
    ra >>= k = Reader (\e -> runReader (k (runReader ra e)) e)
    return x = Reader (\e -> x)
```

### 21.2.4  Write-Only State

This is just our initial logging example. The embellishment is given by the `Writer` functor:

```
newtype Writer w a = Writer (a, w)
```

For completeness, there's also a trivial helper `runWriter` that unpacks the data constructor:

```
runWriter :: Writer w a -> (a, w)
runWriter (Writer (a, w)) = (a, w)
```

As we've seen before, in order to make `Writer` composable, w has to be a monoid. Here's the monad instance for `Writer` written in terms of the bind operator:

```
instance (Monoid w) => Monad (Writer w) where
    (Writer (a, w)) >>= k = let (a', w') = runWriter (k a)
                            in Writer (a', w `mappend` w')
    return a = Writer (a, mempty)
```

### 21.2.5 State

Functions that have read/write access to state combine the embellishments of the `Reader` and the `Writer`. You may think of them as pure functions that take the state as an extra argument and produce a pair value/state as a result: `(a, s) -> (b, s)`. After currying, we get them into the form of Kleisli arrows `a -> (s -> (b, s))`, with the embellishment abstracted in the `State` functor:

```
newtype State s a = State (s -> (a, s))
```

Again, we can look at a Kleisli arrow as returning an action, which can be executed using the helper function:

```
runState :: State s a -> s -> (a, s)
runState (State f) s = f s
```

Different initial states may not only produce different results, but also different final states.

The implementation of bind for the `State` monad is very similar to that of the `Reader` monad, except that care has to be taken to pass the correct state at each step:

```
sa >>= k = State (\s -> let (a, s') = runState sa s
                            sb = k a
                        in runState sb s')
```

Here's the full instance:

```
instance Monad (State s) where
    sa >>= k = State (\s -> let (a, s') = runState sa s
                            in runState (k a) s')
    return a = State (\s -> (a, s))
```

There are also two helper Kleisli arrows that may be used to manipulate the state. One of them retrieves the state for inspection:

```
get :: State s s
get = State (\s -> (s, s))
```

and the other replaces it with a completely new state:

```
put :: s -> State s ()
put s' = State (\s -> ((), s'))
```

### 21.2.6 Exceptions

An imperative function that throws an exception is really a partial function — it's a function that's not defined for some values of its arguments. The simplest implementation of exceptions in terms of pure total functions uses the Maybe functor. A partial function is extended to a total function that returns Just a whenever it makes sense, and Nothing when it doesn't. If we want to also return some information about the cause of the failure, we can use the Either functor instead (with the first type fixed, for instance, to String).

Here's the Monad instance for Maybe:

```
instance Monad Maybe where
    Nothing >>= k = Nothing
    Just a  >>= k = k a
    return a = Just a
```

Notice that monadic composition for Maybe correctly short-circuits the computation (the continuation k is never called) when an error is detected. That's the behavior we expect from exceptions.

### 21.2.7 Continuations

It's the "Don't call us, we'll call you!" situation you may experience after a job interview. Instead of getting a direct answer, you are supposed to provide a handler, a function to be called with the result. This style of

```
```

programming is especially useful when the result is not known at the time of the call because, for instance, it's being evaluated by another thread or delivered from a remote web site. A Kleisli arrow in this case returns a function that accepts a handler, which represents "the rest of the computation":

```
data Cont r a = Cont ((a -> r) -> r)
```

The handler a -> r, when it's eventually called, produces the result of type r, and this result is returned at the end. A continuation is parameterized by the result type. (In practice, this is often some kind of status indicator.)

There is also a helper function for executing the action returned by the Kleisli arrow. It takes the handler and passes it to the continuation:

```
runCont :: Cont r a -> (a -> r) -> r
runCont (Cont k) h = k h
```

The composition of continuations is notoriously difficult, so its handling through a monad and, in particular, the do notation, is of extreme advantage.

Let's figure out the implementation of bind. First let's look at the stripped down signature:

```
(>>=) :: ((a -> r) -> r) ->
  (a -> (b -> r) -> r) ->
  ((b -> r) -> r)
```

Our goal is to create a function that takes the handler (b -> r) and produces the result r. So that's our starting point:

```
ka >>= kab = Cont (\hb -> ...)
```

Inside the lambda, we want to call the function ka with the appropriate handler that represents the rest of the computation. We'll implement this handler as a lambda:

```
runCont ka (\a -> ...)
```

In this case, the rest of the computation involves first calling kab with a, and then passing hb to the resulting action kb:

```
runCont ka (\a -> let kb = kab a
                  in runCont kb hb)
```

As you can see, continuations are composed inside out. The final handler hb is called from the innermost layer of the computation. Here's
the full instance:

```
instance Monad (Cont r) where
  ka >>= kab = Cont (\hb -> runCont ka (\a -> runCont (kab a)
  ↪  hb))
  return a = Cont (\ha -> ha a)
```

## 21.2.8  Interactive Input

This is the trickiest problem and a source of a lot of confusion. Clearly,
a function like getChar, if it were to return a character typed at the
keyboard, couldn't be pure. But what if it returned the character inside
a container? As long as there was no way of extracting the character
from this container, we could claim that the function is pure. Every
time you call getChar it would return exactly the same container. Conceptually, this container would contain the superposition of all possible
characters.

If you're familiar with quantum mechanics, you should have no
problem understanding this analogy. It's just like the box with the Schrödinger's
cat inside — except that there is no way to open or peek inside the box.
The box is defined using the special built-in IO functor. In our example,
getChar could be declared as a Kleisli arrow:

```
getChar :: () -> IO Char
```

(Actually, since a function from the unit type is equivalent to picking
a value of the return type, the declaration of getChar is simplified to
getChar :: IO Char.)

Being a functor, IO lets you manipulate its contents using fmap. And,
as a functor, it can store the contents of any type, not just a character.
The real utility of this approach comes to light when you consider that,
in Haskell, IO is a monad. It means that you are able to compose Kleisli
arrows that produce IO objects.

You might think that Kleisli composition would allow you to peek
at the contents of the IO object (thus "collapsing the wave function," if
we were to continue the quantum analogy). Indeed, you could compose

getChar with another Kleisli arrow that takes a character and, say, converts it to an integer. The catch is that this second Kleisli arrow could only return this integer as an (IO Int). Again, you'll end up with a superposition of all possible integers. And so on. The Schrödinger's cat is never out of the bag. Once you are inside the IO monad, there is no way out of it. There is no equivalent of runState or runReader for the IO monad. There is no runIO!

So what can you do with the result of a Kleisli arrow, the IO object, other than compose it with another Kleisli arrow? Well, you can return it from main. In Haskell, main has the signature:

```
main :: IO ()
```

and you are free to think of it as a Kleisli arrow:

```
main :: () -> IO ()
```

From that perspective, a Haskell program is just one big Kleisli arrow in the IO monad. You can compose it from smaller Kleisli arrows using monadic composition. It's up to the runtime system to do something with the resulting IO object (also called IO action).

Notice that the arrow itself is a pure function — it's pure functions all the way down. The dirty work is relegated to the system. When it finally executes the IO action returned from main, it does all kinds of nasty things like reading user input, modifying files, printing obnoxious messages, formatting a disk, and so on. The Haskell program never dirties its hands (well, except when it calls unsafePerformIO, but that's a different story).

Of course, because Haskell is lazy, main returns almost immediately, and the dirty work begins right away. It's during the execution of the IO action that the results of pure computations are requested and evaluated on demand. So, in reality, the execution of a program is an interleaving of pure (Haskell) and dirty (system) code.

There is an alternative interpretation of the IO monad that is even more bizarre but makes perfect sense as a mathematical model. It treats the whole Universe as an object in a program. Notice that, conceptually, the imperative model treats the Universe as an external global object, so procedures that perform I/O have side effects by virtue of interacting with that object. They can both read and modify the state of the Universe.

We already know how to deal with state in functional programming — we use the state monad. Unlike simple state, however, the state of the Universe cannot be easily described using standard data structures. But we don't have to, as long as we never directly interact with it. It's enough that we assume that there exists a type RealWorld and, by some miracle of cosmic engineering, the runtime is able to provide an object of this type. An IO action is just a function:

```
type IO a = RealWorld -> (a, RealWorld)
```

Or, in terms of the State monad:

```
type IO = State RealWorld
```

However, >=> and return for the IO monad have to be built into the language.

### 21.2.9 Interactive Output

The same IO monad is used to encapsulate interactive output. RealWorld is supposed to contain all output devices. You might wonder why we can't just call output functions from Haskell and pretend that they do nothing. For instance, why do we have:

```
putStr :: String -> IO ()
```

rather than the simpler:

```
putStr :: String -> ()
```

Two reasons: Haskell is lazy, so it would never call a function whose output — here, the unit object — is not used for anything. And, even if it weren't lazy, it could still freely change the order of such calls and thus garble the output. The only way to force sequential execution of two functions in Haskell is through data dependency. The input of one function must depend on the output of another. Having RealWorld passed between IO actions enforces sequencing.

Conceptually, in this program:

```
main :: IO ()
main = do
    putStr "Hello "
    putStr "World!"
```

the action that prints "World!" receives, as input, the Universe in which "Hello " is already on the screen. It outputs a new Universe, with "Hello World!" on the screen.

## 21.3 Conclusion

Of course I have just scratched the surface of monadic programming. Monads not only accomplish, with pure functions, what normally is done with side effects in imperative programming, but they also do it with a high degree of control and type safety. They are not without drawbacks, though. The major complaint about monads is that they don't easily compose with each other. Granted, you can combine most of the basic monads using the monad transformer library. It's relatively easy to create a monad stack that combines, say, state with exceptions, but there is no formula for stacking arbitrary monads together.

# 22

## Monads Categorically

IF YOU MENTION MONADS to a programmer, you'll probably end up talking about effects. To a mathematician, monads are about algebras. We'll talk about algebras later — they play an important role in programming — but first I'd like to give you a little intuition about their relation to monads. For now, it's a bit of a hand-waving argument, but bear with me.

Algebra is about creating, manipulating, and evaluating expressions. Expressions are built using operators. Consider this simple expression:

$$x^2 + 2x + 1$$

This expression is formed using variables like $x$, and constants like 1 or 2, bound together with operators like plus or times. As programmers, we often think of expressions as trees.

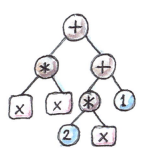

Trees are containers so, more generally, an expression is a container for storing variables. In category theory, we represent containers as endofunctors. If we assign the type $a$ to the variable $x$, our expression will have the type $m\,a$, where $m$ is an endofunctor that builds expression trees. (Nontrivial branching expressions are usually created using recursively defined endofunctors.)

What's the most common operation that can be performed on an expression? It's substitution: replacing variables with expressions. For instance, in our example, we could replace $X$ with $y - 1$ to get:

$$(y - 1)^2 + 2(y - 1) + 1$$

Here's what happened: We took an expression of type $m\,a$ and applied a transformation of type $a \rightarrow m\,b$ ($b$ represents the type of $y$). The result is an expression of type $m\,b$. Let me spell it out:

$$m\,a \rightarrow (a \rightarrow m\,b) \rightarrow m\,b$$

Yes, that's the signature of monadic bind.

That was a bit of motivation. Now let's get to the math of the monad. Mathematicians use different notation than programmers. They prefer to use the letter $T$ for the endofunctor, and Greek letters: $\mu$ for `join` and $\eta$ for `return`. Both `join` and `return` are polymorphic functions, so we can guess that they correspond to natural transformations.

Therefore, in category theory, a monad is defined as an endofunctor $T$ equipped with a pair of natural transformations $\mu$ and $\eta$.

$\mu$ is a natural transformation from the square of the functor $T^2$ back to $T$. The square is simply the functor composed with itself, $T \circ T$ (we can only do this kind of squaring for endofunctors).

$$\mu :: T^2 \rightarrow T$$

The component of this natural transformation at an object $a$ is the morphism:

$$\mu_a :: T(Ta) \rightarrow Ta$$

which, in Hask, translates directly to our definition of `join`.

$\eta$ is a natural transformation between the identity functor $I$ and $T$:

$$\eta :: I \rightarrow T$$

Considering that the action of $I$ on the object $a$ is just $a$, the component of $\eta$ is given by the morphism:

$$\eta_a :: a \rightarrow Ta$$

which translates directly to our definition of `return`.

These natural transformations must satisfy some additional laws. One way of looking at it is that these laws let us define a Kleisli category for the endofunctor $T$. Remember that a Kleisli arrow between $a$ and $b$ is defined as a morphism $a \to Tb$. The composition of two such arrows (I'll write it as a circle with the subscript $T$) can be implemented using $\mu$:

$$g \circ_T f = \mu_c \circ (T\,g) \circ f$$

where

$$f :: a \to T\,b$$
$$g :: b \to T\,c$$

Here $T$, being a functor, can be applied to the morphism $g$. It might be easier to recognize this formula in Haskell notation:

```
f >=> g = join . fmap g . f
```

or, in components:

```
(f >=> g) a = join (fmap g (f a))
```

In terms of the algebraic interpretation, we are just composing two successive substitutions.

For Kleisli arrows to form a category we want their composition to be associative, and $\eta_a$ to be the identity Kleisli arrow at $a$. This requirement can be translated to monadic laws for $\mu$ and $\eta$. But there is another way of deriving these laws that makes them look more like monoid laws. In fact $\mu$ is often called *multiplication*, and $\eta$ – *unit*.

Roughly speaking, the associativity law states that the two ways of reducing the cube of $T$, $T^3$, down to $T$ must give the same result. Two unit laws (left and right) state that when $\eta$ is applied to $T$ and then reduced by $\mu$, we get back $T$.

Things are a little tricky because we are composing natural transformations and functors. So a little refresher on horizontal composition is in order. For instance, $T^3$ can be seen as a composition of $T$ after $T^2$. We can apply to it the horizontal composition of two natural transformations:

$$I_T \circ \mu$$

and get $T \circ T$; which can be further reduced to $T$ by applying $\mu$. $I_T$ is the identity natural transformation from $T$ to $T$. You will often see the notation for this type of horizontal composition $I_T \circ \mu$ shortened to $T \circ \mu$. This nota-

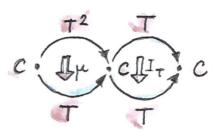

tion is unambiguous because it makes no sense to compose a functor with a natural transformation, therefore $T$ must mean $I_T$ in this context.

We can also draw the diagram in the (endo-) functor category $[C, C]$:

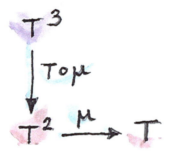

Alternatively, we can treat $T^3$ as the composition of $T^2 \circ T$ and apply $\mu \circ T$ to it. The result is also $T \circ T$ which, again, can be reduced to $T$ using $\mu$. We require that the two paths produce the same result.

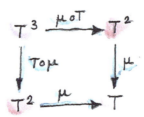

Similarly, we can apply the horizontal composition $\eta \circ T$ to the composition of the identity functor $I$ after $T$ to obtain $T^2$, which can then be reduced using $\mu$. The result should be the same as if we applied the identity natural transformation directly to $T$. And, by analogy, the same should be true for $T \circ \eta$.

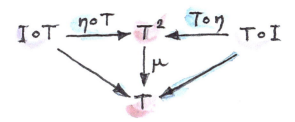

You can convince yourself that these laws guarantee that the composition of Kleisli arrows indeed satisfies the laws of a category.

The similarities between a monad and a monoid are striking. We have multiplication $\mu$, unit $\eta$, associativity, and unit laws. But our definition of a monoid is too narrow to describe a monad as a monoid. So let's generalize the notion of a monoid.

## 22.1 Monoidal Categories

Let's go back to the conventional definition of a monoid. It's a set with a binary operation and a special element called unit. In Haskell, this can be expressed as a typeclass:

```
class Monoid m where
    mappend :: m -> m -> m
    mempty  :: m
```

The binary operation mappend must be associative and unital (i.e., multiplication by the unit mempty is a no-op).

Notice that, in Haskell, the definition of mappend is curried. It can be interpreted as mapping every element of m to a function:

```
mappend :: m -> (m -> m)
```

It's this interpretation that gives rise to the definition of a monoid as a single-object category where endomorphisms (m -> m) represent the elements of the monoid. But because currying is built into Haskell, we could as well have started with a different definition of multiplication:

```
mu :: (m, m) -> m
```

Here, the Cartesian product (m, m) becomes the source of pairs to be multiplied.

This definition suggests a different path to generalization: replacing the Cartesian product with categorical product. We could start with a category where products are globally defined, pick an object m there, and define multiplication as a morphism:

$$\mu :: m \times m \longrightarrow m$$

We have one problem though: In an arbitrary category we can't peek inside an object, so how do we pick the unit element? There is a trick to it. Remember how element selection is equivalent to a function from the singleton set? In Haskell, we could replace the definition of mempty with a function:

```
eta :: () -> m
```

The singleton is the terminal object in **Set**, so it's natural to generalize this definition to any category that has a terminal object $t$:

$$\eta :: t \longrightarrow m$$

This lets us pick the unit "element" without having to talk about elements.

Unlike in our previous definition of a monoid as a single-object category, monoidal laws here are not automatically satisfied — we have to impose them. But in order to formulate them we have to establish the monoidal structure of the underlying categorical product itself. Let's recall how monoidal structure works in Haskell first.

We start with associativity. In Haskell, the corresponding equational law is:

```
mu (x, mu (y, z)) = mu (mu (x, y), z)
```

Before we can generalize it to other categories, we have to rewrite it as an equality of functions (morphisms). We have to abstract it away from its action on individual variables — in other words, we have to use point-free notation. Knowing that the Cartesian product is a bifunctor, we can write the left hand side as:

```
(mu . bimap id mu)(x, (y, z))
```

and the right hand side as:

```
(mu . bimap mu id)((x, y), z)
```

This is almost what we want. Unfortunately, the Cartesian product is not strictly associative — (x, (y, z)) is not the same as ((x, y), z) — so we can't just write point-free:

```
mu . bimap id mu = mu . bimap mu id
```

On the other hand, the two nestings of pairs are isomorphic. There is an invertible function called the associator that converts between them:

```
alpha :: ((a, b), c) -> (a, (b, c))
alpha ((x, y), z) = (x, (y, z))
```

With the help of the associator, we can write the point-free associativity law for mu:

```
mu . bimap id mu . alpha = mu . bimap mu id
```

We can apply a similar trick to unit laws which, in the new notation, take the form:

```
mu (eta (), x) = x
mu (x, eta ()) = x
```

They can be rewritten as:

```
(mu . bimap eta id) ((), x) = lambda((), x)
(mu . bimap id eta) (x, ()) = rho (x, ())
```

The isomorphisms lambda and rho are called the left and right unitor, respectively. They witness the fact that the unit () is the identity of the Cartesian product up to isomorphism:

```
lambda :: ((), a) -> a
lambda ((), x) = x

rho :: (a, ()) -> a
rho (x, ()) = x
```

The point-free versions of the unit laws are therefore:

```
mu . bimap id eta = rho
mu . bimap eta id = lambda
```

We have formulated point-free monoidal laws for mu and eta using the fact that the underlying Cartesian product itself acts like a monoidal multiplication in the category of types. Keep in mind though that the associativity and unit laws for the Cartesian product are valid only up to isomorphism.

It turns out that these laws can be generalized to any category with products and a terminal object. Categorical products are indeed associative up to isomorphism and the terminal object is the unit, also up to isomorphism. The associator and the two unitors are natural isomorphisms. The laws can be represented by commuting diagrams.

$$
\begin{array}{ccc}
(a \times a) \times a & \xrightarrow{\ \alpha\ } & a \times (a \times a) \\[4pt]
\Big\downarrow{\scriptstyle \mu \times id} & & \Big\downarrow{\scriptstyle id \times \mu} \\[4pt]
a \times a \quad \underset{\mu}{\searrow} & \quad & \underset{\mu}{\swarrow} \quad a \times a \\
& a &
\end{array}
$$

Notice that, because the product is a bifunctor, it can lift a pair of morphisms — in Haskell this was done using bimap.

We could stop here and say that we can define a monoid on top of any category with categorical products and a terminal object. As long as we can pick an object $m$ and two morphisms $\mu$ and $\eta$ that satisfy monoidal laws, we have a monoid. But we can do better than that. We don't need a full-blown categorical product to formulate the laws for $\mu$ and $\eta$. Recall that a product is defined through a universal construction that uses projections. We haven't used any projections in our formulation of monoidal laws.

A bifunctor that behaves like a product without being a product is called a *tensor product*, often denoted by the infix operator ⊗. A definition of a tensor product in general is a bit tricky, but we won't worry about it. We'll just list its properties — the most important being associativity up to isomorphism.

Similarly, we don't need the object $t$ to be terminal. We never used its terminal property — namely, the existence of a unique morphism from any object to it. What we require is that it works well in concert with the tensor product. Which means that we want it to be the unit of the tensor product, again, up to isomorphism. Let's put it all together:

A monoidal category is a category C equipped with a bifunctor called the tensor product:

$$\otimes :: C \times C \to C$$

and a distinct object $i$ called the unit object, together with three natural isomorphisms called, respectively, the associator and the left and right unitors:

$$\alpha_{abc} :: (a \otimes b) \otimes c \to a \otimes (b \otimes c)$$
$$\lambda_a :: i \otimes a \to a$$
$$\rho_a :: a \otimes i \to a$$

(There is also a coherence condition for simplifying a quadruple tensor product.)

What's important is that a tensor product describes many familiar bifunctors. In particular, it works for a product, a coproduct and, as we'll see shortly, for the composition of endofunctors (and also for some more esoteric products like Day convolution). Monoidal categories will play an essential role in the formulation of enriched categories.

## 22.2 Monoid In a Monoidal Category

We are now ready to define a monoid in a more general setting of a monoidal category. We start by picking an object $m$. Using the tensor product we can form powers of $m$. The square of $m$ is $m \otimes m$. There are two ways of forming the cube of $m$, but they are isomorphic through the associator. Similarly for higher powers of $m$ (that's where we need the coherence conditions). To form a monoid we need to pick two morphisms:

$$\mu :: m \otimes m \to m$$
$$\eta :: i \to m$$

where $i$ is the unit object for our tensor product.

These morphisms have to satisfy associativity and unit laws, which can be expressed in terms of the following commuting diagrams:

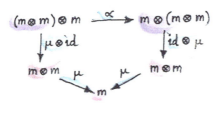

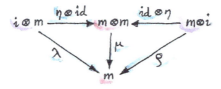

Notice that it's essential that the tensor product be a bifunctor because we need to lift pairs of morphisms to form products such as $\mu \otimes$ id or $\eta \otimes$ id. These diagrams are just a straightforward generalization of our previous results for categorical products.

## 22.3  Monads as Monoids

Monoidal structures pop up in unexpected places. One such place is the functor category. If you squint a little, you might be able to see functor composition as a form of multiplication. The problem is that not any two functors can be composed — the target category of one has to be the source category of the other. That's just the usual rule of composition of morphisms — and, as we know, functors are indeed morphisms in the category **Cat**. But just like endomorphisms (morphisms that loop back to the same object) are always composable, so are endofunctors.

For any given category **C**, endofunctors from **C** to **C** form the functor category [**C**, **C**]. Its objects are endofunctors, and morphisms are natural transformations between them. We can take any two objects from this category, say endofunctors $F$ and $G$, and produce a third object $F \circ G$ — an endofunctor that's their composition.

Is endofunctor composition a good candidate for a tensor product? First, we have to establish that it's a bifunctor. Can it be used to lift a pair of morphisms — here, natural transformations? The signature of the analog of `bimap` for the tensor product would look something like this:

$$bimap :: (a \rightarrow b) \rightarrow (c \rightarrow d) \rightarrow (a \otimes c \rightarrow b \otimes d)$$

If you replace objects by endofunctors, arrows by natural transformations, and tensor products by composition, you get:

$$(F \rightarrow F') \rightarrow (G \rightarrow G') \rightarrow (F \circ G \rightarrow F' \circ G')$$

which you may recognize as the special case of horizontal composition.

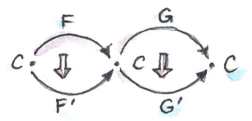

We also have at our disposal the identity endofunctor $I$, which can serve as the identity for endofunctor composition — our new tensor product. Moreover, functor composition is associative. In fact associativity and unit laws are strict — there's no need for the associator or the two unitors. So endofunctors form a strict monoidal category with functor composition as tensor product.

What's a monoid in this category? It's an object — that is an endofunctor $T$; and two morphisms — that is natural transformations:

$$\mu :: T \circ T \rightarrow T$$
$$\eta :: I \rightarrow T$$

Not only that, here are the monoid laws:

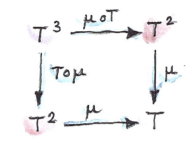

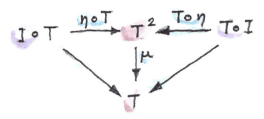

They are exactly the monad laws we've seen before. Now you understand the famous quote from Saunders Mac Lane:

> All told, monad is just a monoid in the category of endofunctors.

You might have seen it emblazoned on some t-shirts at functional programming conferences.

## 22.4 Monads from Adjunctions

An adjunction[1] $L \dashv R$, is a pair of functors going back and forth between two categories **C** and **D**. There are two ways of composing them giving rise to two endofunctors, $R \circ L$ and $L \circ R$. As per an adjunction, these endofunctors are related to identity functors through two natural transformations called unit and counit:

$$\eta :: I_D \rightarrow R \circ L$$
$$\varepsilon :: L \circ R \rightarrow I_C$$

Immediately we see that the unit of an adjunction looks just like the unit of a monad. It turns out that the endofunctor $R \circ L$ is indeed a

---

[1] See ch.18 on adjunctions.

monad. All we need is to define the appropriate μ to go with the η. That's a natural transformation between the square of our endofunctor and the endofunctor itself or, in terms of the adjoint functors:

$$R \circ L \circ R \circ L \to R \circ L$$

And, indeed, we can use the counit to collapse the $L \circ R$ in the middle. The exact formula for $\mu$ is given by the horizontal composition:

$$\mu = R \circ \varepsilon \circ L$$

Monadic laws follow from the identities satisfied by the unit and counit of the adjunction and the interchange law.

We don't see a lot of monads derived from adjunctions in Haskell, because an adjunction usually involves two categories. However, the definitions of an exponential, or a function object, is an exception. Here are the two endofunctors that form this adjunction:

$$L\, z = z \times s$$
$$R\, b = s \Rightarrow b$$

You may recognize their composition as the familiar state monad:

$$R\, (L\, z) = s \Rightarrow (z \times s)$$

We've seen this monad before in Haskell:

```haskell
newtype State s a = State (s -> (a, s))
```

Let's also translate the adjunction to Haskell. The left functor is the product functor:

```haskell
newtype Prod s a = Prod (a, s)
```

and the right functor is the reader functor:

```haskell
newtype Reader s a = Reader (s -> a)
```

They form the adjunction:

```haskell
instance Adjunction (Prod s) (Reader s) where
    counit (Prod (Reader f, s)) = f s
    unit a = Reader (\s -> Prod (a, s))
```

You can easily convince yourself that the composition of the reader functor after the product functor is indeed equivalent to the state functor:

```
newtype State s a = State (s -> (a, s))
```

As expected, the unit of the adjunction is equivalent to the return function of the state monad. The counit acts by evaluating a function acting on its argument. This is recognizable as the uncurried version of the function runState:

```
runState :: State s a -> s -> (a, s)
runState (State f) s = f s
```

(uncurried, because in counit it acts on a pair).

We can now define join for the state monad as a component of the natural transformation $\mu$. For that we need a horizontal composition of three natural transformations:

$$\mu = R \circ \varepsilon \circ L$$

In other words, we need to sneak the counit $\varepsilon$ across one level of the reader functor. We can't just call fmap directly, because the compiler would pick the one for the State functor, rather than the Reader functor. But recall that fmap for the reader functor is just left function composition. So we'll use function composition directly.

We have to first peel off the data constructor State to expose the function inside the State functor. This is done using runState:

```
ssa :: State s (State s a)
runState ssa :: s -> (State s a, s)
```

Then we left-compose it with the counit, which is defined by uncurry runState. Finally, we clothe it back in the State data constructor:

```
join :: State s (State s a) -> State s a
join ssa = State (uncurry runState . runState ssa)
```

This is indeed the implementation of join for the State monad.

It turns out that not only every adjunction gives rise to a monad, but the converse is also true: every monad can be factorized into a composition of two adjoint functors. Such factorization is not unique though.

We'll talk about the other endofunctor $L \circ R$ in the next section.

# 23
# Comonads

Now that we have covered monads, we can reap the benefits of duality and get comonads for free simply by reversing the arrows and working in the opposite category.

Recall that, at the most basic level, monads are about composing Kleisli arrows:

```
a -> m b
```

where m is a functor that is a monad. If we use the letter w (upside down m) for the comonad, we can define co-Kleisli arrows as morphism of the type:

```
w a -> b
```

The analog of the fish operator for co-Kleisli arrows is defined as:

```
(=>=) :: (w a -> b) -> (w b -> c) -> (w a -> c)
```

For co-Kleisli arrows to form a category we also have to have an identity co-Kleisli arrow, which is called extract:

```
extract :: w a -> a
```

This is the dual of return. We also have to impose the laws of associativity as well as left- and right-identity. Putting it all together, we could define a comonad in Haskell as:

```
class Functor w => Comonad w where
    (=>=) :: (w a -> b) -> (w b -> c) -> (w a -> c)
    extract :: w a -> a
```

In practice, we use slightly different primitives, as we'll see shortly.

The question is, what's the use for comonads in programming?

## 23.1   Programming with Comonads

Let's compare the monad with the comonad. A monad provides a way of putting a value in a container using `return`. It doesn't give you access to a value or values stored inside. Of course, data structures that implement monads might provide access to their contents, but that's considered a bonus. There is no common interface for extracting values from a monad. And we've seen the example of the `IO` monad that prides itself in never exposing its contents.

A comonad, on the other hand, provides the means of extracting a single value from it. It does not give the means to insert values. So if you want to think of a comonad as a container, it always comes pre-filled with contents, and it lets you peek at it.

Just as a Kleisli arrow takes a value and produces some embellished result — it embellishes it with context — a co-Kleisli arrow takes a value together with a whole context and produces a result. It's an embodiment of *contextual computation*.

## 23.2   The Product Comonad

Remember the reader monad? We introduced it to tackle the problem of implementing computations that need access to some read-only environment e. Such computations can be represented as pure functions of the form:

```
(a, e) -> b
```

We used currying to turn them into Kleisli arrows:

```
a -> (e -> b)
```

But notice that these functions already have the form of co-Kleisli arrows. Let's massage their arguments into the more convenient functor form:

```
data Product e a = P e a deriving Functor
```

We can easily define the composition operator by making the same
environment available to the arrows that we are composing:

```
(=>=) :: (Product e a -> b) -> (Product e b -> c) -> (Product e
 ↪  a -> c)
f =>= g = \(P e a) -> let b = f (P e a)
                          c = g (P e b)
                      in c
```

The implementation of extract simply ignores the environment:

```
extract (P e a) = a
```

Not surprisingly, the product comonad can be used to perform exactly
the same computations as the reader monad. In a way, the comonadic
implementation of the environment is more natural — it follows the
spirit of "computation in context." On the other hand, monads come
with the convenient syntactic sugar of the do notation.

    The connection between the reader monad and the product comonad
goes deeper, having to do with the fact that the reader functor is the
right adjoint of the product functor. In general, though, comonads cover
different notions of computation than monads. We'll see more examples later.

    It's easy to generalize the Product comonad to arbitrary product
types including tuples and records.

## 23.3  Dissecting the Composition

Continuing the process of dualization, we could go ahead and dualize
monadic bind and join. Alternatively, we can repeat the process we
used with monads, where we studied the anatomy of the fish operator.
This approach seems more enlightening.

    The starting point is the realization that the composition operator
must produce a co-Kleisli arrow that takes w a and produces a c. The
only way to produce a c is to apply the second function to an argument
of the type w b:

```
(=>=) :: (w a -> b) -> (w b -> c) -> (w a -> c)
f =>= g = g ...
```

269

But how can we produce a value of type w b that could be fed to g? We have at our disposal the argument of type w a and the function f :: w a -> b. The solution is to define the dual of bind, which is called extend:

```
extend :: (w a -> b) -> w a -> w b
```

Using extend we can implement composition:

```
f =>= g = g . extend f
```

Can we next dissect extend? You might be tempted to say, why not just apply the function w a -> b to the argument w a, but then you quickly realize that you'd have no way of converting the resulting b to w b. Remember, the comonad provides no means of lifting values. At this point, in the analogous construction for monads, we used fmap. The only way we could use fmap here would be if we had something of the type w (w a) at our disposal. If we could only turn w a into w (w a). And, conveniently, that would be exactly the dual of join. We call it duplicate:

```
duplicate :: w a -> w (w a)
```

So, just like with the definitions of the monad, we have three equivalent definitions of the comonad: using co-Kleisli arrows, extend, or duplicate. Here's the Haskell definition taken directly from Control.Comonad library:

```
class Functor w => Comonad w where
    extract :: w a -> a
    duplicate :: w a -> w (w a)
    duplicate = extend id
    extend :: (w a -> b) -> w a -> w b
    extend f = fmap f . duplicate
```

Provided are the default implementations of extend in terms of duplicate and vice versa, so you only need to override one of them.

The intuition behind these functions is based on the idea that, in general, a comonad can be thought of as a container filled with values of type a (the product comonad was a special case of just one value). There is a notion of the "current" value, one that's easily accessible through extract. A co-Kleisli arrow performs some computation that

270

is focused on the current value, but it has access to all the surrounding values. Think of the Conway's game of life. Each cell contains a value (usually just True or False). A comonad corresponding to the game of life would be a grid of cells focused on the "current" cell.

So what does duplicate do? It takes a comonadic container w a and produces a container of containers w (w a). The idea is that each of these containers is focused on a different a inside w a. In the game of life, you would get a grid of grids, each cell of the outer grid containing an inner grid that's focused on a different cell.

Now look at extend. It takes a co-Kleisli arrow and a comonadic container w a filled with as. It applies the computation to all of these as, replacing them with bs. The result is a comonadic container filled with bs. extend does it by shifting the focus from one a to another and applying the co-Kleisli arrow to each of them in turn. In the game of life, the co-Kleisli arrow would calculate the new state of the current cell. To do that, it would look at its context — presumably its nearest neighbors. The default implementation of extend illustrates this process. First we call duplicate to produce all possible foci and then we apply f to each of them.

## 23.4  The Stream Comonad

This process of shifting the focus from one element of the container to another is best illustrated with the example of an infinite stream. Such a stream is just like a list, except that it doesn't have the empty constructor:

```
data Stream a = Cons a (Stream a)
```

It's trivially a Functor:

```
instance Functor Stream where
    fmap f (Cons a as) = Cons (f a) (fmap f as)
```

The focus of a stream is its first element, so here's the implementation of extract:

```
extract (Cons a _) = a
```

duplicate produces a stream of streams, each focused on a different element.

```
duplicate (Cons a as) = Cons (Cons a as) (duplicate as)
```

The first element is the original stream, the second element is the tail of the original stream, the third element is its tail, and so on, ad infinitum.

Here's the complete instance:

```
instance Comonad Stream where
    extract (Cons a _) = a
    duplicate (Cons a as) = Cons (Cons a as) (duplicate as)
```

This is a very functional way of looking at streams. In an imperative language, we would probably start with a method advance that shifts the stream by one position. Here, duplicate produces all shifted streams in one fell swoop. Haskell's laziness makes this possible and even desirable. Of course, to make a Stream practical, we would also implement the analog of advance:

```
tail :: Stream a -> Stream a
tail (Cons a as) = as
```

but it's never part of the comonadic interface.

If you had any experience with digital signal processing, you'll see immediately that a co-Kleisli arrow for a stream is just a digital filter, and extend produces a filtered stream.

As a simple example, let's implement the moving average filter. Here's a function that sums n elements of a stream:

```
sumS :: Num a => Int -> Stream a -> a
sumS n (Cons a as) = if n <= 0 then 0 else a + sumS (n - 1) as
```

Here's the function that calculates the average of the first n elements of the stream:

```
average :: Fractional a => Int -> Stream a -> a
average n stm = (sumS n stm) / (fromIntegral n)
```

Partially applied average n is a co-Kleisli arrow, so we can extend it over the whole stream:

```
movingAvg :: Fractional a => Int -> Stream a -> Stream a
movingAvg n = extend (average n)
```

The result is the stream of running averages.

A stream is an example of a unidirectional, one-dimensional comonad. It can be easily made bidirectional or extended to two or more dimensions.

## 23.5 Comonad Categorically

Defining a comonad in category theory is a straightforward exercise in duality. As with the monad, we start with an endofunctor $T$. The two natural transformations, $\eta$ and $\mu$, that define the monad are simply reversed for the comonad:

$$\varepsilon :: T \to I$$
$$\delta :: T \to T^2$$

The components of these transformations correspond to extract and duplicate. Comonad laws are the mirror image of monad laws. No big surprise here.

Then there is the derivation of the monad from an adjunction. Duality reverses an adjunction: the left adjoint becomes the right adjoint and vice versa. And, since the composition $R \circ L$ defines a monad, $L \circ R$ must define a comonad. The counit of the adjunction:

$$\varepsilon :: L \circ R \to I$$

is indeed the same $\varepsilon$ that we see in the definition of the comonad — or, in components, as Haskell's extract. We can also use the unit of the adjunction:

$$\eta :: I \to R \circ L$$

to insert an $R \circ L$ in the middle of $L \circ R$ and produce $L \circ R \circ L \circ R$. Making $T^2$ from $T$ defines the $\delta$, and that completes the definition of the comonad.

We've also seen that the monad is a monoid. The dual of this statement would require the use of a comonoid, so what's a comonoid? The original definition of a monoid as a single-object category doesn't dualize to anything interesting. When you reverse the direction of all endomorphisms, you get another monoid. Recall, however, that in our approach to a monad, we used a more general definition of a monoid as an object in a monoidal category. The construction was based on two morphisms:

$$\mu :: m \otimes m \to m$$
$$\eta :: i \to m$$

The reversal of these morphisms produces a comonoid in a monoidal category:

$$\delta :: m \longrightarrow m \otimes m$$

$$\varepsilon :: m \longrightarrow i$$

One can write a definition of a comonoid in Haskell:

```
class Comonoid m where
    split :: m -> (m, m)
    destroy :: m -> ()
```

but it is rather trivial. Obviously `destroy` ignores its argument.

```
destroy _ = ()
```

`split` is just a pair of functions:

```
split x = (f x, g x)
```

Now consider comonoid laws that are dual to the monoid unit laws.

```
lambda . bimap destroy id . split = id
rho . bimap id destroy . split = id
```

Here, `lambda` and `rho` are the left and right unitors, respectively (see the definition of monoidal categories). Plugging in the definitions, we get:

```
lambda (bimap destroy id (split x))
= lambda (bimap destroy id (f x, g x))
= lambda ((), g x)
= g x
```

which proves that `g = id`. Similarly, the second law expands to `f = id`. In conclusion:

```
split x = (x, x)
```

which shows that in Haskell (and, in general, in the category **Set**) every object is a trivial comonoid.

Fortunately there are other more interesting monoidal categories in which to define comonoids. One of them is the category of endofunctors. And it turns out that, just like the monad is a monoid in the category of endofunctors,

> The comonad is a comonoid in the category of endofunctors.

## 23.6  The Store Comonad

Another important example of a comonad is the dual of the state monad. It's called the costate comonad or, alternatively, the store comonad.

We've seen before that the state monad is generated by the adjunction that defines the exponentials:

$$L\,z = z \times s$$
$$R\,a = s \Rightarrow a$$

We'll use the same adjunction to define the costate comonad. A comonad is defined by the composition $L \circ R$:

$$L\,(R\,a) = (s \Rightarrow a) \times s$$

Translating this to Haskell, we start with the adjunction between the `Prod` functor on the left and the `Reader` functor or the right. Composing `Prod` after `Reader` is equivalent to the following definition:

```
data Store s a = Store (s -> a) s
```

The counit of the adjunction taken at the object $a$ is the morphism:

$$\varepsilon_a :: ((s \Rightarrow a) \times s) \longrightarrow a$$

or, in Haskell notation:

```
counit (Prod (Reader f, s)) = f s
```

This becomes our `extract`:

```
extract (Store f s) = f s
```

The unit of the adjunction:

```
unit a = Reader (\s -> Prod (a, s))
```

can be rewritten as partially applied data constructor:

```
Store f :: s -> Store f s
```

We construct $\delta$, or `duplicate`, as the horizontal composition:

$$\delta :: L \circ R \rightarrow L \circ R \circ L \circ R$$
$$\delta = L \circ \eta \circ R$$

We have to sneak $\eta$ through the leftmost $L$, which is the `Prod` functor. It means acting with $\eta$, or `Store f`, on the left component of the pair (that's what `fmap` for `Prod` would do). We get:

```
duplicate (Store f s) = Store (Store f) s
```

(Remember that, in the formula for $\delta$, $L$ and $R$ stand for identity natural transformations whose components are identity morphisms.)

Here's the complete definition of the `Store` comonad:

```
instance Comonad (Store s) where
    extract (Store f s) = f s
    duplicate (Store f s) = Store (Store f) s
```

You may think of the `Reader` part of `Store` as a generalized container of as that are keyed using elements of the type s. For instance, if s is `Int`, `Reader Int a` is an infinite bidirectional stream of as. `Store` pairs this container with a value of the key type. For instance, `Reader Int a` is paired with an `Int`. In this case, `extract` uses this integer to index into the infinite stream. You may think of the second component of `Store` as the current position.

Continuing with this example, `duplicate` creates a new infinite stream indexed by an `Int`. This stream contains streams as its elements. In particular, at the current position, it contains the original stream. But if you use some other `Int` (positive or negative) as the key, you'd obtain a shifted stream positioned at that new index.

In general, you can convince yourself that when `extract` acts on the duplicated `Store` it produces the original `Store` (in fact, the identity law for the comonad states that `extract . duplicate = id`).

The `Store` comonad plays an important role as the theoretical basis for the `Lens` library. Conceptually, the `Store s` a comonad encapsulates the idea of "focusing" (like a lens) on a particular substructure of the date type a using the type s as an index. In particular, a function of the type:

```
a -> Store s a
```

is equivalent to a pair of functions:

```
set :: a -> s -> a
get :: a -> s
```

If a is a product type, **Set** could be implemented as setting the field of type s inside of a while returning the modified version of a. Similarly, get could be implemented to read the value of the s field from a. We'll explore these ideas more in the next section.

## 23.7 **Challenges**

1. Implement the Conway's Game of Life using the Store comonad. Hint: What type do you pick for s?

# 24

# F-Algebras

W E'VE SEEN SEVERAL FORMULATIONS of a monoid: as a set, as a single-object category, as an object in a monoidal category. How much more juice can we squeeze out of this simple concept?

Let's try. Take this definition of a monoid as a set $m$ with a pair of functions:

$$\mu :: m \times m \to m$$
$$\eta :: 1 \to m$$

Here, 1 is the terminal object in **Set** — the singleton set. The first function defines multiplication (it takes a pair of elements and returns their product), the second selects the unit element from $m$. Not every choice of two functions with these signatures results in a monoid. For that we need to impose additional conditions: associativity and unit laws. But let's forget about that for a moment and just consider "potential monoids." A pair of functions is an element of a Cartesian product of two sets of functions. We know that these sets may be represented as exponential objects:

$$\mu \in m^{m \times m}$$
$$\eta \in m^1$$

The Cartesian product of these two sets is:

$$m^{m \times m} \times m^1$$

Using some high-school algebra (which works in every Cartesian closed category), we can rewrite it as:

$$m^{m \times m+1}$$

The + sign stands for the coproduct in **Set**. We have just replaced a pair of functions with a single function — an element of the set:

$$m \times m + 1 \to m$$

Any element of this set of functions is a potential monoid.

The beauty of this formulation is that it leads to interesting generalizations. For instance, how would we describe a group using this language? A group is a monoid with one additional function that assigns the inverse to every element. The latter is a function of the type $m \to m$. As an example, integers form a group with addition as a binary operation, zero as the unit, and negation as the inverse. To define a group we would start with a triple of functions:

$$m \times m \to m$$

$$m \to m$$

$$1 \to m$$

As before, we can combine all these triples into one set of functions:

$$m \times m + m + 1 \to m$$

We started with one binary operator (addition), one unary operator (negation), and one nullary operator (identity — here zero). We combined them into one function. All functions with this signature define potential groups.

We can go on like this. For instance, to define a ring, we would add one more binary operator and one nullary operator, and so on. Each time we end up with a function type whose left-hand side is a sum of powers (possibly including the zeroth power — the terminal object), and the right-hand side being the set itself.

Now we can go crazy with generalizations. First of all, we can replace sets with objects and functions with morphisms. We can define n-ary operators as morphisms from n-ary products. It means that we need a category that supports finite products. For nullary operators we require the existence of the terminal object. So we need a Cartesian category. In order to combine these operators we need exponentials, so that's a Cartesian closed category. Finally, we need coproducts to complete our algebraic shenanigans.

Alternatively, we can just forget about the way we derived our formulas and concentrate on the final product. The sum of products on the left hand side of our morphism defines an endofunctor. What if we pick an arbitrary endofunctor $F$ instead? In that case we don't have to impose any constraints on our category. What we obtain is called an F-algebra.

An F-algebra is a triple consisting of an endofunctor $F$, an object $a$, and a morphism

$$F\ a \to a$$

The object is often called the carrier, an underlying object or, in the context of programming, the carrier *type*. The morphism is often called the evaluation function or the structure map. Think of the functor $F$ as forming expressions and the morphism as evaluating them.

Here's the Haskell definition of an F-algebra:

```
type Algebra f a = f a -> a
```

It identifies the algebra with its evaluation function.

In the monoid example, the functor in question is:

```
data MonF a = MEmpty | MAppend a a
```

This is Haskell for $1 + a \times a$ (remember algebraic data structures).

A ring would be defined using the following functor:

```
data RingF a = RZero
             | ROne
             | RAdd a a
             | RMul a a
             | RNeg a
```

which is Haskell for $1 + 1 + a \times a + a \times a + a$.

An example of a ring is the set of integers. We can choose `Integer` as the carrier type and define the evaluation function as:

```
evalZ :: Algebra RingF Integer
evalZ RZero      = 0
evalZ ROne       = 1
evalZ (RAdd m n) = m + n
evalZ (RMul m n) = m * n
evalZ (RNeg n)   = -n
```

There are more F-algebras based on the same functor RingF. For instance, polynomials form a ring and so do square matrices.

As you can see, the role of the functor is to generate expressions that can be evaluated using the evaluator of the algebra. So far we've only seen very simple expressions. We are often interested in more elaborate expressions that can be defined using recursion.

## 24.1 Recursion

One way to generate arbitrary expression trees is to replace the variable a inside the functor definition with recursion. For instance, an arbitrary expression in a ring is generated by this tree-like data structure:

```
data Expr = RZero
          | ROne
          | RAdd Expr Expr
          | RMul Expr Expr
          | RNeg Expr
```

We can replace the original ring evaluator with its recursive version:

```
evalZ :: Expr -> Integer
evalZ RZero       = 0
evalZ ROne        = 1
evalZ (RAdd e1 e2) = evalZ e1 + evalZ e2
evalZ (RMul e1 e2) = evalZ e1 * evalZ e2
evalZ (RNeg e)    = -(evalZ e)
```

This is still not very practical, since we are forced to represent all integers as sums of ones, but it will do in a pinch.

But how can we describe expression trees using the language of F-algebras? We have to somehow formalize the process of replacing the free type variable in the definition of our functor, recursively, with the result of the replacement. Imagine doing this in steps. First, define a depth-one tree as:

```
type RingF1 a = RingF (RingF a)
```

We are filling the holes in the definition of RingF with depth-zero trees generated by RingF a. Depth-2 trees are similarly obtained as:

```
type RingF2 a = RingF (RingF (RingF a))
```

which we can also write as:

```
type RingF2 a = RingF (RingF1 a)
```

Continuing this process, we can write a symbolic equation:

```
type RingF_{n+1} a = RingF (RingF_n a)
```

Conceptually, after repeating this process infinitely many times, we end up with our Expr. Notice that Expr does not depend on a. The starting point of our journey doesn't matter, we always end up in the same place. This is not always true for an arbitrary endofunctor in an arbitrary category, but in the category **Set** things are nice.

Of course, this is a hand-waving argument, and I'll make it more rigorous later.

Applying an endofunctor infinitely many times produces a *fixed point*, an object defined as:

$$Fix\ f = f\ (Fix\ f)$$

The intuition behind this definition is that, since we applied $f$ infinitely many times to get $Fix\ f$, applying it one more time doesn't change anything. In Haskell, the definition of a fixed point is:

```
newtype Fix f = Fix (f (Fix f))
```

Arguably, this would be more readable if the constructor's name were different than the name of the type being defined, as in:

```
newtype Fix f = In (f (Fix f))
```

but I'll stick with the accepted notation. The constructor Fix (or In, if you prefer) can be seen as a function:

```
Fix :: f (Fix f) -> Fix f
```

There is also a function that peels off one level of functor application:

```
unFix :: Fix f -> f (Fix f)
unFix (Fix x) = x
```

The two functions are the inverse of each other. We'll use these functions later.

## 24.2  Category of F-Algebras

Here's the oldest trick in the book: Whenever you come up with a way of constructing some new objects, see if they form a category. Not surprisingly, algebras over a given endofunctor $F$ form a category. Objects in that category are algebras — pairs consisting of a carrier object $a$ and a morphism $F\,a \to a$, both from the original category C.

To complete the picture, we have to define morphisms in the category of F-algebras. A morphism must map one algebra $(a, f)$ to another algebra $(b, g)$. We'll define it as a morphism $m$ that maps the carriers — it goes from $a$ to $b$ in the original category. Not any morphism will do: we want it to be compatible with the two evaluators. (We call such a structure-preserving morphism a *homomorphism*.) Here's how you define a homomorphism of F-algebras. First, notice that we can lift $m$ to the mapping:

$$F\,m :: F\,a \to F\,b$$

we can then follow it with $g$ to get to $b$. Equivalently, we can use $f$ to go from $F\,a$ to $a$ and then follow it with $m$. We want the two paths to be equal:

$$g \circ F\,m = m \circ f$$

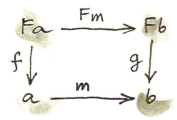

It's easy to convince yourself that this is indeed a category (hint: identity morphisms from C work just fine, and a composition of homomorphisms is a homomorphism).

An initial object in the category of F-algebras, if it exists, is called the *initial algebra*. Let's call the carrier of this initial algebra $i$ and its evaluator $j :: F\,i \to i$. It turns out that $j$, the evaluator of the initial algebra, is an isomorphism. This result is known as Lambek's theorem. The proof relies on the definition of the initial object, which requires that there be a unique homomorphism $m$ from it to any other F-algebra. Since $m$ is a homomorphism, the following diagram must commute:

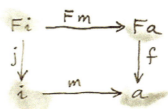

Now let's construct an algebra whose carrier is $F\ i$. The evaluator of such an algebra must be a morphism from $F\ (F\ i)$ to $F\ i$. We can easily construct such an evaluator simply by lifting $j$:

$$F\ j :: F\ (F\ i) \rightarrow F\ i$$

Because $(i, j)$ is the initial algebra, there must be a unique homomorphism $m$ from it to $(F\ i, F\ j)$. The following diagram must commute:

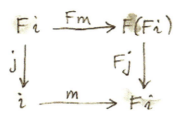

But we also have this trivially commuting diagram (both paths are the same!):

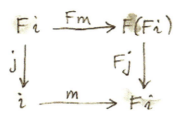

which can be interpreted as showing that $j$ is a homomorphism of algebras, mapping $(F\ i, F\ j)$ to $(i, j)$. We can glue these two diagrams together to get:

285

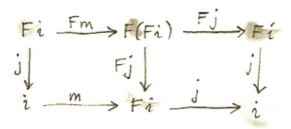

This diagram may, in turn, be interpreted as showing that $j \circ m$ is a homomorphism of algebras. Only in this case the two algebras are the same. Moreover, because $(i, j)$ is initial, there can only be one homomorphism from it to itself, and that's the identity morphism $\mathrm{id}_i$ — which we know is a homomorphism of algebras. Therefore $j \circ m = \mathrm{id}_i$. Using this fact and the commuting property of the left diagram we can prove that $m \circ j = \mathrm{id}_{Fi}$. This shows that $m$ is the inverse of $j$ and therefore $j$ is an isomorphism between $F\ i$ and $i$:

$$F\ i \cong i$$

But that is just saying that $i$ is a fixed point of $F$. That's the formal proof behind the original hand-waving argument.

Back to Haskell: We recognize $i$ as our `Fix f`, $j$ as our constructor `Fix`, and its inverse as `unFix`. The isomorphism in Lambek's theorem tells us that, in order to get the initial algebra, we take the functor $f$ and replace its argument $a$ with `Fix f`. We also see why the fixed point does not depend on $a$.

## 24.3 Natural Numbers

Natural numbers can also be defined as an F-algebra. The starting point is the pair of morphisms:

$$zero :: 1 \to N$$
$$succ :: N \to N$$

The first one picks the zero, and the second one maps all numbers to their successors. As before, we can combine the two into one:

$$1 + N \to N$$

The left hand side defines a functor which, in Haskell, can be written like this:

```
data NatF a = ZeroF | SuccF a
```

The fixed point of this functor (the initial algebra that it generates) can be encoded in Haskell as:

```
data Nat = Zero | Succ Nat
```

A natural number is either zero or a successor of another number. This is known as the Peano representation for natural numbers.

## 24.4 Catamorphisms

Let's rewrite the initiality condition using Haskell notation. We call the initial algebra `Fix f`. Its evaluator is the constructor `Fix`. There is a unique morphism `m` from the initial algebra to any other algebra over the same functor. Let's pick an algebra whose carrier is `a` and the evaluator is `alg`.

By the way, notice what `m` is: It's an evaluator for the fixed point, an evaluator for the whole recursive expression tree. Let's find a general way of implementing it.

Lambek's theorem tells us that the constructor `Fix` is an isomorphism. We called its inverse `unFix`. We can therefore flip one arrow in this diagram to get:

Let's write down the commutation condition for this diagram:

287

```
m = alg . fmap m . unFix
```

We can interpret this equation as a recursive definition of m. The recursion is bound to terminate for any finite tree created using the functor f. We can see that by noticing that fmap m operates underneath the top layer of the functor f. In other words, it works on the children of the original tree. The children are always one level shallower than the original tree.

Here's what happens when we apply m to a tree constructed using Fix f. The action of unFix peels off the constructor, exposing the top level of the tree. We then apply m to all the children of the top node. This produces results of type a. Finally, we combine those results by applying the non-recursive evaluator alg. The key point is that our evaluator alg is a simple non-recursive function.

Since we can do this for any algebra alg, it makes sense to define a higher order function that takes the algebra as a parameter and gives us the function we called m. This higher order function is called a catamorphism:

```
cata :: Functor f => (f a -> a) -> Fix f -> a
cata alg = alg . fmap (cata alg) . unFix
```

Let's see an example of that. Take the functor that defines natural numbers:

```
data NatF a = ZeroF | SuccF a
```

Let's pick (Int, Int) as the carrier type and define our algebra as:

```
fib :: NatF (Int, Int) -> (Int, Int)
fib ZeroF = (1, 1)
fib (SuccF (m, n)) = (n, m + n)
```

You can easily convince yourself that the catamorphism for this algebra, cata fib, calculates Fibonacci numbers.

In general, an algebra for NatF defines a recurrence relation: the value of the current element in terms of the previous element. A catamorphism then evaluates the n-th element of that sequence.

288

## 24.5  Folds

A list of e is the initial algebra of the following functor:

```
data ListF e a = NilF | ConsF e a
```

Indeed, replacing the variable a with the result of recursion, which we'll call List e, we get:

```
data List e = Nil | Cons e (List e)
```

An algebra for a list functor picks a particular carrier type and defines a function that does pattern matching on the two constructors. Its value for NilF tells us how to evaluate an empty list, and its value for ConsF tells us how to combine the current element with the previously accumulated value.

For instance, here's an algebra that can be used to calculate the length of a list (the carrier type is Int):

```
lenAlg :: ListF e Int -> Int
lenAlg (ConsF e n) = n + 1
lenAlg NilF = 0
```

Indeed, the resulting catamorphism cata lenAlg calculates the length of a list. Notice that the evaluator is a combination of (1) a function that takes a list element and an accumulator and returns a new accumulator, and (2) a starting value, here zero. The type of the value and the type of the accumulator are given by the carrier type.

Compare this to the traditional Haskell definition:

```
length = foldr (\e n -> n + 1) 0
```

The two arguments to foldr are exactly the two components of the algebra.

Let's try another example:

```
sumAlg :: ListF Double Double -> Double
sumAlg (ConsF e s) = e + s
sumAlg NilF = 0.0
```

Again, compare this with:

```
sum = foldr (\e s -> e + s) 0.0
```

As you can see, foldr is just a convenient specialization of a catamorphism to lists.

## 24.6 Coalgebras

As usual, we have a dual construction of an F-coagebra, where the direction of the morphism is reversed:

$$a \to F\, a$$

Coalgebras for a given functor also form a category, with homomorphisms preserving the coalgebraic structure. The terminal object $(t, u)$ in that category is called the terminal (or final) coalgebra. For every other algebra $(a, f)$ there is a unique homomorphism $m$ that makes the following diagram commute:

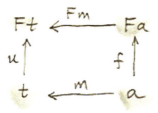

A terminal colagebra is a fixed point of the functor, in the sense that the morphism $u :: t \to F\, t$ is an isomorphism (Lambek's theorem for coalgebras):

$$F\, t \cong t$$

A terminal coalgebra is usually interpreted in programming as a recipe for generating (possibly infinite) data structures or transition systems.

Just like a catamorphism can be used to evaluate an initial algebra, an anamorphism can be used to coevaluate a terminal coalgebra:

```
ana :: Functor f => (a -> f a) -> a -> Fix f
ana coalg = Fix . fmap (ana coalg) . coalg
```

A canonical example of a coalgebra is based on a functor whose fixed point is an infinite stream of elements of type e. This is the functor:

```
data StreamF e a = StreamF e a
  deriving Functor
```

and this is its fixed point:

```
data Stream e = Stream e (Stream e)
```

A coalgebra for StreamF e is a function that takes the seed of type a and produces a pair (StreamF is a fancy name for a pair) consisting of an element and the next seed.

You can easily generate simple examples of coalgebras that produce infinite sequences, like the list of squares, or reciprocals.

A more interesting example is a coalgebra that produces a list of primes. The trick is to use an infinite list as a carrier. Our starting seed will be the list [2..]. The next seed will be the tail of this list with all multiples of 2 removed. It's a list of odd numbers starting with 3. In the next step, we'll take the tail of this list and remove all multiples of 3, and so on. You might recognize the makings of the sieve of Eratosthenes. This coalgebra is implemented by the following function:

```
era :: [Int] -> StreamF Int [Int]
era (p : ns) = StreamF p (filter (notdiv p) ns)
    where notdiv p n = n `mod` p /= 0
```

The anamorphism for this coalgebra generates the list of primes:

```
primes = ana era [2..]
```

A stream is an infinite list, so it should be possible to convert it to a Haskell list. To do that, we can use the same functor StreamF to form an algebra, and we can run a catamorphism over it. For instance, this is a catamorphism that converts a stream to a list:

```
toListC :: Fix (StreamF e) -> [e]
toListC = cata al
    where al :: StreamF e [e] -> [e]
          al (StreamF e a) = e : a
```

Here, the same fixed point is simultaneously an initial algebra and a terminal coalgebra for the same endofunctor. It's not always like this, in an arbitrary category. In general, an endofunctor may have many (or no) fixed points. The initial algebra is the so called least fixed point, and the terminal coalgebra is the greatest fixed point. In Haskell, though, both are defined by the same formula, and they coincide.

The anamorphism for lists is called unfold. To create finite lists, the functor is modified to produce a Maybe pair:

```
unfoldr :: (b -> Maybe (a, b)) -> b -> [a]
```

The value of `Nothing` will terminate the generation of the list.

An interesting case of a coalgebra is related to lenses. A lens can be represented as a pair of a getter and a setter:

```
set :: a -> s -> a
get :: a -> s
```

Here, `a` is usually some product data type with a field of type `s`. The getter retrieves the value of that field and the setter replaces this field with a new value. These two functions can be combined into one:

```
a -> (s, s -> a)
```

We can rewrite this function further as:

```
a -> Store s a
```

where we have defined a functor:

```
data Store s a = Store (s -> a) s
```

Notice that this is not a simple algebraic functor constructed from sums of products. It involves an exponential $a^s$.

A lens is a coalgebra for this functor with the carrier type `a`. We've seen before that `Store s` is also a comonad. It turns out that a well-behaved lens corresponds to a coalgebra that is compatible with the comonad structure. We'll talk about this in the next section.

## 24.7 Challenges

1. Implement the evaluation function for a ring of polynomials of one variable. You can represent a polynomial as a list of coefficients in front of powers of $x$. For instance, $4x^2 - 1$ would be represented as (starting with the zero'th power) `[-1, 0, 4]`.
2. Generalize the previous construction to polynomials of many independent variables, like $x^2y - 3y^3z$.
3. Implement the algebra for the ring of $2 \times 2$ matrices.
4. Define a coalgebra whose anamorphism produces a list of squares of natural numbers.
5. Use `unfoldr` to generate a list of the first $n$ primes.

# 25

# Algebras for Monads

IF WE INTERPRET endofunctors as ways of defining expressions, algebras let us evaluate them and monads let us form and manipulate
them. By combining algebras with monads we not only gain a lot of
functionality but we can also answer a few interesting questions.

One such question concerns the relation
between monads and adjunctions. As we've
seen, every adjunction defines a monad (and a
comonad). The question is: Can every monad
(comonad) be derived from an adjunction? The
answer is positive. There is a whole family of
adjunctions that generate a given monad. I'll
show you two such adjunction. Let's review the

definitions. A monad is an endofunctor $m$ equipped with two natural
transformations that satisfy some coherence conditions. The components of these transformations at $a$ are:

$$\eta_a :: a \to m\, a$$
$$\mu_a :: m\,(m\, a) \to m\, a$$

An algebra for the same endofunctor is a selection of a particular object
— the carrier $a$ — together with the morphism:

$$alg :: m\, a \to a$$

The first thing to notice is that the algebra goes in the opposite direction to $\eta_a a$. The intuition is that $\eta_a$ creates a trivial expression from

a value of type *a*. The first coherence condition that makes the algebra compatible with the monad ensures that evaluating this expression using the algebra whose carrier is *a* gives us back the original value:

$$alg \circ \eta_a = \mathrm{id}_a$$

The second condition arises from the fact that there are two ways of evaluating the doubly nested expression *m* (*m a*). We can first apply $\mu_a$ to flatten the expression, and then use the evaluator of the algebra; or we can apply the lifted evaluator to evaluate the inner expressions, and then apply the evaluator to the result. We'd like the two strategies to be equivalent:

$$alg \circ \mu_a = alg \circ m\ alg$$

Here, m alg is the morphism resulting from lifting *alg* using the functor *m*. The following commuting diagrams describe the two conditions (I replaced *m* with *T* in anticipation of what follows):

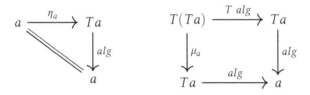

We can also express these conditions in Haskell:

```
alg . return = id
alg . join = alg . fmap alg
```

Let's look at a small example. An algebra for a list endofunctor consists of some type a and a function that produces an a from a list of a. We can express this function using foldr by choosing both the element type and the accumulator type to be equal to a:

```
foldr :: (a -> a -> a) -> a -> [a] -> a
```

This particular algebra is specified by a two-argument function, let's call it f, and a value z. The list functor happens to also be a monad, with return turning a value into a singleton list. The composition of the algebra, here foldr f z, after return takes x to:

```
foldr f z [x] = x `f` z
```

where the action of f is written in the infix notation. The algebra is compatible with the monad if the following coherence condition is satisfied for every x:

```
x `f` z = x
```

If we look at f as a binary operator, this condition tells us that z is the right unit.

The second coherence condition operates on a list of lists. The action of `join` concatenates the individual lists. We can then fold the resulting list. On the other hand, we can first fold the individual lists, and then fold the resulting list. Again, if we interpret f as a binary operator, this condition tells us that this binary operation is associative. These conditions are certainly fulfilled when (a, f, z) is a monoid.

## 25.1 T-algebras

Since mathematicians prefer to call their monads $T$, they call algebras compatible with them T-algebras. T-algebras for a given monad $T$ in a category C form a category called the Eilenberg-Moore category, often denoted by $C^T$. Morphisms in that category are homomorphisms of algebras. These are the same homomorphisms we've seen defined for F-algebras.

A T-algebra is a pair consisting of a carrier object and an evaluator, $(a, f)$. There is an obvious forgetful functor $U^T$ from $C^T$ to C, which maps $(a, f)$ to $a$. It also maps a homomorphism of T-algebras to a corresponding morphism between carrier objects in C. You may remember from our discussion of adjunctions that the left adjoint to a forgetful functor is called a free functor.

The left adjoint to $U^T$ is called $F^T$. It maps an object $A$ in C to a free algebra in $C^T$. The carrier of this free algebra is $T\ a$. Its evaluator is a morphism from $T\ (T\ a)$ back to $T\ a$. Since $T$ is a monad, we can use the monadic $\mu_a$ (`join` in Haskell) as the evaluator.

We still have to show that this is a T-algebra. For that, two coherence conditions must be satisfied:

$$alg \circ \eta_{Ta} = \mathrm{id}_{Ta}$$
$$alg \circ \mu_a = alg \circ T\ alg$$

But these are just monadic laws, if you plug in $\mu$ for the algebra.

As you may recall, every adjunction defines a monad. It turns out that the adjunction between $F^T$ and $U^T$ defines the very monad $T$ that was used in the construction of the Eilenberg-Moore category. Since we can perform this construction for every monad, we conclude that every monad can be generated from an adjunction. Later I'll show you that there is another adjunction that generates the same monad.

Here's the plan: First I'll show you that $F^T$ is indeed the left adjoint of $U^T$. I'll do it by defining the unit and the counit of this adjunction and proving that the corresponding triangular identities are satisfied. Then I'll show you that the monad generated by this adjunction is indeed our original monad.

The unit of the adjunction is the natural transformation:

$$\eta :: I \rightarrow U^T \circ F^T$$

Let's calculate the $a$ component of this transformation. The identity functor gives us $a$. The free functor produces the free algebra $(T\,a, \mu_a)$, and the forgetful functor reduces it to $T\,a$. Altogether we get a mapping from $a$ to $T\,a$. We'll simply use the unit of the monad $T$ as the unit of this adjunction.

Let's look at the counit:

$$\varepsilon :: F^T \circ U^T \rightarrow I$$

Let's calculate its component at some T-algebra $(a, f)$. The forgetful functor forgets the $f$, and the free functor produces the pair $(T\,a, \mu_a)$. So in order to define the component of the counit $\varepsilon$ at $(a, f)$, we need the right morphism in the Eilenberg-Moore category, or a homomorphism of T-algebras:

$$(T\,a, \mu_a) \rightarrow (a, f)$$

Such homomorphism should map the carrier $T\,a$ to $a$. Let's just resurrect the forgotten evaluator $f$. This time we'll use it as a homomorphism of T-algebras. Indeed, the same commuting diagram that makes $f$ a T-algebra may be re-interpreted to show that it's a homomorphism of T-algebras:

$$
\begin{array}{ccc}
T(T\,a) & \xrightarrow{\;Tf\;} & T\,a \\
\downarrow{\scriptstyle \mu_a} & & \downarrow{\scriptstyle f} \\
T\,a & \xrightarrow{\;f\;} & a
\end{array}
$$

We have thus defined the component of the counit natural transformation $\varepsilon$ at $(a, f)$ (an object in the category of T-algebras) to be $f$.

To complete the adjunction we also need to show that the unit and
the counit satisfy triangular identities. These are:

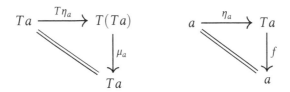

The first one holds because of the unit law for the monad $T$. The second
is just the law of the T-algebra $(a, f)$.

We have established that the two functors form an adjunction:

$$F^T \dashv U^T$$

Every adjunction gives rise to a monad. The round trip

$$U^T \circ F^T$$

is the endofunctor in C that gives rise to the corresponding monad.
Let's see what its action on an object $a$ is. The free algebra created by
$F^T$ is $(T a, \mu_a)$. The forgetful functor $F^T$ drops the evaluator. So, indeed,
we have:

$$U^T \circ F^T = T$$

As expected, the unit of the adjunction is the unit of the monad $T$.

You may remember that the counint of the adjunction produces
monadic multiplication through the following formula:

$$\mu = R \circ \varepsilon \circ L$$

This is a horizontal composition of three natural transformations, two
of them being identity natural transformations mapping, respectively,
$L$ to $L$ and $R$ to $R$. The one in the middle, the counit, is a natural transformation whose component at an algebra $(a, f)$ is $f$.

Let's calculate the component $\mu_a$. We first horizontally compose $\varepsilon$
after $F^T$, which results in the component of $\varepsilon$ at $F^T a$. Since $F^T$ takes $a$
to the algebra $(T a, \mu_a)$, and $\varepsilon$ picks the evaluator, we end up with $\mu_a$.
Horizontal composition on the left with $U^T$ doesn't change anything,
since the action of $U^T$ on morphisms is trivial. So, indeed, the $\mu$ obtained from the adjunction is the same as the $\mu$ of the original monad
$T$.

## 25.2 The Kleisli Category

We've seen the Kleisli category before. It's a category constructed from another category C and a monad $T$. We'll call this category $C^T$. The objects in the Kleisli category $C^T$ are the objects of C, but the morphisms are different. A morphism $f_K$ from $a$ to $b$ in the Kleisli category corresponds to a morphism $f$ from $a$ to $T$ $b$ in the original category. We call this morphism a Kleisli arrow from $a$ to $b$.

Composition of morphisms in the Kleisli category is defined in terms of monadic composition of Kleisli arrows. For instance, let's compose $g_K$ after $f_K$. In the Kleisli category we have:

$$f_K :: a \to b$$
$$g_K :: b \to c$$

which, in the category C, corresponds to:

$$f :: a \to T\ b$$
$$g :: b \to T\ c$$

We define the composition:

$$h_K = g_K \circ f_K$$

as a Kleisli arrow in C

$$h :: a \to T\ c$$
$$h = \mu \circ (T\ g) \circ f$$

In Haskell we would write it as:

```
h = join . fmap g . f
```

There is a functor $F$ from C to $C_T$ which acts trivially on objects. On morphims, it maps $f$ in C to a morphism in $C_T$ by creating a Kleisli arrow that embellishes the return value of $f$. Given a morphism:

$$f :: a \to b$$

it creates a morphism in $C_T$ with the corresponding Kleisli arrow:

$$\eta \circ f$$

In Haskell we'd write it as:

```
return . f
```

We can also define a functor $G$ from $\mathbf{C}_T$ back to C. It takes an object $a$ from the Kleisli category and maps it to an object $T\,a$ in C. Its action on a morphism $f_K$ corresponding to a Kleisli arrow:

$$f :: a\text{-}> T\ b$$

is a morphism in C:

$$T\ a \rightarrow T\ b$$

given by first lifting $f$ and then applying $\mu$:

$$\mu_{T\ b} \circ T\ f$$

In Haskell notation this would read:

```
G fT = join . fmap f
```

You may recognize this as the definition of monadic bind in terms of join.

It's easy to see that the two functors form an adjunction:

$$F \dashv G$$

and their composition $G \circ F$ reproduces the original monad $T$.

So this is the second adjunction that produces the same monad. In fact there is a whole category of adjunctions $\mathbf{Adj}(\mathbf{C}, T)$ that result in the same monad $T$ on C. The Kleisli adjunction we've just seen is the initial object in this category, and the Eilenberg-Moore adjunction is the terminal object.

## 25.3 Coalgebras for Comonads

Analogous constructions can be done for any comonad $W$. We can define a category of coalgebras that are compatible with a comonad. They make the following diagrams commute:

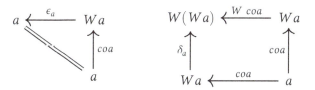

where *coa* is the coevaluation morphism of the coalgebra whose carrier is *a*:

$$coa :: a \to W\ a$$

and $\varepsilon$ and $\delta$ are the two natural transformations defining the comonad (in Haskell, their components are called `extract` and `duplicate`).

There is an obvious forgetful functor $U^W$ from the category of these coalgebras to **C**. It just forgets the coevaluation. We'll consider its right adjoint $F^W$.

$$U^W \dashv F^W$$

The right adjoint to a forgetful functor is called a cofree functor. $F^W$ generates cofree coalgebras. It assigns, to an object *a* in **C**, the coalgebra $(W\ a, \delta_a)$. The adjunction reproduces the original comonad as the composite $F^W \circ U^W$.

Similarly, we can construct a co-Kleisli category with co-Kleisli arrows and regenerate the comonad from the corresponding adjunction.

## 25.4 Lenses

Let's go back to our discussion of lenses. A lens can be written as a coalgebra:

$$coalg_s :: a \to Store\ s\ a$$

for the functor *Store s*:

```
data Store s a = Store (s -> a) s
```

This coalgebra can be also expressed as a pair of functions:

$$set :: a \to s \to a$$
$$get :: a \to s$$

(Think of *a* as standing for "all," and *s* as a "small" part of it.) In terms of this pair, we have:

$$coalg_s\ a = Store\ (set\ a)\ (get\ a)$$

Here, *a* is a value of type *a*. Notice that partially applied **Set** is a function $s \to a$.

We also know that *Store s* is a comonad:

```
instance Comonad (Store s) where
    extract (Store f s) = f s
    duplicate (Store f s) = Store (Store f) s
```

The question is: Under what conditions is a lens a coalgebra for this comonad? The first coherence condition:

$$\varepsilon_a \circ coalg = \mathrm{id}_a$$

translates to:

$$set\ a\ (get\ a) = a$$

This is the lens law that expresses the fact that if you set a field of the structure $a$ to its previous value, nothing changes.

The second condition:

$$fmap\ coalg \circ coalg = \delta_a \circ coalg$$

requires a little more work. First, recall the definition of `fmap` for the Store functor:

```
fmap g (Store f s) = Store (g . f) s
```

Applying `fmap coalg` to the result of `coalg` gives us:

```
Store (coalg . set a) (get a)
```

On the other hand, applying `duplicate` to the result of `coalg` produces:

```
Store (Store (set a)) (get a)
```

For these two expressions to be equal, the two functions under `Store` must be equal when acting on an arbitrary s:

```
coalg (set a s) = Store (set a) s
```

Expanding `coalg`, we get:

```
Store (set (set a s)) (get (set a s)) = Store (set a) s
```

This is equivalent to two remaining lens laws. The first one:

```
set (set a s) = set a
```

tells us that setting the value of a field twice is the same as setting it once. The second law:

```
get (set a s) = s
```

tells us that getting a value of a field that was set to s gives s back.

In other words, a well-behaved lens is indeed a comonad coalgebra for the Store functor.

## 25.5 Challenges

1. What is the action of the free functor $F :: C \to C^T$ on morphisms. Hint: use the naturality condition for monadic $\mu$.
2. Define the adjunction:

$$U^W \dashv F^W$$

3. Prove that the above adjunction reproduces the original comonad.

# 26

## Ends and Coends

THERE ARE MANY INTUITIONS that we may attach to morphisms in a category, but we can all agree that if there is a morphism from the object $a$ to the object $b$ than the two objects are in some way "related." A morphism is, in a sense, the proof of this relation. This is clearly visible in any poset category, where a morphism *is* a relation. In general, there may be many "proofs" of the same relation between two objects. These proofs form a set that we call the hom-set. When we vary the objects, we get a mapping from pairs of objects to sets of "proofs." This mapping is functorial — contravariant in the first argument and covariant in the second. We can look at it as establishing a global relationship between objects in the category. This relationship is described by the hom-functor:

$$\mathbf{C}(-,=) :: \mathbf{C}^{op} \times \mathbf{C} \to \mathbf{Set}$$

In general, any functor like this may be interpreted as establishing a relation between objects in a category. A relation may also involve two different categories $C$ and $D$. A functor, which describes such a relation, has the following signature and is called a profunctor:

$$p :: \mathbf{D}^{op} \times \mathbf{C} \to \mathbf{Set}$$

Mathematicians say that it's a profunctor from $\mathbf{C}$ to $\mathbf{D}$ (notice the inversion), and use a slashed arrow as a symbol for it:

$$\mathbf{C} \nrightarrow \mathbf{D}$$

You may think of a profunctor as a *proof-relevant relation* between objects of **C** and objects of **D**, where the elements of the set symbolize proofs of the relation. Whenever $p$ $a$ $b$ is empty, there is no relation between $a$ and $b$. Keep in mind that relations don't have to be symmetric.

Another useful intuition is the generalization of the idea that an endofunctor is a container. A profunctor value of the type $p$ $a$ $b$ could then be considered a container of $bs$ that are keyed by elements of type $a$. In particular, an element of the hom-profunctor is a function from $a$ to $b$.

In Haskell, a profunctor is defined as a two-argument type constructor p equipped with the method called dimap, which lifts a pair of functions, the first going in the "wrong" direction:

```
class Profunctor p where
    dimap :: (c -> a) -> (b -> d) -> p a b -> p c d
```

The functoriality of the profunctor tells us that if we have a proof that a is related to b, then we get the proof that c is related to d, as long as there is a morphism from c to a and another from b to d. Or, we can think of the first function as translating new keys to the old keys, and the second function as modifying the contents of the container.

For profunctors acting within one category, we can extract quite a lot of information from diagonal elements of the type $p$ $a$ $a$. We can prove that $b$ is related to $c$ as long as we have a pair of morphisms $b \rightarrow a$ and $a \rightarrow c$. Even better, we can use a single morphism to reach off-diagonal values. For instance, if we have a morphism $f :: a \rightarrow b$, we can lift the pair $\langle f, \mathrm{id}_b \rangle$ to go from $p$ $b$ $b$ to $p$ $a$ $b$:

```
dimap f id (p b b) :: p a b
```

Or we can lift the pair $\langle \mathrm{id}_a, f \rangle$ to go from $p$ $a$ $a$ to $p$ $a$ $b$:

```
dimap id f (p a a) :: p a b
```

## 26.1 Dinatural Transformations

Since profunctors are functors, we can define natural transformations between them in the standard way. In many cases, though, it's enough to define the mapping between diagonal elements of two profunctors. Such a transformation is called a dinatural transformation, provided it satisfies the commuting conditions that reflect the two ways we can connect diagonal elements to non-diagonal ones. A dinatural transformation between two profunctors $p$ and $q$, which are members of the functor category $[C^{op} \times C, \mathbf{Set}]$, is a family of morphisms:

$$\alpha_a :: p\, a\, a \to q\, a\, a$$

for which the following diagram commutes, for any $f :: a \to b$:

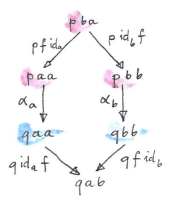

Notice that this is strictly weaker than the naturality condition. If $\alpha$ were a natural transformation in $[C^{op} \times C, \mathbf{Set}]$, the above diagram could be constructed from two naturality squares and one functoriality condition (profunctor $q$ preserving composition):

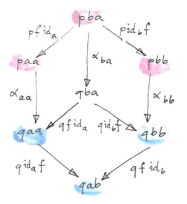

Notice that a component of a natural transformation $\alpha$ in $[C^{op} \times C, \mathbf{Set}]$ is indexed by a pair of objects $\alpha_{a\,b}$. A dinatural transformation, on the other hand, is indexed by one object, since it only maps diagonal elements of the respective profunctors.

305

## 26.2 Ends

We are now ready to advance from "algebra" to what could be considered the "calculus" of category theory. The calculus of ends (and coends) borrows ideas and even some notation from traditional calculus. In particular, the coend may be understood as an infinite sum or an integral, whereas the end is similar to an infinite product. There is even something that resembles the Dirac delta function.

An end is a generalization of a limit, with the functor replaced by a profunctor. Instead of a cone, we have a wedge. The base of a wedge is formed by diagonal elements of a profunctor $p$. The apex of the wedge is an object (here, a set, since we are considering **Set**-valued profunctors), and the sides are a family of functions mapping the apex to the sets in the base. You may think of this family as one polymorphic function — a function that's polymorphic in its return type:

$$\alpha :: \forall a \,.\, apex\!-\!>p\ a\ a$$

Unlike in cones, within a wedge we don't have any functions that would connect vertices of the base. However, as we've seen earlier, given any morphism $f :: a \rightarrow b$ in C, we can connect both $p\ a\ a$ and $p\ b\ b$ to the common set $p\ a\ b$. We therefore insist that the following diagram commute:

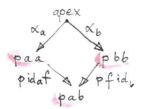

This is called the *wedge condition*. It can be written as:

$$p\ \mathrm{id}_a\ f \circ \alpha_a = p\ f\ \mathrm{id}_b \circ \alpha_b$$

Or, using Haskell notation:

```
dimap id f . alpha = dimap f id . alpha
```

We can now proceed with the universal construction and define the end of $p$ as the universal wedge — a set $e$ together with a family of functions

$\pi$ such that for any other wedge with the apex $a$ and a family $\alpha$ there is a unique function $h :: a \rightarrow e$ that makes all triangles commute:

$$\pi_a \circ h = \alpha_a$$

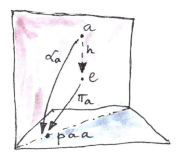

The symbol for the end is the integral sign, with the "integration variable" in the subscript position:

$$\int_c p\, c\, c$$

Components of $\pi$ are called projection maps for the end:

$$\pi_a :: \int_c p\, c\, c \rightarrow p\, a\, a$$

Note that if C is a discrete category (no morphisms other than the identitico) the end is just a global product of all diagonal entries of $p$ across the whole category C. Later I'll show you that, in the more general case, there is a relationship between the end and this product through an equalizer.

In Haskell, the end formula translates directly to the universal quantifier:

```
forall a. p a a
```

Strictly speaking, this is just a product of all diagonal elements of $p$, but the wedge condition is satisfied automatically due to parametricity[1]. For any function $f :: a \rightarrow b$, the wedge condition reads:

```
dimap f id . pi = dimap id f . pi
```

---

[1]https://bartoszmilewski.com/2017/04/11/profunctor-parametricity/

or, with type annotations:

```
dimap f id_b . pi_b = dimap id_a f . pi_a
```

where both sides of the equation have the type:

```
Profunctor p => (forall c. p c c) -> p a b
```

and pi is the polymorphic projection:

```
pi :: Profunctor p => forall c. (forall a. p a a) -> p c c
pi e = e
```

Here, type inference automatically picks the right component of e.

Just as we were able to express the whole set of commutation conditions for a cone as one natural transformation, likewise we can group all the wedge conditions into one dinatural transformation. For that we need the generalization of the constant functor $\Delta_c$ to a constant profunctor that maps all pairs of objects to a single object $c$, and all pairs of morphisms to the identity morphism for this object. A wedge is a dinatural transformation from that functor to the profunctor $p$. Indeed, the dinaturality hexagon shrinks down to the wedge diamond when we realize that $\Delta_c$ lifts all morphisms to one identity function.

Ends can also be defined for target categories other than **Set**, but here we'll only consider **Set**-valued profunctors and their ends.

## 26.3 Ends as Equalizers

The commutation condition in the definition of the end can be written using an equalizer. First, let's define two functions (I'm using Haskell notation, because mathematical notation seems to be less user-friendly in this case). These functions correspond to the two converging branches of the wedge condition:

```
lambda :: Profunctor p => p a a -> (a -> b) -> p a b
lambda paa f = dimap id f paa

rho :: Profunctor p => p b b -> (a -> b) -> p a b
rho pbb f = dimap f id pbb
```

Both functions map diagonal elements of the profunctor p to polymorphic functions of the type:

```
type ProdP p = forall a b. (a -> b) -> p a b
```

These functions have different types. However, we can unify their types, if we form one big product type, gathering together all diagonal elements of p:

```
newtype DiaProd p = DiaProd (forall a. p a a)
```

The functions `lambda` and `rho` induce two mappings from this product type:

```
lambdaP :: Profunctor p => DiaProd p -> ProdP p
lambdaP (DiaProd paa) = lambda paa

rhoP :: Profunctor p => DiaProd p -> ProdP p
rhoP (DiaProd pbb) = rho pbb
```

The end of p is the equalizer of these two functions. Remember that the equalizer picks the largest subset on which two functions are equal. In this case it picks the subset of the product of all diagonal elements for which the wedge diagrams commute.

## 26.4   Natural Transformations as Ends

The most important example of an end is the set of natural transformations. A natural transformation between two functors $F$ and $G$ is a family of morphisms picked from hom-sets of the form $C(F\, a, G\, a)$. If it weren't for the naturality condition, the set of natural transformations would be just the product of all these hom-sets. In fact, in Haskell, it is:

```
forall a. f a -> g a
```

The reason it works in Haskell is because naturality follows from parametricity. Outside of Haskell, though, not all diagonal sections across such hom-sets will yield natural transformations. But notice that the mapping:

$$\langle a, b \rangle \rightarrow C(F\, a, G\, b)$$

is a profunctor, so it makes sense to study its end. This is the wedge condition:

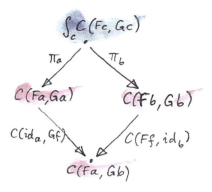

Let's just pick one element from the set $\int_c C(F\,c, G\,c)$. The two projections will map this element to two components of a particular transformation, let's call them:

$$\tau_a :: F\,a \to G\,a$$
$$\tau_b :: F\,b \to G\,b$$

In the left branch, we lift a pair of morphisms $\langle \mathrm{id}_a, G\,f \rangle$ using the hom-functor. You may recall that such lifting is implemented as simultaneous pre- and post-composition. When acting on $\tau_a$ the lifted pair gives us:

$$G\,f \circ \tau_a \circ \mathrm{id}_a$$

The other branch of the diagram gives us:

$$\mathrm{id}_b \circ \tau_b \circ F\,f$$

Their equality, demanded by the wedge condition, is nothing but the naturality condition for $\tau$.

## 26.5 Coends

As expected, the dual to an end is called a coend. It is constructed from a dual to a wedge called a cowedge (pronounced co-wedge, not cow-edge).

The symbol for a coend is the integral sign with the "integration variable" in the superscript position:

$$\int^c p\,c\,c$$

Just like the end is related to a product, the coend is related to a co-product, or a sum (in this respect, it resembles an integral, which is a limit of a sum). Rather than having projections, we have injections going from the diagonal elements of the profunctor down to the coend. If it weren't for the cowedge conditions, we could say that the coend of the profunctor $p$ is either $p\ a\ a$, or $p\ b\ b$, or $p\ c\ c$, and so on. Or we could say that there exists such an $a$ for which the coend is just the set $p\ a\ a$. The universal quantifier that we used in the definition of the end turns into an existential quantifier for the coend.

This is why, in pseudo-Haskell, we would define the coend as:

```
exists a. p a a
```

An edgy cow?

The standard way of encoding existential quantifiers in Haskell is to use universally quantified data constructors. We can thus define:

```
data Coend p = forall a. Coend (p a a)
```

The logic behind this is that it should be possible to construct a coend using a value of any of the family of types $p\ a\ a$, no matter what $a$ we chose.

Just like an end can be defined using an equalizer, a coend can be described using a *coequalizer*. All the cowedge conditions can be summarized by taking one gigantic coproduct of $p\ a\ b$ for all possible functions $b \rightarrow a$. In Haskell, that would be expressed as an existential type.

```
data SumP p = forall a b. SumP (b -> a) (p a b)
```

There are two ways of evaluating this sum type, by lifting the function using `dimap` and applying it to the profunctor $p$:

```
lambda, rho :: Profunctor p => SumP p -> DiagSum p
lambda (SumP f pab) = DiagSum (dimap f id pab)
rho    (SumP f pab) = DiagSum (dimap id f pab)
```

where `DiagSum` is the sum of diagonal elements of $p$:

```
data DiagSum p = forall a. DiagSum (p a a)
```

311

The coequalizer of these two functions is the coend. A coequilizer is obtained from `DiagSum p` by identifying values that are obtained by applying `lambda` or `rho` to the same argument. Here, the argument is a pair consisting of a function $b \rightarrow a$ and an element of $p\ a\ b$. The application of `lambda` and `rho` produces two potentially different values of the type `DiagSum p`. In the coend, these two values are identified, making the cowedge condition automatically satisfied.

The process of identification of related elements in a set is formally known as taking a quotient. To define a quotient we need an *equivalence relation* ~, a relation that is reflexive, symmetric, and transitive:

$$a \sim a$$
$$\text{if } a \sim b \text{ then } b \sim a$$
$$\text{if } a \sim b \text{ and } b \sim c \text{ then } a \sim c$$

Such a relation splits the set into equivalence classes. Each class consists of elements that are related to each other. We form a quotient set by picking one representative from each class. A classic example is the definition of rational numbers as pairs of whole numbers with the following equivalence relation:

$$(a, b) \sim (c, d) \text{ iff } a * d = b * c$$

It's easy to check that this is an equivalence relation. A pair $(a, b)$ is interpreted as a fraction $\frac{a}{b}$, and fractions that have a common divisor are identified. A rational number is an equivalence class of such fractions.

You might recall from our earlier discussion of limits and colimits that the hom-functor is continuous, that is, it preserves limits. Dually, the contravariant hom-functor turns colimits into limits. These properties can be generalized to ends and coends, which are a generalization of limits and colimits, respectively. In particular, we get a very useful identity for converting coends to ends:

$$\text{Set}\left(\int^x p\ x\ x, c\right) \cong \int_x \text{Set}(p\ x\ x, c)$$

Let's have a look at it in pseudo-Haskell:

```
(exists x. p x x) -> c ≅ forall x. p x x -> c
```

It tells us that a function that takes an existential type is equivalent to a polymorphic function. This makes perfect sense, because such a function must be prepared to handle any one of the types that may be encoded in the existential type. It's the same principle that tells us that a function that accepts a sum type must be implemented as a case statement, with a tuple of handlers, one for every type present in the sum. Here, the sum type is replaced by a coend, and a family of handlers becomes an end, or a polymorphic function.

## 26.6  Ninja Yoneda Lemma

The set of natural transformations that appears in the Yoneda lemma may be encoded using an end, resulting in the following formulation:

$$\int_z \mathbf{Set}(C(a, z), F\, z) \cong F\, a$$

There is also a dual formula:

$$\int^z C(a, z) \times F\, z \cong F\, a$$

This identity is strongly reminiscent of the formula for the Dirac delta function (a function $\delta(a - z)$, or rather a distribution, that has an infinite peak at $a = z$). Here, the hom-functor plays the role of the delta function.

Together these two identities are sometimes called the Ninja Yoneda lemma.

To prove the second formula, we will use the consequence of the Yoneda embedding, which states that two objects are isomorphic if and only if their hom-functors are isomorphic. In other words $a \cong b$ if and only if there is a natural transformation of the type:

$$[C, \mathbf{Set}](C(a, -), C(b, =))$$

that is an isomorphism.

We start by inserting the left-hand side of the identity we want to prove inside a hom-functor that's going to some arbitrary object $c$:

$$\mathbf{Set}\left(\int^z C(a, z) \times F\, z, c\right)$$

Using the continuity argument, we can replace the coend with the end:

$$\int_z \mathbf{Set}(C(a, z) \times F\, z, c)$$

We can now take advantage of the adjunction between the product and the exponential:

$$\int_z \mathbf{Set}(\mathbf{C}(a, z), c^{(F\,z)})$$

We can "perform the integration" by using the Yoneda lemma to get:

$$c^{(F\,a)}$$

This exponential object is isomorphic to the hom-set:

$$\mathbf{Set}(F\,a, c)$$

Finally, we take advantage of the Yoneda embedding to arrive at the isomorphism:

$$\int^z \mathbf{C}(a, z) \times F\,z \cong F\,a$$

## 26.7 Profunctor Composition

Let's explore further the idea that a profunctor describes a relation — more precisely, a proof-relevant relation, meaning that the set $p\,a\,b$ represents the set of proofs that $a$ is related to $b$. If we have two relations $p$ and $q$ we can try to compose them. We'll say that $a$ is related to $b$ through the composition of $q$ after $p$ if there exist an intermediary object $c$ such that both $q\,b\,c$ and $p\,c\,a$ are non-empty. The proofs of this new relation are all pairs of proofs of individual relations. Therefore, with the understanding that the existential quantifier corresponds to a coend, and the Cartesian product of two sets corresponds to "pairs of proofs," we can define composition of profunctors using the following formula:

$$(q \circ p)\,a\,b = \int^c p\,c\,a \times q\,b\,c$$

Here's the equivalent Haskell definition from `Data.Profunctor.Composition`, after some renaming:

```
data Procompose q p a b where
    Procompose :: q a c -> p c b -> Procompose q p a b
```

This is using generalized algebraic data type, or GADT syntax, in which a free type variable (here c) is automatically existentially quantified. The (uncurried) data constructor Procompose is thus equivalent to:

```
exists c. (q a c, p c b)
```

The unit of so defined composition is the hom-functor — this immediately follows from the Ninja Yoneda lemma. It makes sense, therefore, to ask the question if there is a category in which profunctors serve as morphisms. The answer is positive, with the caveat that both associativity and identity laws for profunctor composition hold only up to natural isomorphism. Such a category, where laws are valid up to isomorphism, is called a bicategory (which is more general than a 2-category). So we have a bicategory **Prof**, in which objects are categories, morphisms are profunctors, and morphisms between morphisms (a.k.a., two-cells) are natural transformations. In fact, one can go even further, because beside profunctors, we also have regular functors as morphisms between categories. A category which has two types of morphisms is called a double category.

Profunctors play an important role in the Haskell lens library and in the arrow library.

# 27

# Kan Extensions

S O FAR WE'VE BEEN mostly working with a single category or a pair of categories. In some cases that was a little too constraining.

For instance, when defining a limit in a category C, we introduced an index category I as the template for the pattern that would form the basis for our cones. It would have made sense to introduce another category, a trivial one, to serve as a template for the apex of the cone. Instead we used the constant functor $\Delta_c$ from I to C.

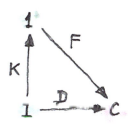

It's time to fix this awkwardness. Let's define a limit using three categories. Let's start with the functor $D$ from the index category I to C. This is the functor that selects the base of the cone — the diagram functor.

The new addition is the category **1** that contains a single object (and a single identity morphism). There is only one possible functor $K$ from I to this category. It maps all objects to the only object in **1**, and all morphisms to the identity morphism. Any functor $F$ from **1** to C picks a potential apex for our cone.

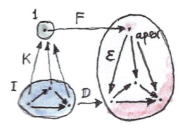

A cone is a natural transformation $\varepsilon$ from $F \circ K$ to $D$. Notice that $F \circ K$ does exactly the same thing as our original $\Delta_c$. The following diagram shows this transformation.

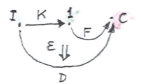

We can now define a universal property that picks the "best" such functor $F$. This $F$ will map $\mathbf{1}$ to the object that is the limit of $D$ in $\mathbf{C}$, and the natural transformation $\varepsilon$ from $F \circ K$ to $D$ will provide the corresponding projections. This universal functor is called the right Kan extension of $D$ along $K$ and is denoted by $\mathrm{Ran}_K D$.

Let's formulate the universal property. Suppose we have another cone — that is another functor $F'$ together with a natural transformation $\varepsilon'$ from $F' \circ K$ to $D$.

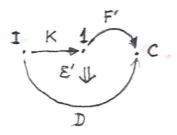

If the Kan extension $F = \mathrm{Ran}_K D$ exists, there must be a unique natural transformation $\sigma$ from $F'$ to it, such that $\varepsilon'$ factorizes through $\varepsilon$, that is:

$$\varepsilon' = \varepsilon . (\sigma \circ K)$$

318

Here, $\sigma \circ K$ is the horizontal composition of two natural transformations (one of them being the identity natural transformation on $K$). This transformation is then vertically composed with $\varepsilon$.

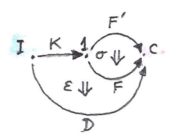

In components, when acting on an object $i$ in I, we get:

$$\varepsilon'_i = \varepsilon_i \circ \sigma_{K\,i}$$

In our case, $\sigma$ has only one component corresponding to the single object of 1. So, indeed, this is the unique morphism from the apex of the cone defined by $F'$ to the apex of the universal cone defined by $\mathrm{Ran}_K D$. The commuting conditions are exactly the ones required by the definition of a limit.

But, importantly, we are free to replace the trivial category 1 with an arbitrary category A, and the definition of the right Kan extension remains valid.

## 27.1 Right Kan Extension

The right Kan extension of the functor $D :: I \to C$ along the functor $K :: I \to A$ is a functor $F :: A \to C$ (denoted $\mathrm{Ran}_K D$) together with a natural transformation

$$\varepsilon :: F \circ K \to D$$

such that for any other functor $F' :: A \to C$ and a natural transformation

$$\varepsilon' :: F' \circ K \to D$$

there is a unique natural transformation

$$\sigma :: F' \to F$$

319

that factorizes $\varepsilon'$:

$$\varepsilon' = \varepsilon . (\sigma \circ K)$$

This is quite a mouthful, but it can be visualized in this nice diagram:

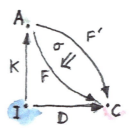

An interesting way of looking at this is to notice that, in a sense, the Kan extension acts like the inverse of "functor multiplication." Some authors go as far as use the notation $D/K$ for $\mathrm{Ran}_K D$. Indeed, in this notation, the definition of $\varepsilon$, which is also called the counit of the right Kan extension, looks like simple cancellation:

$$\varepsilon :: D/K \circ K \to D$$

There is another interpretation of Kan extensions. Consider that the functor $K$ embeds the category $\mathbf{I}$ inside $\mathbf{A}$. In the simplest case $\mathbf{I}$ could just be a subcategory of $\mathbf{A}$. We have a functor $D$ that maps $\mathbf{I}$ to $\mathbf{C}$. Can we extend $D$ to a functor $F$ that is defined on the whole of $\mathbf{A}$? Ideally, such an extension would make the composition $F \circ K$ be isomorphic to $D$. In other words, $F$ would be extending the domain of $D$ to $\mathbf{A}$. But a full-blown isomorphism is usually too much to ask, and we can do with just half of it, namely a one-way natural transformation $\varepsilon$ from $F \circ K$ to $D$. (The left Kan extension picks the other direction.)

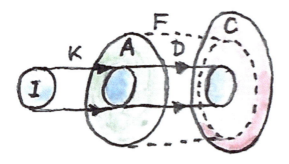

Of course, the embedding picture breaks down when the functor $K$ is not injective on objects or not faithful on hom-sets, as in the example of the limit. In that case, the Kan extension tries its best to extrapolate the lost information.

## 27.2 Kan Extension as Adjunction

Now suppose that the right Kan extension exists for any $D$ (and a fixed $K$). In that case $\mathrm{Ran}_K-$ (with the dash replacing $D$) is a functor from the functor category $[I, C]$ to the functor category $[A, C]$. It turns out that this functor is the right adjoint to the precomposition functor $- \circ K$. The latter maps functors in $[A, C]$ to functors in $[I, C]$. The adjunction is:

$$[I, C](F' \circ K, D) \cong [A, C](F', \mathrm{Ran}_K D)$$

It is just a restatement of the fact that to every natural transformation we called $\varepsilon'$ corresponds a unique natural transformation we called $\sigma$.

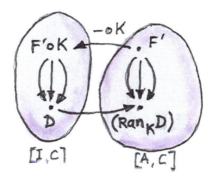

Furthermore, if we chose the category $I$ to be the same as $C$, we can substitute the identity functor $I_C$ for $D$. We get the following identity:

$$[C, C](F' \circ K, I_C) \cong [A, C](F', \mathrm{Ran}_K I_C)$$

We can now chose $F'$ to be the same as $\mathrm{Ran}_K I_C$. In that case the right hand side contains the identity natural transformation and, corresponding to it, the left hand side gives us the following natural transformation:

$$\varepsilon :: \mathrm{Ran}_K I_C \circ K \to I_C$$

This looks very much like the counit of an adjunction:

$$\mathrm{Ran}_K I_C \dashv K$$

Indeed, the right Kan extension of the identity functor along a functor $K$ can be used to calculate the left adjoint of $K$. For that, one more condition is necessary: the right Kan extension must be preserved by the functor $K$. The preservation of the extension means that, if we calculate the Kan extension of the functor precomposed with $K$, we should get the same result as precomposing the original Kan extension with $K$. In our case, this condition simplifies to:

$$K \circ \mathrm{Ran}_K I_{\mathbf{C}} \cong \mathrm{Ran}_K K$$

Notice that, using the division-by-$K$ notation, the adjunction can be written as:

$$I/K \dashv K$$

which confirms our intuition that an adjunction describes some kind of an inverse. The preservation condition becomes:

$$K \circ I/K \cong K/K$$

The right Kan extension of a functor along itself, $K/K$, is called a codensity monad.

The adjunction formula is an important result because, as we'll see soon, we can calculate Kan extensions using ends (coends), thus giving us practical means of finding right (and left) adjoints.

## 27.3  Left Kan Extension

There is a dual construction that gives us the left Kan extension. To build some intuition, we'll can start with the definition of a colimit and restructure it to use the singleton category **1**. We build a cocone by using the functor $D :: \mathbf{I} \rightarrow \mathbf{C}$ to form its base, and the functor $F :: \mathbf{1} \rightarrow \mathbf{C}$ to select its apex.

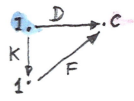

The sides of the cocone, the injections, are components of a natural transformation $\eta$ from $D$ to $F \circ K$.

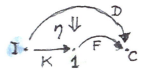

The colimit is the universal cocone. So for any other functor $F'$ and a natural transformation

$$\eta' :: D \to F' \circ K$$

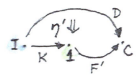

there is a unique natural transformation $\sigma$ from $F$ to $F'$

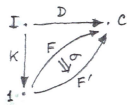

such that:

$$\eta' = (\sigma \circ K) . \eta$$

This is illustrated in the following diagram:

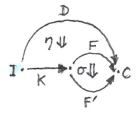

Replacing the singleton category **1** with **A**, this definition naturally generalized to the definition of the left Kan extension, denoted by $\mathrm{Lan}_K D$.

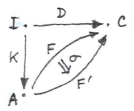

The natural transformation:

$$\eta :: D \to \mathrm{Lan}_K D \circ K$$

is called the unit of the left Kan extension.

As before, we can recast the one-to-one correspondence between natural transformations:

$$\eta' = (\sigma \circ K) \cdot \eta$$

in terms of the adjunction:

$$[\mathbf{A}, \mathbf{C}](\mathrm{Lan}_K D, F') \cong [\mathbf{I}, \mathbf{C}](D, F' \circ K)$$

In other words, the left Kan extension is the left adjoint, and the right Kan extension is the right adjoint of the postcomposition with $K$.

Just like the right Kan extension of the identity functor could be used to calculate the left adjoint of $K$, the left Kan extension of the identity functor turns out to be the right adjoint of $K$ (with $\eta$ being the unit of the adjunction):

$$K \dashv \mathrm{Lan}_K I_{\mathbf{C}}$$

Combining the two results, we get:

$$\mathrm{Ran}_K I_{\mathbf{C}} \dashv K \dashv \mathrm{Lan}_K I_{\mathbf{C}}$$

## 27.4  Kan Extensions as Ends

The real power of Kan extensions comes from the fact that they can be calculated using ends (and coends). For simplicity, we'll restrict our attention to the case where the target category $\mathbf{C}$ is **Set**, but the formulas can be extended to any category.

Let's revisit the idea that a Kan extension can be used to extend the action of a functor outside of its original domain. Suppose that $K$

embeds **I** inside **A**. Functor $D$ maps **I** to **Set**. We could just say that for any object $a$ in the image of $K$, that is $a = K\,i$, the extended functor maps $a$ to $D\,i$. The problem is, what to do with those objects in **A** that are outside of the image of $K$? The idea is that every such object is potentially connected through lots of morphisms to every object in the image of $K$. A functor must preserve these morphisms. The totality of morphisms from an object $a$ to the image of $K$ is characterized by the hom-functor:

$$\mathbf{A}(a, K\,-)$$

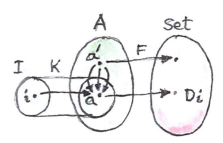

Notice that this hom-functor is a composition of two functors:

$$\mathbf{A}(a, K\,-) = \mathbf{A}(a, -) \circ K$$

The right Kan extension is the right adjoint of functor composition:

$$[\mathbf{I}, \mathbf{Set}](F' \circ K, D) \cong [\mathbf{A}, \mathbf{Set}](F', \mathrm{Ran}_K D)$$

Let's see what happens when we replace $F'$ with the hom functor:

$$[\mathbf{I}, \mathbf{Set}](\mathbf{A}(a, -) \circ K, D) \cong [\mathbf{A}, \mathbf{Set}](\mathbf{A}(a, -), \mathrm{Ran}_K D)$$

and then inline the composition:

$$[\mathbf{I}, \mathbf{Set}](\mathbf{A}(a, K\,-), D) \cong [\mathbf{A}, \mathbf{Set}](\mathbf{A}(a, -), \mathrm{Ran}_K D)$$

The right hand side can be reduced using the Yoneda lemma:

$$[\mathbf{I}, \mathbf{Set}](\mathbf{A}(a, K\,-), D) \cong \mathrm{Ran}_K D\,a$$

We can now rewrite the set of natural transformations as the end to get this very convenient formula for the right Kan extension:

$$\mathrm{Ran}_K D\,a \cong \int_i \mathbf{Set}(\mathbf{A}(a, K\,i), D\,i)$$

325

There is an analogous formula for the left Kan extension in terms of a coend:

$$\mathrm{Lan}_K D \, a = \int^i \mathbf{A}(K \, i, a) \times D \, i$$

To see that this is the case, we'll show that this is indeed the left adjoint to functor composition:

$$[\mathbf{A}, \mathbf{Set}](\mathrm{Lan}_K D, F') \cong [\mathbf{I}, \mathbf{Set}](D, F' \circ K)$$

Let's substitute our formula in the left hand side:

$$[\mathbf{A}, \mathbf{Set}](\int^i \mathbf{A}(K \, i, -) \times D \, i, F')$$

This is a set of natural transformations, so it can be rewritten as an end:

$$\int_a \mathbf{Set}(\int^i \mathbf{A}(K \, i, a) \times D \, i, F' \, a)$$

Using the continuity of the hom-functor, we can replace the coend with the end:

$$\int_a \int_i \mathbf{Set}(\mathbf{A}(K \, i, a) \times D \, i, F' \, a)$$

We can use the product-exponential adjunction:

$$\int_a \int_i \mathbf{Set}(\mathbf{A}(K \, i, a), (F' \, a)^{D \, i})$$

The exponential is isomorphic to the corresponding hom-set:

$$\int_a \int_i \mathbf{Set}(\mathbf{A}(K \, i, a), \mathbf{A}(D \, i, F' \, a))$$

There is a theorem called the Fubini theorem that allows us to swap the two ends:

$$\int_i \int_a \mathbf{Set}(\mathbf{A}(K \, i, a), \mathbf{A}(D \, i, F' \, a))$$

The inner end represents the set of natural transformations between two functors, so we can use the Yoneda lemma:

$$\int_i \mathbf{A}(D \, i, F' \, (K \, i))$$

This is indeed the set of natural transformations that forms the right hand side of the adjunction we set out to prove:

$$[\mathbf{I}, \mathbf{Set}](D, F' \circ K)$$

These kinds of calculations using ends, coends, and the Yoneda lemma are pretty typical for the "calculus" of ends.

## 27.5 Kan Extensions in Haskell

The end/coend formulas for Kan extensions can be easily translated to Haskell. Let's start with the right extension:

$$\mathrm{Ran}_K D \, a \cong \int_i \mathbf{Set}(\mathbf{A}(a, K \, i), D \, i)$$

We replace the end with the universal quantifier, and hom-sets with function types:

```
newtype Ran k d a = Ran (forall i. (a -> k i) -> d i)
```

Looking at this definition, it's clear that `Ran` must contain a value of type `a` to which the function can be applied, and a natural transformation between the two functors `k` and `d`. For instance, suppose that `k` is the tree functor, and `d` is the list functor, and you were given a `Ran Tree [] String`. If you pass it a function:

```
f :: String -> Tree Int
```

you'll get back a list of `Int`, and so on. The right Kan extension will use your function to produce a tree and then repackage it into a list. For instance, you may pass it a parser that generates a parsing tree from a string, and you'll get a list that corresponds to the depth-first traversal of this tree.

The right Kan extension can be used to calculate the left adjoint of a given functor by replacing the functor `d` with the identity functor. This leads to the left adjoint of a functor `k` being represented by the set of polymorphic functions of the type:

```
forall i. (a -> k i) -> i
```

Suppose that `k` is the forgetful functor from the category of monoids. The universal quantifier then goes over all monoids. Of course, in Haskell we cannot express monoidal laws, but the following is a decent approximation of the resulting free functor (the forgetful functor `k` is an identity on objects):

```
type Lst a = forall i. Monoid i => (a -> i) -> i
```

As expected, it generates free monoids, or Haskell lists:

```
toLst :: [a] -> Lst a
toLst as = \f -> foldMap f as

fromLst :: Lst a -> [a]
fromLst f = f (\a -> [a])
```

The left Kan extension is a coend:

$$\mathrm{Lan}_K D \; a = \int^i \mathbf{A}(K \; i, a) \times D \; i$$

so it translates to an existential quantifier. Symbolically:

```
Lan k d a = exists i. (k i -> a, d i)
```

This can be encoded in Haskell using GADTs, or using a universally quantified data constructor:

```
data Lan k d a = forall i. Lan (k i -> a) (d i)
```

The interpretation of this data structure is that it contains a function that takes a container of some unspecified `is` and produces an `a`. It also has a container of those `is`. Since you have no idea what `is` are, the only thing you can do with this data structure is to retrieve the container of `is`, repack it into the container defined by the functor `k` using a natural transformation, and call the function to obtain the `a`. For instance, if `d` is a tree, and `k` is a list, you can serialize the tree, call the function with the resulting list, and obtain an `a`.

The left Kan extension can be used to calculate the right adjoint of a functor. We know that the right adjoint of the product functor is the exponential, so let's try to implement it using the Kan extension:

```
type Exp a b = Lan ((,) a) I b
```

This is indeed isomorphic to the function type, as witnessed by the following pair of functions:

```
toExp :: (a -> b) -> Exp a b
toExp f = Lan (f . fst) (I ())

fromExp :: Exp a b -> (a -> b)
fromExp (Lan f (I x)) = \a -> f (a, x)
```

Notice that, as described earlier in the general case, we performed the following steps:

1. Retrieved the container of x (here, it's just a trivial identity container), and the function f.
2. Repackaged the container using the natural transformation between the identity functor and the pair functor.
3. Called the function f.

## 27.6 Free Functor

An interesting application of Kan extensions is the construction of a free functor. It's the solution to the following practical problem: suppose you have a type constructor — that is a mapping of objects. Is it possible to define a functor based on this type constructor? In other words, can we define a mapping of morphisms that would extend this type constructor to a full-blown endofunctor?

The key observation is that a type constructor can be described as a functor whose domain is a discrete category. A discrete category has no morphisms other than the identity morphisms. Given a category C, we can always construct a discrete category |C| by simply discarding all non-identity morphisms. A functor F from |C| to C is then a simple mapping of objects, or what we call a type constructor in Haskell. There is also a canonical functor J that injects |C| into C: it's an identity on objects (and on identity morphisms). The left Kan extension of F along J, if it exists, is then a functor for C to C:

$$\mathrm{Lan}_J F\ a = \int^{i} C(J\ i, a) \times F\ i$$

It's called a free functor based on F.

In Haskell, we would write it as:

```
data FreeF f a = forall i. FMap (i -> a) (f i)
```

Indeed, for any type constructor f, FreeF f is a functor:

```
instance Functor (FreeF f) where
    fmap g (FMap h fi) = FMap (g . h) fi
```

As you can see, the free functor fakes the lifting of a function by recording both the function and its argument. It accumulates the lifted functions by recording their composition. Functor rules are automatically satisfied. This construction was used in a paper Freer Monads, More Extensible Effects[1].

Alternatively, we can use the right Kan extension for the same purpose:

```
newtype FreeF f a = FreeF (forall i. (a -> i) -> f i)
```

It's easy to check that this is indeed a functor:

```
instance Functor (FreeF f) where
    fmap g (FreeF r) = FreeF (\bi -> r (bi . g))
```

---

[1]http://okmij.org/ftp/Haskell/extensible/more.pdf

# 28

# Enriched Categories

A CATEGORY IS SMALL if its objects form a set. But we know that there are things larger than sets. Famously, a set of all sets cannot be formed within the standard set theory (the Zermelo-Fraenkel theory, optionally augmented with the Axiom of Choice). So a category of all sets must be large. There are mathematical tricks like Grothendieck universes that can be used to define collections that go beyond sets. These tricks let us talk about large categories.

A category is *locally small* if morphisms between any two objects form a set. If they don't form a set, we have to rethink a few definitions. In particular, what does it mean to compose morphisms if we can't even pick them from a set? The solution is to bootstrap ourselves by replacing hom-sets, which are objects in **Set**, with *objects* from some other category **V**. The difference is that, in general, objects don't have elements, so we are no longer allowed to talk about individual morphisms. We have to define all properties of an *enriched* category in terms of operations that can be performed on hom-objects as a whole. In order to do that, the category that provides hom-objects must have additional structure — it must be a monoidal category. If we call this monoidal category **V**, we can talk about a category **C** enriched over **V**.

Beside size reasons, we might be interested in generalizing hom-sets to something that has more structure than mere sets. For instance, a traditional category doesn't have the notion of a distance between objects. Two objects are either connected by morphisms or not. All objects that are connected to a given object are its neighbors. Unlike in real life; in a category, a friend of a friend of a friend is as close to me as my bosom buddy. In a suitably enriched category, we can define distances between objects.

There is one more very practical reason to get some experience with enriched categories, and that's because a very useful online source of categorical knowledge, the nLab[1], is written mostly in terms of enriched categories.

## 28.1 Why Monoidal Category?

When constructing an enriched category we have to keep in mind that we should be able to recover the usual definitions when we replace the monoidal category with **Set** and hom-objects with hom-sets. The best way to accomplish this is to start with the usual definitions and keep reformulating them in a point-free manner — that is, without naming elements of sets.

Let's start with the definition of composition. Normally, it takes a pair of morphisms, one from $C(b, c)$ and one from $C(a, b)$ and maps it to a morphism from $C(a, c)$. In other words it's a mapping:

$$C(b, c) \times C(a, b) \longrightarrow C(a, c)$$

This is a function between sets — one of them being the Cartesian product of two hom-sets. This formula can be easily generalized by replacing Cartesian product with something more general. A categorical product would work, but we can go even further and use a completely general tensor product.

Next come the identity morphisms. Instead of picking individual elements from hom-sets, we can define them using functions from the singleton set **1**:

$$j_a :: \mathbf{1} \longrightarrow C(a, a)$$

Again, we could replace the singleton set with the terminal object, but we can go even further by replacing it with the unit $i$ of the tensor product.

As you can see, objects taken from some monoidal category **V** are good candidates for hom-set replacement.

---

[1]https://ncatlab.org/

## 28.2  Monoidal Category

We've talked about monoidal categories before, but it's worth restating
the definition. A monoidal category defines a tensor product that is a
bifunctor:

$$\otimes :: \mathbf{V} \times \mathbf{V} \to \mathbf{V}$$

We want the tensor product to be associative, but it's enough to satisfy
associativity up to natural isomorphism. This isomorphism is called the
associator. Its components are:

$$\alpha_{a\ b\ c} :: (a \otimes b) \otimes c \to a \otimes (b \otimes c)$$

It must be natural in all three arguments.

A monoidal category must also define a special unit object $i$ that
serves as the unit of the tensor product; again, up to natural isomorphism. The two isomorphisms are called, respectively, the left and the
right unitor, and their components are:

$$\lambda_a :: i \otimes a \to a$$
$$\rho_a :: a \otimes i \to a$$

The associator and the unitors must satisfy coherence conditions:

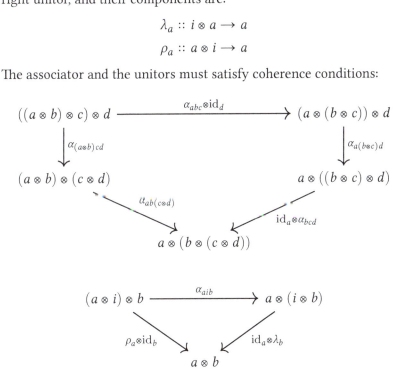

A monoidal category is called *symmetric* if there is a natural isomorphism with components:

$$\gamma_{a\ b} :: a \otimes b \to b \otimes a$$

whose "square is one":

$$\gamma_{b\,a} \circ \gamma_{a\,b} = \mathrm{id}_{a\otimes b}$$

and which is consistent with the monoidal structure.

An interesting thing about monoidal categories is that you may be able to define the internal hom (the function object) as the right adjoint to the tensor product. You may recall that the standard definition of the function object, or the exponential, was through the right adjoint to the categorical product. A category in which such an object existed for any pair of objects was called Cartesian closed. Here is the adjunction that defines the internal hom in a monoidal category:

$$\mathbf{V}(a \otimes b, c) \sim \mathbf{V}(a, [b, c])$$

Following G. M. Kelly[2], I'm using the notation $[b, c]$ for the internal hom. The counit of this adjunction is the natural transformation whose components are called evaluation morphisms:

$$\varepsilon_{a\,b} :: ([a, b] \otimes a) \rightarrow b$$

Notice that, if the tensor product is not symmetric, we may define another internal hom, denoted by $[[a, c]]$, using the following adjunction:

$$\mathbf{V}(a \otimes b, c) \sim \mathbf{V}(b, [[a, c]])$$

A monoidal category in which both are defined is called *biclosed*. An example of a category that is not biclosed is the category of endofunctors in **Set**, with functor composition serving as tensor product. That's the category we used to define monads.

## 28.3  Enriched Category

A category **C** enriched over a monoidal category **V** replaces hom-sets with hom-objects. To every pair of objects $a$ and $b$ in **C** we associate an object $\mathbf{C}(a, b)$ in **V**. We use the same notation for hom-objects as we used for hom-sets, with the understanding that they don't contain morphisms. On the other hand, **V** is a regular (non-enriched) category with hom-sets and morphisms. So we are not entirely rid of sets — we just swept them under the rug.

---

[2]http://www.tac.mta.ca/tac/reprints/articles/10/tr10.pdf

Since we cannot talk about individual morphisms in C, composition of morphisms is replaced by a family of morphisms in **V**:

$$\circ :: C(b, c) \otimes C(a, b) \to C(a, c)$$

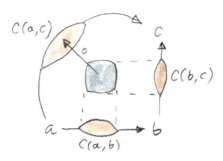

Similarly, identity morphisms are replaced by a family of morphisms in **V**:

$$j_a :: i \to C(a, a)$$

where $i$ is the tensor unit in **V**.

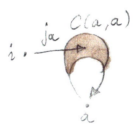

Associativity of composition is defined in terms of the associator in **V**:

$$
\begin{array}{ccc}
(C(c, d) \otimes C(b, c)) \otimes C(a, b) & \xrightarrow{\;\circ \otimes id\;} & C(b, d) \otimes C(a, b) \\
\downarrow{\scriptstyle \alpha} & & \searrow{\scriptstyle \circ} \\
& & \qquad C(a, d) \\
C(c, d) \otimes (C(b, c) \otimes C(a, b)) & \xrightarrow{\;id \otimes \circ\;} & C(c, d) \otimes C(a, c) \nearrow{\scriptstyle \circ}
\end{array}
$$

Unit laws are likewise expressed in terms of unitors:

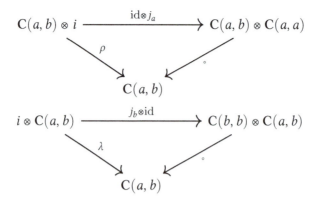

## 28.4 Preorders

A preorder is defined as a thin category, one in which every hom-set is either empty or a singleton. We interpret a non-empty set $C(a, b)$ as the proof that $a$ is less than or equal to $b$. Such a category can be interpreted as enriched over a very simple monoidal category that contains just two objects, 0 and 1 (sometimes called *False* and *True*). Besides the mandatory identity morphisms, this category has a single morphism going from 0 to 1, let's call it $0 \to 1$. A simple monoidal structure can be established in it, with the tensor product modeling the simple arithmetic of 0 and 1 (i.e., the only non-zero product is $1 \otimes 1$). The identity object in this category is 1. This is a strict monoidal category, that is, the associator and the unitors are identity morphisms.

Since in a preorder the-hom set is either empty or a singleton, we can easily replace it with a hom-object from our tiny category. The enriched preorder $C$ has a hom-object $C(a, b)$ for any pair of objects $a$ and $b$. If $a$ is less than or equal to $b$, this object is 1; otherwise it's 0.

Let's have a look at composition. The tensor product of any two objects is 0, unless both of them are 1, in which case it's 1. If it's 0, then we have two options for the composition morphism: it could be either $\text{id}_0$ or $0 \to 1$. But if it's 1, then the only option is $\text{id}_1$. Translating this back to relations, this says that if $a \le b$ and $b \le c$ then $a \le c$, which is exactly the transitivity law we need.

What about the identity? It's a morphism from 1 to $C(a, a)$. There is only one morphism going from 1, and that's the identity $\text{id}_1$, so $C(a, a)$ must be 1. It means that $a \le a$, which is the reflexivity law for a preorder. So both transitivity and reflexivity are automatically enforced, if we implement a preorder as an enriched category.

## 28.5  Metric Spaces

An interesting example is due to William Lawvere[3]. He noticed that metric spaces can be defined using enriched categories. A metric space defines a distance between any two objects. This distance is a non-negative real number. It's convenient to include infinity as a possible value. If the distance is infinite, there is no way of getting from the starting object to the target object.

There are some obvious properties that have to be satisfied by distances. One of them is that the distance from an object to itself must be zero. The other is the triangle inequality: the direct distance is no larger than the sum of distances with intermediate stops. We don't require the distance to be symmetric, which might seem weird at first but, as Lawvere explained, you can imagine that in one direction you're walking uphill, while in the other you're going downhill. In any case, symmetry may be imposed later as an additional constraint.

So how can a metric space be cast into a categorical language? We have to construct a category in which hom-objects are distances. Mind you, distances are not morphisms but hom-objects. How can a hom-object be a number? Only if we can construct a monoidal category $\mathbf{V}$ in which these numbers are objects. Non-negative real numbers (plus infinity) form a total order, so they can be treated as a thin category. A morphism between two such numbers $x$ and $y$ exists if and only if $x \geqslant y$ (note: this is the opposite direction to the one traditionally used in the definition of a preorder). The monoidal structure is given by addition, with zero serving as the unit object. In other words, the tensor product of two numbers is their sum.

A metric space is a category enriched over such monoidal category. A hom-object $\mathbf{C}(a, b)$ from object $a$ to $b$ is a non-negative (possibly infinite) number that we will call the distance from $a$ to $b$. Let's see what we get for identity and composition in such a category.

By our definitions, a morphism from the tensorial unit, which is the number zero, to a hom-object $\mathbf{C}(a, a)$ is the relation:

$$0 \geqslant \mathbf{C}(a, a)$$

[3]http://www.tac.mta.ca/tac/reprints/articles/1/tr1.pdf

Since $C(a, a)$ is a non-negative number, this condition tells us that the distance from $a$ to $a$ is always zero. Check!

Now let's talk about composition. We start with the tensor product of two abutting hom-objects, $C(b, c) \otimes C(a, b)$. We have defined the tensor product as the sum of the two distances. Composition is a morphism in $V$ from this product to $C(a, c)$. A morphism in $V$ is defined as the greater-or-equal relation. In other words, the sum of distances from $a$ to $b$ and from $b$ to $c$ is greater than or equal to the distance from $a$ to $c$. But that's just the standard triangle inequality. Check!

By re-casting the metric space in terms of an enriched category, we get the triangle inequality and the zero self-distance "for free."

## 28.6  Enriched Functors

The definition of a functor involves the mapping of morphisms. In the enriched setting, we don't have the notion of individual morphisms, so we have to deal with hom-objects in bulk. Hom-objects are objects in a monoidal category $V$, and we have morphisms between them at our disposal. It therefore makes sense to define enriched functors between categories when they are enriched over the same monoidal category $V$. We can then use morphisms in $V$ to map the hom-objects between two enriched categories.

An *enriched functor* $F$ between two categories $C$ and $D$, besides mapping objects to objects, also assigns, to every pair of objects in $C$, a morphism in $V$:

$$F_{a\ b} :: C(a, b) \rightarrow D(F\ a, F\ b)$$

A functor is a structure-preserving mapping. For regular functors it meant preserving composition and identity. In the enriched setting, the preservation of composition means that the following diagram commute:

$$
\begin{array}{ccc}
C(b, c) \otimes C(a, b) & \xrightarrow{\ \circ\ } & C(a, c) \\
\downarrow{\scriptstyle F_{bc} \otimes F_{ab}} & & \downarrow{\scriptstyle F_{ac}} \\
D(F\ b, F\ c) \otimes D(F\ a, F\ b) & \xrightarrow{\ \circ\ } & D(F\ a, F\ c)
\end{array}
$$

The preservation of identity is replaced by the preservation of the morphisms in $V$ that "select" the identity:

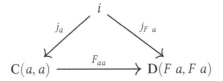

## 28.7 Self Enrichment

A closed symmetric monoidal category may be self-enriched by replacing hom-sets with internal homs (see the definition above). To make this work, we have to define the composition law for internal homs. In other words, we have to implement a morphism with the following signature:

$$[b, c] \otimes [a, b] \rightarrow [a, c]$$

This is not much different from any other programming task, except that, in category theory, we usually use point free implementations. We start by specifying the set whose element it's supposed to be. In this case, it's a member of the hom-set:

$$\mathbf{V}([b, c] \otimes [a, b], [a, c])$$

This hom-set is isomorphic to:

$$\mathbf{V}(([b, c] \otimes [a, b]) \otimes a, c)$$

I just used the adjunction that defined the internal hom $[a, c]$. If we can build a morphism in this new set, the adjunction will point us at the morphism in the original set, which we can then use as composition. We construct this morphism by composing several morphisms that are at our disposal. To begin with, we can use the associator $\alpha_{[b,c]\,[a,b]\,a}$ to reassociate the expression on the left:

$$([b, c] \otimes [a, b]) \otimes a \rightarrow [b, c] \otimes ([a, b] \otimes a)$$

We can follow it with the co-unit of the adjunction $\varepsilon_{a\,b}$:

$$[b, c] \otimes ([a, b] \otimes a) \rightarrow [b, c] \otimes b$$

And use the counit $\varepsilon_{b\,c}$ again to get to $c$. We have thus constructed a morphism:

$$\varepsilon_{b\,c} \cdot (\mathrm{id}_{[b,c]} \otimes \varepsilon_{a\,b}) \cdot \alpha_{[b,c]\,[a,b]\,a}$$

339

that is an element of the hom-set:

$$\mathbf{V}(([b, c] \otimes [a, b]) \otimes a, c)$$

The adjunction will give us the composition law we were looking for.

Similarly, the identity:

$$j_a :: i \rightarrow [a, a]$$

is a member of the following hom-set:

$$\mathbf{V}(i, [a, a])$$

which is isomorphic, through adjunction, to:

$$\mathbf{V}(i \otimes a, a)$$

We know that this hom-set contains the left identity $\lambda_a$. We can define $j_a$ as its image under the adjunction.

A practical example of self-enrichment is the category **Set** that serves as the prototype for types in programming languages. We've seen before that it's a closed monoidal category with respect to Cartesian product. In **Set**, the hom-set between any two sets is itself a set, so it's an object in **Set**. We know that it's isomorphic to the exponential set, so the external and the internal homs are equivalent. Now we also know that, through self-enrichment, we can use the exponential set as the hom-object and express composition in terms of Cartesian products of exponential objects.

## 28.8   Relation to 2-Categories

I talked about 2-categories in the context of **Cat**, the category of (small) categories. The morphisms between categories are functors, but there is an additional structure: natural transformations between functors. In a 2-category, the objects are often called zero-cells; morphisms, 1-cells; and morphisms between morphisms, 2-cells. In **Cat** the 0-cells are categories, 1-cells are functors, and 2-cells are natural transformations.

But notice that functors between two categories form a category too; so, in **Cat**, we really have a *hom-category* rather than a hom-set. It turns out that, just like **Set** can be treated as a category enriched over **Set**, **Cat** can be treated as a category enriched over **Cat**. Even more generally, just like every category can be treated as enriched over **Set**, every 2-category can be considered enriched over **Cat**.

340

# 29

# Topoi

I REALIZE THAT WE MIGHT be getting away from programming and diving into hard-core math. But you never know what the next big revolution in programming might bring and what kind of math might be necessary to understand it. There are some very interesting ideas going around, like functional reactive programming with its continuous time, the extension of Haskell's type system with dependent types, or the exploration on homotopy type theory in programming.

So far I've been casually identifying types with *sets* of values. This is not strictly correct, because such approach doesn't take into account the fact that, in programming, we *compute* values, and the computation is a process that takes time and, in extreme cases, might not terminate. Divergent computations are part of every Turing-complete language.

There are also foundational reasons why set theory might not be the best fit as the basis for computer science or even math itself. A good analogy is that of set theory being the assembly language that is tied to a particular architecture. If you want to run your math on different architectures, you have to use more general tools.

One possibility is to use spaces in place of sets. Spaces come with more structure, and may be defined without recourse to sets. One thing usually associated with spaces is topology, which is necessary to define things like continuity. And the conventional approach to topology is, you guessed it, through set theory. In particular, the notion of a subset is central to topology. Not surprisingly, category theorists generalized this idea to categories other than **Set**. The type of category that has just the right properties to serve as a replacement for set theory is called a *topos* (plural: topoi), and it provides, among other things, a generalized notion of a subset.

## 29.1  Subobject Classifier

Let's start by trying to express the idea of a subset using functions rather than elements. Any function $f$ from some set $a$ to $b$ defines a subset of $b$–that of the image of $a$ under $f$. But there are many functions that define the same subset. We need to be more specific. To begin with, we might focus on functions that are injective — ones that don't smush multiple elements into one. Injective functions "inject" one set into another. For finite sets, you may visualize injective functions as parallel arrows connecting elements of one set to elements of another. Of course, the first set cannot be larger than the second set, or the arrows would necessarily converge. There is still some ambiguity left: there may be another set $a'$ and another injective function $f'$ from that set to $b$ that picks the same subset. But you can easily convince yourself that such a set would have to be isomorphic to $a$. We can use this fact to define a subset as a family of injective functions that are related by isomorphisms of their domains. More precisely, we say that two injective functions:

$$f :: a \rightarrow b$$
$$f' :: a' \rightarrow b$$

are equivalent if there is an isomorphism:

$$h :: a \rightarrow a'$$

such that:

$$f = f' \cdot h$$

Such a family of equivalent injections defines a subset of $b$.

342

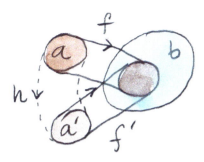

This definition can be lifted to an arbitrary category if we replace injective functions with monomorphism. Just to remind you, a monomorphism $m$ from $a$ to $b$ is defined by its universal property. For any object $c$ and any pair of morphisms:

$$g :: c \rightarrow a$$
$$g' :: c \rightarrow a$$

such that:

$$m \cdot g = m \cdot g'$$

it must be that $g = g'$.

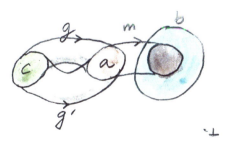

On sets, this definition is easier to understand if we consider what it would mean for a function $m$ *not* to be a monomorphism. It would map two different elements of $a$ to a single element of $b$. We could then find two functions $g$ and $g'$ that differ only at those two elements. The postcomposition with $m$ would then mask this difference.

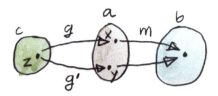

There is another way of defining a subset: using a single function called the characteristic function. It's a function $\chi$ from the set $b$ to a two-element set $\Omega$. One element of this set is designated as "true" and the other as "false." This function assigns "true" to those elements of $b$ that are members of the subset, and "false" to those that aren't.

It remains to specify what it means to designate an element of $\Omega$ as "true." We can use the standard trick: use a function from a singleton set to $\Omega$. We'll call this function *true*:

$$true :: 1 \to \Omega$$

These definitions can be combined in such a way that they not only define what a subobject is, but also define the special object $\Omega$ without talking about elements. The idea is that we want the morphism *true* to represent a "generic" subobject. In **Set**, it picks a single-element subset from a two-element set $\Omega$. This is as generic as it gets. It's clearly a proper subset, because $\Omega$ has one more element that's *not* in that subset.

In a more general setting, we define *true* to be a monomorphism from the terminal object to the *classifying object* $\Omega$. But we have to define the classifying object. We need a universal property that links this object to the characteristic function. It turns out that, in **Set**, the pullback of *true* along the characteristic function $\chi$ defines both the subset $a$ and the injective function that embeds it in $b$. Here's the pullback diagram:

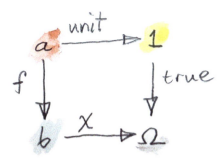

Let's analyze this diagram. The pullback equation is:

$$true \cdot unit = \chi \cdot f$$

The function $true \cdot unit$ maps every element of $a$ to "true." Therefore $f$ must map all elements of $a$ to those elements of $b$ for which $\chi$ is "true." These are, by definition, the elements of the subset that is specified by the characteristic function $\chi$. So the image of $f$ is indeed the subset in question. The universality of the pullback guarantees that $f$ is injective.

This pullback diagram can be used to define the classifying object in categories other than **Set**. Such a category must have a terminal object, which will let us define the monomorphism $true$. It must also have pullbacks — the actual requirement is that it must have all finite limits (a pullback is an example of a finite limit). Under those assumptions, we define the classifying object $\Omega$ by the property that, for every monomorphism $f$ there is a unique morphism $\chi$ that completes the pullback diagram.

Let's analyze the last statement. When we construct a pullback, we are given three objects $\Omega$, $b$ and 1; and two morphisms, $true$ and $\chi$. The existence of a pullback means that we can find the best such object $a$, equipped with two morphisms $f$ and $unit$ (the latter is uniquely determined by the definition of the terminal object), that make the diagram commute.

Here we are solving a different system of equations. We are solving for $\Omega$ and $true$ while varying both $a$ and $b$. For a given $a$ and $b$ there may or may not be a monomorphism $f :: a \rightarrow b$. But if there is one, we want it to be a pullback of some $\chi$. Moreover, we want this $\chi$ to be uniquely determined by $f$.

We can't say that there is a one-to-one correspondence between monomorphisms $f$ and characteristic functions $\chi$, because a pullback is only unique up to isomorphism. But remember our earlier definition of a subset as a family of equivalent injections. We can generalize it by defining a subobject of $b$ as a family of equivalent monomorphisms to $b$. This family of monomorphisms is in one-to-one correspondence with the family of equivalent pullbacks of our diagram.

We can thus define a set of subobjects of $b$, $Sub(b)$, as a family of monomorphisms, and see that it is isomorphic to the set of morphisms from $b$ to $\Omega$:

$$Sub(b) \cong C(b, \Omega)$$

This happens to be a natural isomorphism of two functors. In other words, $Sub(-)$ is a representable (contravariant) functor whose representation is the object $\Omega$.

## 29.2 Topos

A topos is a category that:

1. Is Cartesian closed: It has all products, the terminal object, and exponentials (defined as right adjoints to products),
2. Has limits for all finite diagrams,
3. Has a subobject classifier $\Omega$.

This set of properties makes a topos a shoe-in for **Set** in most applications. It also has additional properties that follow from its definition. For instance, a topos has all finite colimits, including the initial object.

It would be tempting to define the subobject classifier as a coproduct (sum) of two copies of the terminal object –that's what it is in **Set**– but we want to be more general than that. Topoi in which this is true are called Boolean.

## 29.3 Topoi and Logic

In set theory, a characteristic function may be interpreted as defining a property of the elements of a set — a *predicate* that is true for some elements and false for others. The predicate *isEven* selects a subset of even numbers from the set of natural numbers. In a topos, we can generalize the idea of a predicate to be a morphism from object $a$ to $\Omega$. This is why $\Omega$ is sometimes called the truth object.

Predicates are the building blocks of logic. A topos contains all the necessary instrumentation to study logic. It has products that correspond to logical conjunctions (logical *and*), coproducts for disjunctions (logical *or*), and exponentials for implications. All standard axioms of logic hold in a topos except for the law of excluded middle (or, equivalently, double negation elimination). That's why the logic of a topos corresponds to constructive or intuitionistic logic.

Intuitionistic logic has been steadily gaining ground, finding unexpected support from computer science. The classical notion of excluded middle is based on the belief that there is absolute truth: Any statement is either true or false or, as Ancient Romans would say, *tertium non datur* (there is no third option). But the only way we can know whether something is true or false is if we can prove or disprove it. A proof is a process, a computation — and we know that computations take time and resources. In some cases, they may never terminate. It doesn't make sense to claim that a statement is true if we cannot prove it in finite amount of time. A topos with its more nuanced truth object provides a more general framework for modeling interesting logics.

## 29.4 Challenges

1. Show that the function $f$ that is the pullback of *true* along the characteristic function must be injective.

# 30

# Lawvere Theories

NOWADAYS YOU CAN'T talk about functional programming without mentioning monads. But there is an alternative universe in which, by chance, Eugenio Moggi turned his attention to Lawvere theories rather than monads. Let's explore that universe.

## 30.1 Universal Algebra

There are many ways of describing algebras at various levels of abstraction. We try to find a general language to describe things like monoids, groups, or rings. At the simplest level, all these constructions define *operations* on elements of a set, plus some *laws* that must be satisfied by these operations. For instance, a monoid can be defined in terms of a binary operation that is associative. We also have a unit element and unit laws. But with a little bit of imagination we can turn the unit element to a nullary operation — an operation that takes no arguments and returns a special element of the set. If we want to talk about groups, we add a unary operator that takes an element and returns its inverse. There are corresponding left and right inverse laws to go with it. A ring defines two binary operators plus some more laws. And so on.

The big picture is that an algebra is defined by a set of $n$-ary operations for various values of $n$, and a set of equational identities. These identities are all universally quantified. The associativity equation must be satisfied for all possible combinations of three elements, and so on.

Incidentally, this eliminates fields from consideration, for the simple reason that zero (unit with respect to addition) has no inverse with respect to multiplication. The inverse law for a field can't be universally quantified.

This definition of a universal algebra can be extended to categories other than **Set**, if we replace operations (functions) with morphisms. Instead of a set, we select an object $a$ (called a generic object). A unary operation is just an endomorphism of $a$. But what about other arities (*arity* is the number of arguments for a given operation)? A binary operation (arity 2) can be defined as a morphism from the product $a \times a$ back to $a$. A general $n$-ary operation is a morphism from the $n^{th}$ power of $a$ to $a$:

$$\alpha_n :: a^n \to a$$

A nullary operation is a morphism from the terminal object (the zeroth power of $a$). So all we need in order to define any algebra is a category whose objects are powers of one special object $a$. The specific algebra is encoded in the hom-sets of this category. This is a Lawvere theory in a nutshell.

The derivation of Lawvere theories goes through many steps, so here's the roadmap:

1. Category of finite sets **FinSet**.
2. Its skeleton **F**.
3. Its opposite $\mathbf{F}^{op}$.
4. Lawvere theory **L**: an object in the category **Law**.
5. Model $M$ of a Lawvere category: an object in the category **Mod(Law, Set)**.

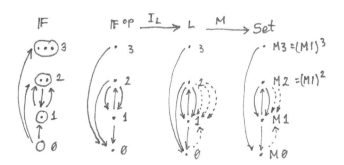

## 30.2 Lawvere Theories

All Lawvere theories share a common backbone. All objects in a Lawvere theory are generated from just one object using products (really, just powers). But how do we define these products in a general category? It turns out that we can define products using a mapping from a simpler category. In fact this simpler category may define coproducts instead of products, and we'll use a *contravariant* functor to embed them in our target category. A contravariant functor turns coproducts into products and injections to projections.

The natural choice for the backbone of a Lawvere category is the category of finite sets, **FinSet**. It contains the empty set $\emptyset$, a singleton set 1, a two-element set 2, and so on. All objects in this category can be generated from the singleton set using coproducts (treating the empty set as a special case of a nullary coproduct). For instance, a two-element set is a sum of two singletons, $2 = 1 + 1$, as expressed in Haskell:

```haskell
type Two = Either () ()
```

However, even though it's natural to think that there's only one empty set, there may be many distinct singleton sets. In particular, the set $1+\emptyset$ is different from the set $\emptyset + 1$, and different from 1 — even though they are all isomorphic. The coproduct in the category of sets is not associative. We can remedy that situation by building a category that identifies all isomorphic sets. Such a category is called a *skeleton*. In other words, the backbone of any Lawvere theory is the skeleton **F** of **FinSet**. The objects in this category can be identified with natural numbers (including zero) that correspond to the element count in **FinSet**. Coproduct plays the role of addition. Morphisms in **F** correspond to functions between finite sets. For instance, there is a unique morphism from $\emptyset$ to $n$ (empty set being the initial object), no morphisms from $n$ to $\emptyset$ (except $\emptyset \to \emptyset$), $n$ morphisms from 1 to $n$ (the injections), one morphism from $n$ to 1, and so on. Here, $n$ denotes an object in **F** corresponding to all $n$-element sets in **FinSet** that have been identified through isomorphisms.

Using the category **F** we can formally define a *Lawvere theory* as a category **L** equipped with a special functor

$$I_L :: F^{op} \to L$$

351

This functor must be a bijection on objects and it must preserve finite products (products in $F^{op}$ are the same as coproducts in $F$):

$$I_L (m \times n) = I_L \, m \times I_L \, n$$

You may sometimes see this functor characterized as identity-on-objects, which means that the objects in $F$ and $L$ are the same. We will therefore use the same names for them — we'll denote them by natural numbers. Keep in mind though that objects in $F$ are not the same as sets (they are classes of isomorphic sets).

The hom-sets in $L$ are, in general, richer than those in $F^{op}$. They may contain morphisms other than the ones corresponding to functions in **FinSet** (the latter are sometimes called *basic product operations*). Equational laws of a Lawvere theory are encoded in those morphisms.

The key observation is that the singleton set 1 in $F$ is mapped to some object that we also call 1 in $L$, and all the other objects in $L$ are automatically powers of this object. For instance, the two-element set 2 in $F$ is the coproduct $1 + 1$, so it must be mapped to a product $1 \times 1$ (or $1^2$) in $L$. In this sense, the category $F$ behaves like the logarithm of $L$.

Among morphisms in $L$ we have those transferred by the functor $I_L$ from $F$. They play structural role in $L$. In particular coproduct injections $i_k$ become product projections $p_k$. A useful intuition is to imagine the projection:

$$p_k :: 1^n \rightarrow 1$$

as the prototype for a function of $n$ variables that ignores all but the $k^{th}$ variable. Conversely, constant morphisms $n \rightarrow 1$ in $F$ become diagonal morphisms $1 \rightarrow 1^n$ in $L$. They correspond to duplication of variables.

The interesting morphisms in $L$ are the ones that define $n$-ary operations other than projections. It's those morphisms that distinguish one Lawvere theory from another. These are the multiplications, the additions, the selections of unit elements, and so on, that define the algebra. But to make $L$ a full category, we also need compound operations $n \rightarrow m$ (or, equivalently, $1^n \rightarrow 1^m$). Because of the simple structure of the category, they turn out to be products of simpler morphisms of the type $n \rightarrow 1$. This is a generalization of the statement that a function that returns a product is a product of functions (or, as we've seen earlier, that the hom-functor is continuous).

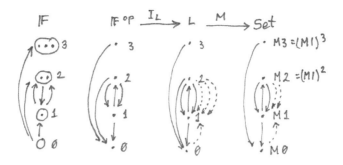

Lawvere theory **L** is based on $F^{op}$, from which it inherits the "boring" morphisms that define the products. It adds the "interesting" morphisms that describe the $n$-ary operations (dotted arrows).

Lawvere theories form a category **Law**, in which morphisms are functors that preserve finite products and commute with the functors $I$. Given two such theories, $(L, I_L)$ and $(L', I'_{L'})$, a morphism between them is a functor $F :: L \to L'$ such that:

$$F\,(m \times n) = F\,m \times F\,n$$
$$F \circ I_L = I'_{L'}$$

Morphisms between Lawvere theories encapsulate the idea of the interpretation of one theory inside another. For instance, group multiplication may be interpreted as monoid multiplication if we ignore inverses.

The simplest trivial example of a Lawvere category is $F^{op}$ itself (corresponding to the choice of the identity functor for $I_L$). This Lawvere theory that has no operations or laws happens to be the initial object in **Law**.

At this point it would be very helpful to present a non-trivial example of a Lawvere theory, but it would be hard to explain it without first understanding what models are.

## 30.3  Models of Lawvere Theories

The key to understand Lawvere theories is to realize that one such theory generalizes a lot of individual algebras that share the same structure. For instance, the Lawvere theory of monoids describes the essence of being a monoid. It must be valid for all monoids. A particular monoid becomes a model of such a theory. A model is defined as a functor from the Lawvere theory **L** to the category of sets **Set**. (There are generalizations of Lawvere theories that use other categories for models but here

I'll just concentrate on **Set**.) Since the structure of **L** depends heavily on products, we require that such a functor preserve finite products. A model of **L**, also called the algebra over the Lawvere theory **L**, is therefore defined by a functor:

$$M :: \mathbf{L} \to \mathbf{Set}$$
$$M\,(a \times b) \cong M\,a \times M\,b$$

Notice that we require the preservation of products only *up to isomorphism*. This is very important, because strict preservation of products would eliminate most interesting theories.

The preservation of products by models means that the image of $M$ in **Set** is a sequence of sets generated by powers of the set $M\,1$ — the image of the object 1 from **L**. Let's call this set $a$. (This set is sometimes called a *sort*, and such algebra is called *single-sorted*. There exist generalizations of Lawvere theories to multi-sorted algebras.) In particular, binary operations from **L** are mapped to functions:

$$a \times a \to a$$

As with any functor, it's possible that multiple morphisms in **L** are collapsed to the same function in **Set**.

Incidentally, the fact that all laws are universally quantified equalities means that every Lawvere theory has a trivial model: a constant functor mapping all objects to the singleton set, and all morphisms to the identity function on it.

A general morphism in **L** of the form $m \to n$ is mapped to a function:

$$a^m \to a^n$$

If we have two different models, $M$ and $N$, a natural transformation between them is a family of functions indexed by $n$:

$$\mu_n :: M\,n \to N\,n$$

or, equivalently:

$$\mu_n :: a^n \to b^n$$

where $b = N\,1$.

Notice that the naturality condition guarantees the preservation of $n$-ary operations:

$$N\,f \circ \mu_n = \mu_1 \circ M\,f$$

where $f :: n \to 1$ is an $n$-ary operation in **L**.

The functors that define models form a category of models, **Mod**(**L**, **Set**), with natural transformations as morphisms.

Consider a model for the trivial Lawvere category $\mathbf{F}^{op}$. Such model is completely determined by its value at 1, $M\,1$. Since $M\,1$ can be any set, there are as many of these models as there are sets in **Set**. Moreover, every morphism in **Mod**($\mathbf{F}^{op}$, **Set**) (a natural transformation between functors $M$ and $N$) is uniquely determined by its component at $M\,1$. Conversely, every function $M\,1 \to N\,1$ induces a natural transformation between the two models $M$ and $N$. Therefore **Mod**($\mathbf{F}^{op}$, **Set**) is equivalent to **Set**.

## 30.4  The Theory of Monoids

The simplest nontrivial example of a Lawvere theory describes the structure of monoids. It is a single theory that distills the structure of all possible monoids, in the sense that the models of this theory span the whole category **Mon** of monoids. We've already seen a universal construction, which showed that every monoid can be obtained from an appropriate free monoid by identifying a subset of morphisms. So a single free monoid already generalizes a whole lot of monoids. There are, however, infinitely many free monoids. The Lawvere theory for monoids $\mathbf{L_{Mon}}$ combines all of them in one elegant construction.

Every monoid must have a unit, so we have to have a special morphism $\eta$ in $\mathbf{L_{Mon}}$ that goes from 0 to 1. Notice that there can be no corresponding morphism in **F**. Such morphism would go in the opposite direction, from 1 to 0 which, in **FinSet**, would be a function from the singleton set to the empty set. No such function exists.

Next, consider morphisms $2 \to 1$, members of $\mathbf{L_{Mon}}(2, 1)$, which must contain prototypes of all binary operations. When constructing models in **Mod**($\mathbf{L_{Mon}}$, **Set**), these morphisms will be mapped to functions from the Cartesian product $M\,1 \times M\,1$ to $M\,1$. In other words, functions of two arguments.

The question is: how many functions of two arguments can one implement using only the monoidal operator. Let's call the two arguments $a$ and $b$. There is one function that ignores both arguments and returns the monoidal unit. Then there are two projections that return $a$ and $b$, respectively. They are followed by functions that return $ab$, $ba$, $aa$, $bb$, $aab$, and so on... In fact there are as many such functions of two arguments as there are elements in the free monoid with generators $a$ and $b$. Notice that $L_{Mon}(2, 1)$ must contain all those morphisms because one of the models is the free monoid. In a free monoid they correspond to distinct functions. Other models may collapse multiple morphisms in $L_{Mon}(2, 1)$ down to a single function, but not the free monoid.

If we denote the free monoid with $n$ generators $n^*$, we may identify the hom-set $L(2, 1)$ with the hom-set $Mon(1^*, 2^*)$ in $Mon$, the category of monoids. In general, we pick $L_{Mon}(m, n)$ to be $Mon(n^*, m^*)$. In other words, the category $L_{Mon}$ is the opposite of the category of free monoids.

The category of *models* of the Lawvere theory for monoids, $Mod(L_{Mon}, Set)$, is equivalent to the category of all monoids, $Mon$.

## 30.5  Lawvere Theories and Monads

As you may remember, algebraic theories can be described using monads — in particular algebras for monads. It should be no surprise then that there is a connection between Lawvere theories and monads.

First, let's see how a Lawvere theory induces a monad. It does it through an adjunction between a forgetful functor and a free functor. The forgetful functor $U$ assigns a set to each model. This set is given by evaluating the functor $M$ from $Mod(L, Set)$ at the object 1 in $L$.

Another way of deriving $U$ is by exploiting the fact that $F^{op}$ is the initial object in $Law$. It means that, for any Lawvere theory $L$, there is a unique functor $F^{op} \rightarrow L$. This functor induces the opposite functor on models (since models are functors *from* theories to sets):

$$Mod(L, Set) \rightarrow Mod(F^{op}, Set)$$

But, as we discussed, the category of models of $F^{op}$ is equivalent to $Set$, so we get the forgetful functor:

$$U :: Mod(L, Set) \rightarrow Set$$

It can be shown that so defined $U$ always has a left adjoint, the free functor $F$.

This is easily seen for finite sets. The free functor $F$ produces free algebras. A free algebra is a particular model in $Mod(L, Set)$ that is generated from a finite set of generators $n$. We can implement $F$ as the representable functor:

$$L(n, -) :: L \rightarrow Set$$

To show that it's indeed free, all we have to do is to prove that it's a left adjoint to the forgetful functor:

$$\mathbf{Mod}(\mathbf{L}(n, -), M) \cong \mathbf{Set}(n, U(M))$$

Let's simplify the right hand side:

$$\mathbf{Set}(n, U(M)) \cong \mathbf{Set}(n, M\ 1) \cong (M\ 1)^n \cong M\ n$$

(I used the fact that a set of morphisms is isomorphic to the exponential which, in this case, is just the iterated product.) The adjunction is the result of the Yoneda lemma:

$$[\mathbf{L}, \mathbf{Set}](\mathbf{L}(n, -), M) \cong M\ n$$

Together, the forgetful and the free functor define a monad $T = U \circ F$ on **Set**. Thus every Lawvere theory generates a monad.

It turns out that the category of algebras for this monad is equivalent to the category of models.

You may recall that monad algebras define ways to evaluate expressions that are formed using monads. A Lawvere theory defines n-ary operations that can be used to generate expressions. Models provide means to evaluate these expressions.

The connection between monads and Lawvere theories doesn't go both ways, though. Only finitary monads lead to Lawvere theories. A finitary monad is based on a finitary functor. A finitary functor on **Set** is fully determined by its action on finite sets. Its action on an arbitrary set $a$ can be evaluated using the following coend:

$$F\ a = \int^n a^n \times (\Gamma\ n)$$

Since the coend generalizes a coproduct, or a sum, this formula is a generalization of a power series expansion. Or we can use the intuition that a functor is a generalized container. In that case a finitary container of *as* can be described as a sum of shapes and contents. Here, $F\ n$ is a set of shapes for storing $n$ elements, and the contents is an $n$-tuple of elements, itself an element of $a^n$. For instance, a list (as a functor) is finitary, with one shape for every arity. A tree has more shapes per arity, and so on.

First off, all monads that are generated from Lawvere theories are finitary and they can be expressed as coends:

$$T_{\mathbf{L}}\ a = \int^n a^n \times \mathbf{L}(n, 1)$$

Conversely, given any finitary monad $T$ on **Set**, we can construct a Lawvere theory. We start by constructing a Kleisli category for $T$. As you may remember, a morphism in a Kleisli category from $a$ to $b$ is given by a morphism in the underlying category:

$$a \to T\ b$$

When restricted to finite sets, this becomes:

$$m \to T\ n$$

The category opposite to this Kleisli category, $\mathbf{Kl}_T^{op}$, restricted to finite sets, is the Lawvere theory in question. In particular, the hom-set $\mathbf{L}(n, 1)$ that describes n-ary operations in **L** is given by the hom-set $\mathbf{Kl}_T(1, n)$.

It turns out that most monads that we encounter in programming are finitary, with the notable exception of the continuation monad. It is possible to extend the notion of Lawvere theory beyond finitary operations.

## 30.6  Monads as Coends

Let's explore the coend formula in more detail.

$$T_L\ a = \int^n a^n \times \mathbf{L}(n, 1)$$

To begin with, this coend is taken over a profunctor $P$ in **F** defined as:

$$P\ n\ m = a^n \times \mathbf{L}(m, 1)$$

This profunctor is contravariant in the first argument, $n$. Consider how it lifts morphisms. A morphism in **FinSet** is a mapping of finite sets $f :: m \to n$. Such a mapping describes a selection of $m$ elements from an $n$-element set (repetitions are allowed). It can be lifted to the mapping of powers of $a$, namely (notice the direction):

$$a^n \to a^m$$

The lifting simply selects $m$ elements from a tuple of $n$ elements $(a_1, a_2, ...a_n)$ (possibly with repetitions).

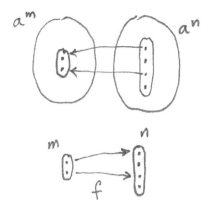

For instance, let's take $f_k :: 1 \rightarrow n$ — a selection of the $k^{th}$ element from an $n$-element set. It lifts to a function that takes a $n$-tuple of elements of $a$ and returns the $k^{th}$ one.

Or let's take $f :: m \rightarrow 1$ — a constant function that maps all $m$ elements to one. Its lifting is a function that takes a single element of $a$ and duplicates it $m$ times:

$$\lambda x \rightarrow \underbrace{(x, x, \ldots, x)}_{m}$$

You might notice that it's not immediately obvious that the profunctor in question is covariant in the second argument. The hom-functor $L(m, 1)$ is actually contravariant in $m$. However, we are taking the co-end not in the category $L$ but in the category $F$. The coend variable $n$ goes over finite sets (or the skeletons of such). The category $L$ contains the opposite of $F$, so a morphism $m \rightarrow n$ in $F$ is a member of $L(n, m)$ in $L$ (the embedding is given by the functor $I_L$).

Let's check the functoriality of $L(m, 1)$ as a functor from $F$ to $\mathbf{Set}$. We want to lift a function $f :: m \rightarrow n$, so our goal is to implement a function from $L(m, 1)$ to $L(n, 1)$. Corresponding to the function $f$ there is a morphism in $L$ from $n$ to $m$ (notice the direction). Precomposing this morphism with $L(m, 1)$ gives us a subset of $L(n, 1)$.

$$L(m, 1) \xrightarrow{\hspace{2cm}} L(n, 1)$$

$$m_\bullet \xrightarrow[\hspace{1cm} f \hspace{1cm}]{} {}_\bullet n$$

Notice that, by lifting a function $1 \to n$ we can go from $L(1,1)$ to $L(n,1)$. We'll use this fact later on.

The product of a contravariant functor $a^n$ and a covariant functor $L(m,1)$ is a profunctor $F^{op} \times F \to Set$. Remember that a coend can be defined as a coproduct (disjoint sum) of all the diagonal members of a profunctor, in which some elements are identified. The identifications correspond to cowedge conditions.

Here, the coend starts as the disjoint sum of sets $a^n \times L(n,1)$ over all $n$s. The identifications can be generated by expressing the coend as a coequilizer. We start with an off-diagonal term $a^n \times L(m,1)$. To get to the diagonal, we can apply a morphism $f :: m \to n$ either to the first or the second component of the product. The two results are then identified.

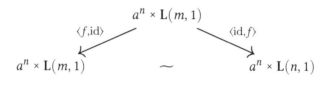

$$f :: m \to n$$

I have shown before that the lifting of $f :: 1 \to n$ results in these two transformations:

$$a^n \to a$$

and:

$$L(1,1) \to L(n,1)$$

Therefore, starting from $a^n \times L(1,1)$ we can reach both:

$$a \times L(1,1)$$

when we lift $\langle f, id \rangle$ and:

$$a^n \times L(n,1)$$

when we lift $\langle id, f \rangle$. This doesn't mean, however, that all elements of $a^n \times L(n,1)$ can be identified with $a \times L(1,1)$. That's because not all elements of $L(n,1)$ can be reached from $L(1,1)$. Remember that we can only lift morphisms from $F$. A non-trivial $n$-ary operation in $L$ cannot be constructed by lifting a morphism $f :: 1 \to n$.

In other words, we can only identify all addends in the coend formula for which $L(n, 1)$ can be reached from $L(1, 1)$ through the application of basic morphisms. They are all equivalent to $a \times L(1, 1)$. Basic morphisms are the ones that are images of morphisms in **F**.

Let's see how this works in the simplest case of the Lawvere theory, the $\mathbf{F}^{op}$ itself. In such a theory, every $L(n, 1)$ can be reached from $L(1, 1)$. This is because $L(1, 1)$ is a singleton containing just the identity morphism, and $L(n, 1)$ only contains morphisms corresponding to injections $1 \rightarrow n$ in **F**, which *are* basic morphisms. Therefore all the addends in the coproduct are equivalent and we get:

$$T\ a = a \times L(1, 1) = a$$

which is the identity monad.

## 30.7  Lawvere Theory of Side Effects

Since there is such a strong connection between monads and Lawvere theories, it's natural to ask the question if Lawvere theories could be used in programming as an alternative to monads. The major problem with monads is that they don't compose nicely. There is no generic recipe for building monad transformers. Lawvere theories have an advantage in this area: they can be composed using coproducts and tensor products. On the other hand, only finitary monads can be easily converted to Lawvere theories. The outlier here is the continuation monad. There is ongoing research in this area (see bibliography).

To give you a taste of how a Lawvere theory can be used to describe side effects, I'll discuss the simple case of exceptions that are traditionally implemented using the Maybe monad.

The Maybe monad is generated by the Lawvere theory with a single nullary operation $0 \rightarrow 1$. A model of this theory is a functor that maps 1 to some set $a$, and maps the nullary operation to a function:

```
raise :: () -> a
```

We can recover the Maybe monad using the coend formula. Let's consider what the addition of the nullary operation does to the hom-sets $L(n, 1)$. Besides creating a new $L(0, 1)$ (which is absent from $\mathbf{F}^{op}$), it also adds new morphisms to $L(n, 1)$. These are the results of composing morphism of the type $n \rightarrow 0$ with our $0 \rightarrow 1$. Such contributions are all identified with $a^0 \times \mathbf{L}(0,1)$ in the coend formula, because they can be obtained from:

$$a^n \times \mathbf{L}(0,1)$$

by lifting $0 \rightarrow n$ in two different ways.

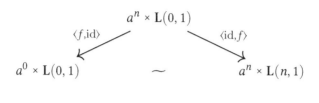

$$f :: 0 \rightarrow n$$

The coend reduces to:

$$T_\mathbf{L}\, a = a^0 + a^1$$

or, using Haskell notation:

```
type Maybe a = Either () a
```

which is equivalent to:

```
data Maybe a = Nothing | Just a
```

Notice that this Lawvere theory only supports the raising of exceptions, not their handling.

## 30.8  Challenges

1. Enumerate all morphisms between 2 and 3 in **F** (the skeleton of **FinSet**).
2. Show that the category of models for the Lawvere theory of monoids is equivalent to the category of monad algebras for the list monad.
3. The Lawvere theory of monoids generates the list monad. Show that its binary operations can be generated using the corresponding Kleisli arrows.
4. **FinSet** is a subcategory of **Set** and there is a functor that embeds it in **Set**. Any functor on **Set** can be restricted to **FinSet**. Show that a finitary functor is the left Kan extension of its own restriction.

## 30.9  Further Reading

1. Functorial Semantics of Algebraic Theories[1], F. William Lawvere
2. Notions of computation determine monads[2], Gordon Plotkin and John Power

---

[1]http://www.tac.mta.ca/tac/reprints/articles/5/tr5.pdf
[2]http://homepages.inf.ed.ac.uk/gdp/publications/Comp_Eff_Monads.pdf

# 31

# Monads, Monoids, and Categories

THERE IS NO GOOD PLACE to end a book on category theory. There's always more to learn. Category theory is a vast subject. At the same time, it's obvious that the same themes, concepts, and patterns keep showing up over and over again. There is a saying that all concepts are Kan extensions and, indeed, you can use Kan extensions to derive limits, colimits, adjunctions, monads, the Yoneda lemma, and much more. The notion of a category itself arises at all levels of abstraction, and so does the concept of a monoid and a monad. Which one is the most basic? As it turns out they are all interrelated, one leading to another in a never-ending cycle of abstractions. I decided that showing these interconnections might be a good way to end this book.

## 31.1  Bicategories

One of the most difficult aspects of category theory is the constant switching of perspectives. Take the category of sets, for instance. We are used to defining sets in terms of elements. An empty set has no elements. A singleton set has one element. A Cartesian product of two sets is a set of pairs, and so on. But when talking about the category **Set** I asked you to forget about the contents of sets and instead concentrate on morphisms (arrows) between them. You were allowed, from time to time, to peek under the covers to see what a particular universal construction in **Set** described in terms of elements. The terminal object turned out to be a set with one element, and so on. But these were just sanity checks.

A functor is defined as a mapping of categories. It's natural to consider a mapping as a morphism in a category. A functor turned out to be a morphism in the category of categories (small categories, if we want to avoid questions about size). By treating a functor as an arrow, we forfeit the information about its action on the internals of a category (its objects and morphisms), just like we forfeit the information about the action of a function on elements of a set when we treat it as an arrow in **Set**. But functors between any two categories also form a category. This time you are asked to consider something that was an arrow in one category to be an object in another. In a functor category functors are objects and natural transformations are morphisms. We have discovered that the same thing can be an arrow in one category and an object in another. The naive view of objects as nouns and arrows as verbs doesn't hold.

Instead of switching between two views, we can try to merge them into one. This is how we get the concept of a 2-category, in which objects are called 0-cells, morphisms are 1-cells, and morphisms between morphisms are 2-cells.

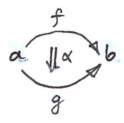

0-cells $a$, $b$; 1-cells $f$, $g$; and a 2-cell $\alpha$.

The category of categories **Cat** is an immediate example. We have categories as 0-cells, functors as 1-cells, and natural transformations as 2-cells. The laws of a 2-category tell us that 1-cells between any two 0-cells form a category (in other words, $C(a, b)$ is a hom-category rather than a hom-set). This fits nicely with our earlier assertion that functors between any two categories form a functor category.

In particular, 1-cells from any 0-cell back to itself also form a category, the hom-category $C(a, a)$; but that category has even more structure. Members of $C(a, a)$ can be viewed as arrows in $C$ or as objects in

C($a$, $a$). As arrows, they can be composed with each other. But when we look at them as objects, the composition becomes a mapping from a pair of objects to an object. In fact it looks very much like a product — a tensor product to be precise. This tensor product has a unit: the identity 1-cell. It turns out that, in any 2-category, a hom-category C($a$, $a$) is automatically a monoidal category with the tensor product defined as composition of 1-cells. Associativity and unit laws simply fall out from the corresponding category laws.

Let's see what this means in our canonical example of a 2-category **Cat**. The hom-category **Cat**($a$, $a$) is the category of endofunctors on $a$. Endofunctor composition plays the role of a tensor product in it. The identity functor is the unit with respect to this product. We've seen before that endofunctors form a monoidal category (we used this fact in the definition of a monad), but now we see that this is a more general phenomenon: endo-1-cells in any 2-category form a monoidal category. We'll come back to it later when we generalize monads.

You might recall that, in a general monoidal category, we did not insist on the monoid laws being satisfied on the nose. It was often enough for the unit laws and the associativity laws to be satisfied up to isomorphism. In a 2-category, monoidal laws in C($a$, $a$) follow from composition laws for 1-cells. These laws are strict, so we will always get a strict monoidal category. It is, however, possible to relax these laws as well. We can say, for instance, that a composition of the identity 1-cell $\mathrm{id}_a$ with another 1-cell, $f :: a \to b$, is isomorphic, rather than equal, to $f$. Isomorphism of 1-cells is defined using 2-cells. In other words, there is a 2-cell:

$$\rho :: f \circ \mathrm{id}_a \to f$$

that has an inverse.

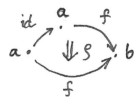

Identity law in a bicategory holds up to isomorphism (an invertible 2-cell ⬚).

We can do the same for the left identity and associativity laws. This kind of relaxed 2-category is called a bicategory (there are some additional coherency laws, which I will omit here).

As expected, endo-1-cells in a bicategory form a general monoidal category with non-strict laws.

An interesting example of a bicategory is the category of spans. A span between two objects $a$ and $b$ is an object $x$ and a pair of morphisms:

$$f :: x \rightarrow a$$
$$g :: x \rightarrow b$$

You might recall that we used spans in the definition of a categorical product. Here, we want to look at spans as 1-cells in a bicategory. The first step is to define a composition of spans. Suppose that we have an adjoining span:

$$f' :: y \rightarrow b$$
$$g' :: y \rightarrow c$$

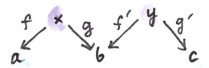

The composition would be a third span, with some apex $z$. The most natural choice for it is the pullback of $g$ along $f'$. Remember that a pullback is the object $z$ together with two morphisms:

$$h :: z \rightarrow x$$
$$h' :: z \rightarrow y$$

such that:

$$g \circ h = f' \circ h'$$

which is universal among all such objects.

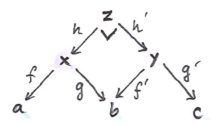

For now, let's concentrate on spans over the category of sets. In that case, the pullback is just a set of pairs $(p, q)$ from the Cartesian product $x \times y$ such that:

$$g\, p = f'\, q$$

A morphism between two spans that share the same endpoints is defined as a morphism $h$ between their apices, such that the appropriate triangles commute.

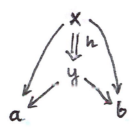

A 2-cell in **Span**.

To summarize, in the bicategory **Span**: 0-cells are sets, 1-cells are spans, 2-cells are span morphisms. An identity 1-cell is a degenerate span in which all three objects are the same, and the two morphisms are identities.

We've seen another example of a bicategory before: the bicategory **Prof** of profunctors, where 0-cells are categories, 1-cells are profunctors, and 2-cells are natural transformations. The composition of profunctors was given by a coend.

## 31.2 Monads

By now you should be pretty familiar with the definition of a monad as a monoid in the category of endofunctors. Let's revisit this definition with the new understanding that the category of endofunctors is just one small hom-category of endo-1-cells in the bicategory **Cat**. We know it's a monoidal category: the tensor product comes from the composition of endofunctors. A monoid is defined as an object in a monoidal category — here it will be an endofunctor $T$ — together with two morphisms. Morphisms between endofunctors are natural transformations. One morphism maps the monoidal unit — the identity endofunctor — to $T$:

$$\eta :: I \to T$$

The second morphism maps the tensor product of $T \otimes T$ to $T$. The tensor product is given by endofunctor composition, so we get:

$$\mu :: T \circ T \to T$$

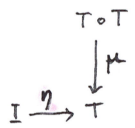

We recognize these as the two operations defining a monad (they are called `return` and `join` in Haskell), and we know that monoid laws turn to monad laws.

Now let's remove all mention of endofunctors from this definition. We start with a bicategory C and pick a 0-cell $a$ in it. As we've seen earlier, the hom-category $C(a, a)$ is a monoidal category. We can therefore define a monoid in $C(a, a)$ by picking a 1-cell, $T$, and two 2-cells:

$$\eta :: I \to T$$
$$\mu :: T \circ T \to T$$

satisfying the monoid laws. We call *this* a monad.

370

That's a much more general definition of a monad using only 0-cells, 1-cells, and 2-cells. It reduces to the usual monad when applied to the bicategory **Cat**. But let's see what happens in other bicategories.

Let's construct a monad in **Span**. We pick a 0-cell, which is a set that, for reasons that will become clear soon, I will call *Ob*. Next, we pick an endo-1-cell: a span from *Ob* back to *Ob*. It has a set at the apex, which I will call *Ar*, equipped with two functions:

$$dom :: Ar \rightarrow Ob$$
$$cod :: Ar \rightarrow Ob$$

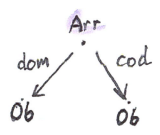

Let's call the elements of the set *Ar* "arrows." If I also tell you to call the elements of *Ob* "objects," you might get a hint where this is leading to. The two functions *dom* and *cod* assign the domain and the codomain to an "arrow."

To make our span into a monad, we need two 2-cells, $\eta$ and $\mu$. The monoidal unit, in this case, is the trivial span from *Ob* to *Ob* with the apex at *Ob* and two identity functions. The 2-cell $\eta$ is a function between the apices *Ob* and *Ar*. In other words, $\eta$ assigns an "arrow" to every "object." A 2-cell in **Span** must satisfy commutation conditions — in this case:

$$dom \circ \eta = \text{id}$$
$$cod \circ \eta = \text{id}$$

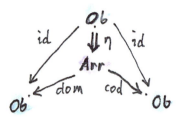

In components, this becomes:

$$dom\,(\eta\,ob) = ob = cod\,(\eta\,ob)$$

where *ob* is an "object" in *Ob*. In other words, $\eta$ assigns to every "object" and "arrow" whose domain and codomain are that "object." We'll call this special "arrow" the "identity arrow."

The second 2-cell $\mu$ acts on the composition of the span *Ar* with itself. The composition is defined as a pullback, so its elements are pairs of elements from *Ar* — pairs of "arrows" $(a_1, a_2)$. The pullback condition is:

$$cod\,a_1 = dom\,a_2$$

We say that $a_1$ and $a_2$ are "composable," because the domain of one is the codomain of the other.

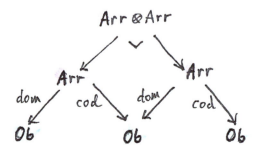

The 2-cell $\mu$ is a function that maps a pair of composable arrows $(a_1, a_2)$ to a single arrow $a_3$ from $Ar$. In other words $\mu$ defines composition of arrows.

It's easy to check that monad laws correspond to identity and associativity laws for arrows. We have just defined a category (a small category, mind you, in which objects and arrows form sets).

So, all told, a category is just a monad in the bicategory of spans.

What is amazing about this result is that it puts categories on the same footing as other algebraic structures like monads and monoids. There is nothing special about being a category. It's just two sets and four functions. In fact we don't even need a separate set for objects, because objects can be identified with identity arrows (they are in one-to-one correspondence). So it's really just a set and a few functions. Considering the pivotal role that category theory plays in all of mathematics, this is a very humbling realization.

## 31.3 Challenges

1. Derive unit and associativity laws for the tensor product defined as composition of endo-1-cells in a bicategory.
2. Check that monad laws for a monad in **Span** correspond to identity and associativity laws in the resulting category.
3. Show that a monad in **Prof** is an identity-on-objects functor.
4. What's a monad algebra for a monad in **Span**?

## 31.4 Bibliography

1. Paweł Sobociński's blog[1].

---

[1]https://graphicallinearalgebra.net/2017/04/16/
a-monoid-is-a-category-a-category-is-a-monad-a-monad-is-a-monoid/

# Index

Any inaccuracies in this index may be explained by the fact that it has been prepared with the help of a computer.

—Donald E. Knuth, *Fundamental Algorithms* (Volume 1 of *The Art of Computer Programming*)

linear order, 24

modus ponens, 117
monad, 231
monoidal category, 59
morphisms, 3

natural, 205
Natural isomorphism, 124
naturality condition, 123
naturally isomorphic, 209

object, 196
objects, 3
one way, 209
one-to-one, 55
onto, 55
operational semantics, 16
opposite category, 44

parametric polymorphism, 99, 125
partial order, 24
point-free, 27
points, 27
poset, 43
predicate, 346
predicates, 21
preorder, 24
profunctor, 101
proof-relevant relation, 304
pure functions, 18

representable, 176, 212

representable presheaf, 154
representation, 176
rig, 66
right adjoint, 219
ring, 66

semiring, 66
side effects, 31
single-sorted, 354
skeleton, 351
surjective, 55, 193
symmetric, 333

template template parameter, 79
tensor product, 260
theorems for free, 99
topos, 342
total, 54
total order, 24
type inference, 12

underlying, 168
underlying set, 221
universal cone, 150
universal construction, 41
up to isomorphism, 42

variant, 52

wedge condition, 306
writer monad, 39

Yoneda embedding, 193

# Acknowledgments

I'd like to thank Edward Kmett and Gershom Bazerman for checking my math and logic, and André van Meulebrouck, who has been volunteering his editing help throughout this series of posts.

I'd like to thank Andrew Sutton for rewriting my C++ monoid concept code according to his and Bjarne Stroustrup's latest proposal.

I'm grateful to Eric Niebler for reading the draft and providing the clever implementation of compose that uses advanced features of C++14 to drive type inference. I was able to cut the whole section of old fashioned template magic that did the same thing using type traits. Good riddance! I'm also grateful to Gershom Bazerman for useful comments that helped me clarify some important points.

# Colophon

THIS BOOK was compiled by Igal Tabachnik[2], by converting the original text by Bartosz Milewski into LaTeX format, by first scraping the original WordPress blog posts using Mercury Web Parser[3] to get a clean HTML content, modifying and tweaking with Beautiful Soup[4], finally, converting to LaTeX with Pandoc[5].

The typefaces are Linux Libertine for body text and Linux Biolinum for headings, both by Philipp H. Poll. Typewriter face is Inconsolata created by Raph Levien and supplemented by Dimosthenis Kaponis and Takashi Tanigawa in the form of Inconsolata LGC. The cover page typeface is Alegreya, designed by Juan Pablo del Peral.

Original book layout design and typography are done by Andres Raba.

---

[2] https://hmemcpy.com
[3] https://mercury.postlight.com/web-parser/
[4] https://www.crummy.com/software/BeautifulSoup/
[5] https://pandoc.org/

# Copyleft notice

THIS BOOK is **Libre** and follows the philosophy of Free Software[6]: you can use this book as you like, the source is available, you can redistribute this book and you can distribute your own version. That means you can print it, photocopy it, e-mail it, upload it to websites, change it, translate it, remix it, delete bits, and draw all over it.

This book is Copyleft: if you change the book and distribute your own version, you must also pass these freedoms to its recipients. This book uses the Creative Commons Attribution-ShareAlike 4.0 International License (CC BY-SA 4.0).

---

[6]https://www.gnu.org/philosophy/free-sw.en.html

CPSIA information can be obtained
at www.ICGtesting.com
Printed in the USA
LVHW070919031118
594556LV00014BH/116/P